¡Brigadistas!

¡Brigadistas!

An American Anti-Fascist in the Spanish Civil War

Written by MIGUEL FERGUSON
Edited by PAUL BUHLE and FRASER OTTANELLI
Art by ANNE TIMMONS

MONTHLY REVIEW PRESS
New York

Library of Congress Cataloging-in-Publication data available from the publisher.

ISBN 978-158367-960-9 paper
ISBN 978-158367-961-6 cloth

MONTHLY REVIEW PRESS, NEW YORK
monthlyreview.org

5 4 3 2 1

Contents

DEDICATION

THIS BOOK IS DEDICATED TO ABE OSHEROFF (1915–2008), carpenter, union organizer, veteran of the Abraham Lincoln Brigade, and the Second World War, filmmaker, lecturer, and lifelong social activist. Whether in Spain in 1937, Normandy in 1944, Mississippi in 1964, or Nicaragua in the 1980s, Abe always took the side of the common person against fascists, racists, and bullies. Over his long and active life, he was a friend and mentor to us and many others, and his words and deeds inspire and challenge us to think deeply about the world around us and act accordingly. This story is based on his experiences as a teenage activist during the Great Depression and on events that he and others experienced in Spain as volunteer soldiers—narrated in such a way, as he explained, that it "bent, but did not break, the rubber band of truth." We hope you enjoy it, and in remembering the heroic sacrifices of the Abraham Lincoln and International Brigades in the Spanish Civil War, find in it the inspiration to make your own world a better place.

—MIGUEL FERGUSON

The Civil War in Spain and the American Volunteers

by Fraser Ottanelli

The Spanish Civil War (1936–1939) began when rebel forces backed by monarchists, large landowners, and the hierarchy of the Catholic Church, and supported with massive military aid provided by Hitler and Mussolini, revolted against the democratically elected Spanish Republican government. This conflict stirred the conscience and imagination of women and men around the world for whom events in Spain came to exemplify the broader global confrontation between fascism and democracy.

Approximately forty thousand anti-fascists from over fifty countries volunteered to fight in Spain. At first, travel into Spain simply meant taking the night train from Paris to Barcelona or the bus from Perpignan to Figueres. After March 1937, when French authorities closed the border, entering Spain involved a perilous nighttime trek over the Pyrenees, or, as described in this graphic novel, on the ill-fated voyage of the *Ciudad de Barcelona*.

Foreign anti-fascist volunteers were "workers of the world," and for them international solidarity with those dispossessed of their democratic rights transcended national boundaries. However, inter-nationalist ideology coexisted with national and cultural identity. In Spain, volunteers were incorporated into separate units divided according to nationality and named after national heroes and Communist icons such as James Connolly, Giuseppe Garibaldi, Abraham Lincoln, or Ernst

Thälmann. These units served to overcome linguistic differences and at the same time affirmed the universal and national character of the struggle against fascism. The link between internationalism and national and ethnic identity took a variety of other forms: German volunteers sang "Today our homeland is before Madrid," and Italian anti-fascists decreed "Today in Spain, tomorrow in Italy." Regardless of their different backgrounds, for all international volunteers the struggle against fascism in Spain reverberated with the promise of ultimate deliverance from oppression everywhere.

Written in concise, accessible language and based on the stories of real-life volunteers—several of which are combined into a main character—*!Brigadistas! An American Anti-Fascist in the Spanish Civil War* provides a vivid and powerful educational resource that brings to life the motivations that led a group of young women and men to join the struggle in defense of democracy in a distant land. In so doing, this graphic novel introduces readers to some of the major historical, political, and cultural issues that defined the history of the United States during the interwar years.

The beliefs of those who volunteered to fight in Spain mirrored the scope of the U.S. left, from Communists and socialists to other shades of radicalism. Most of the volunteers had come of age during the Great Depression, a period marked by widespread hunger and poverty, along with the rise and consolidation of reactionary forces in the United States and around the world. With the conviction that a better world was possible, a world in which common people could enjoy the fruits of their labor and live in harmony as equals, many of those who went to Spain had been active in the struggles of the unemployed and the fight for workers' rights. Similarly, they were also on the forefront of confrontations against homegrown fascist organizations like the KKK, the Silver Shirts, and the German American Bund, participated in the campaigns to save the Scottsboro Boys, and in the demonstrations protesting Fascist Italy's war of aggression against Ethiopia and the arrival in New York's harbor of the German liner *Bremen*.

For most, then, the decision to cross the Atlantic to fight fascism (this time arms in hand) was rooted in the belief that the battle against racism and exploitation for justice and equality in the United States was inseparable from the larger struggle against Franco, Hitler, and Mussolini. While fighting in Spain, Canute Frankson, one of the over eighty African Americans who risked life and limb to serve in the first fully integrated military unit in U.S. history, explained this connection in a letter home:

> Why I, a Negro, who have fought through these years for the rights of my people, am here in Spain today? Once Fascism has been crushed . . . we will build us a new society—a society of peace and plenty. There will be no color line, no jim-crow trains, no lynchings. That is why, my dear, I am here in Spain.

This motivation, rooted in a history of racial persecution and exploitation, mirrored that of Jewish volunteers for whom ethnic and cultural identity constituted an important element of their radical politics and opposition to fascism. Accordingly, the battlefields of Spain provided Jews with the first opportunity to offer armed and organized resistance against fascism and Nazi anti-Semitism. A Jewish volunteer, Hy Katz, who wanted to mollify his mother's obvious disapproval of a decision to risk his life in Spain, had this to say about his choice:

> This is a case where sons must go against their mothers' wishes for the sake of their mothers themselves. So I took up arms against the persecutors of my people—the Jews—and my class— the Oppressed. Are these traits which you admire so much in a Prophet Jeremiah or a Judas Maccabeus bad when your son exhibits them?

The story of the Abraham Lincoln Brigade challenges the traditional narrative of U.S. attitudes toward world affairs during the years leading up to the outbreak of the Second World War. It shows that while the country's foreign policy emphasized isolationism and fear of involvement in world affairs, thousands of Americans were aware of the global threat of fascism. Confronted with their government's unwillingness to stand up to aggression, the volunteers defied neutrality legislation to fight for the Spanish Republican government.

Many more found other ways to contribute and campaign in support of Spanish democracy.

The commitment to social justice, equality, and democracy that motivated the volunteers of the Lincoln Brigade did not end with the defeat of the Spanish Republic in 1939. Those who survived the Spanish Civil War, disparagingly labeled by the right as "premature anti-fascists," continued to uphold the principles of human dignity and social justice as they contributed to the struggle against Nazi Germany, Fascist Italy, and militarist Japan during the Second World War, stood against the repressive policies of the second Red Scare, supported the civil rights movement, and, later, opposed U.S. imperialism in Vietnam, Cuba, Chile, El Salvador, and Nicaragua.

Based on the fictionalized account of the experiences of Spanish Civil War volunteer Abe Osheroff and his comrades, *!Brigadistas!* tells the story of one of the central dramas in the anti-fascist struggle of the 1930s. In so doing, it inspires new generations of activists as they further the principles of social justice and human dignity that motivated the volunteers of the Abraham Lincoln Brigade.

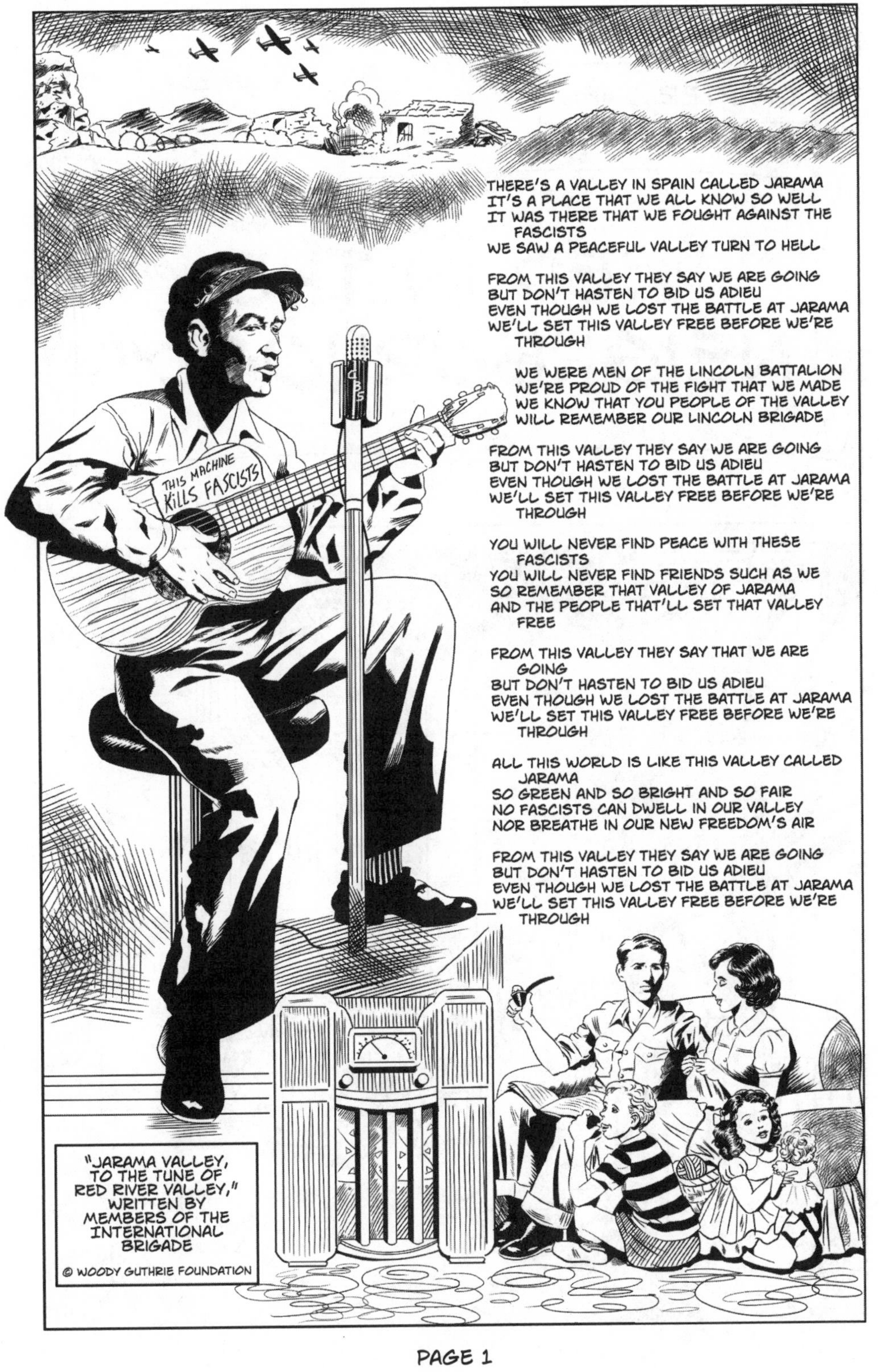
THERE'S A VALLEY IN SPAIN CALLED JARAMA
IT'S A PLACE THAT WE ALL KNOW SO WELL
IT WAS THERE THAT WE FOUGHT AGAINST THE FASCISTS
WE SAW A PEACEFUL VALLEY TURN TO HELL

FROM THIS VALLEY THEY SAY WE ARE GOING
BUT DON'T HASTEN TO BID US ADIEU
EVEN THOUGH WE LOST THE BATTLE AT JARAMA
WE'LL SET THIS VALLEY FREE BEFORE WE'RE THROUGH

WE WERE MEN OF THE LINCOLN BATTALION
WE'RE PROUD OF THE FIGHT THAT WE MADE
WE KNOW THAT YOU PEOPLE OF THE VALLEY
WILL REMEMBER OUR LINCOLN BRIGADE

FROM THIS VALLEY THEY SAY WE ARE GOING
BUT DON'T HASTEN TO BID US ADIEU
EVEN THOUGH WE LOST THE BATTLE AT JARAMA
WE'LL SET THIS VALLEY FREE BEFORE WE'RE THROUGH

YOU WILL NEVER FIND PEACE WITH THESE FASCISTS
YOU WILL NEVER FIND FRIENDS SUCH AS WE
SO REMEMBER THAT VALLEY OF JARAMA
AND THE PEOPLE THAT'LL SET THAT VALLEY FREE

FROM THIS VALLEY THEY SAY THAT WE ARE GOING
BUT DON'T HASTEN TO BID US ADIEU
EVEN THOUGH WE LOST THE BATTLE AT JARAMA
WE'LL SET THIS VALLEY FREE BEFORE WE'RE THROUGH

ALL THIS WORLD IS LIKE THIS VALLEY CALLED JARAMA
SO GREEN AND SO BRIGHT AND SO FAIR
NO FASCISTS CAN DWELL IN OUR VALLEY
NOR BREATHE IN OUR NEW FREEDOM'S AIR

FROM THIS VALLEY THEY SAY WE ARE GOING
BUT DON'T HASTEN TO BID US ADIEU
EVEN THOUGH WE LOST THE BATTLE AT JARAMA
WE'LL SET THIS VALLEY FREE BEFORE WE'RE THROUGH
THIS MACHINE KILLS FASCISTS
CBS
"JARAMA VALLEY, TO THE TUNE OF RED RIVER VALLEY," WRITTEN BY MEMBERS OF THE INTERNATIONAL BRIGADE
© WOODY GUTHRIE FOUNDATION

CHAPTER ONE:

"RED IN THE NEIGHBORHOOD"

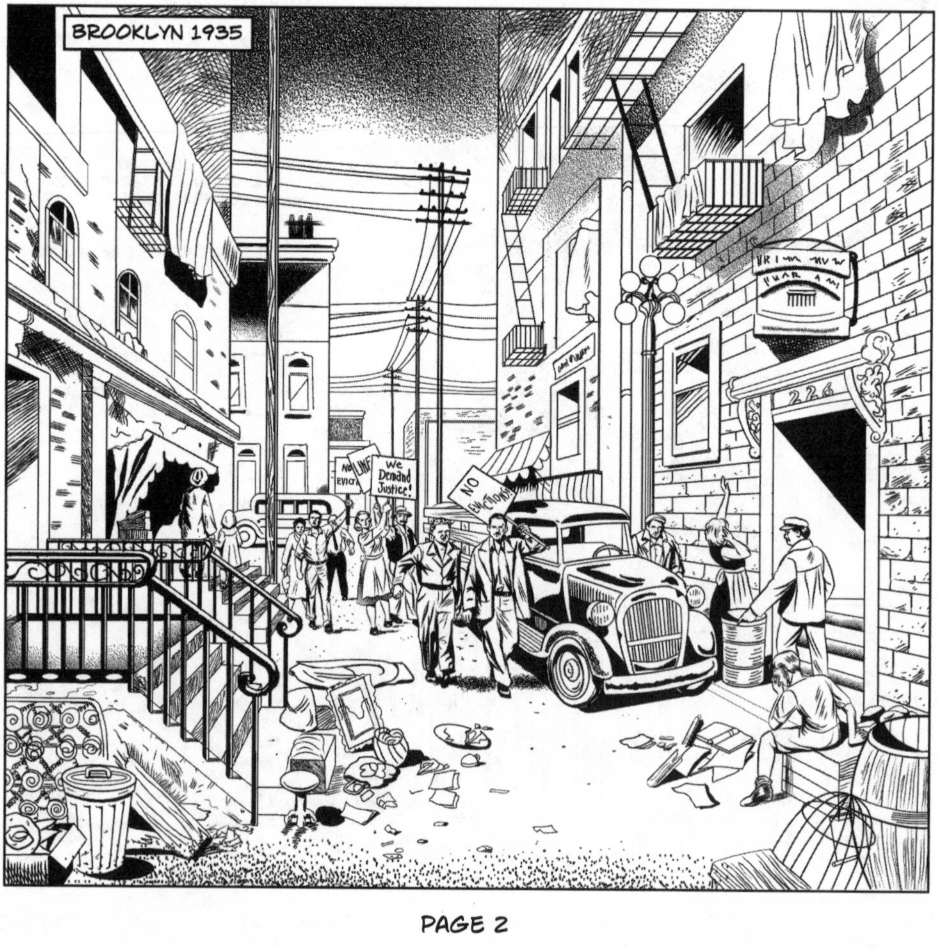
BROOKLYN 1935
We Demand Justice!
NO EVICTIONS
226

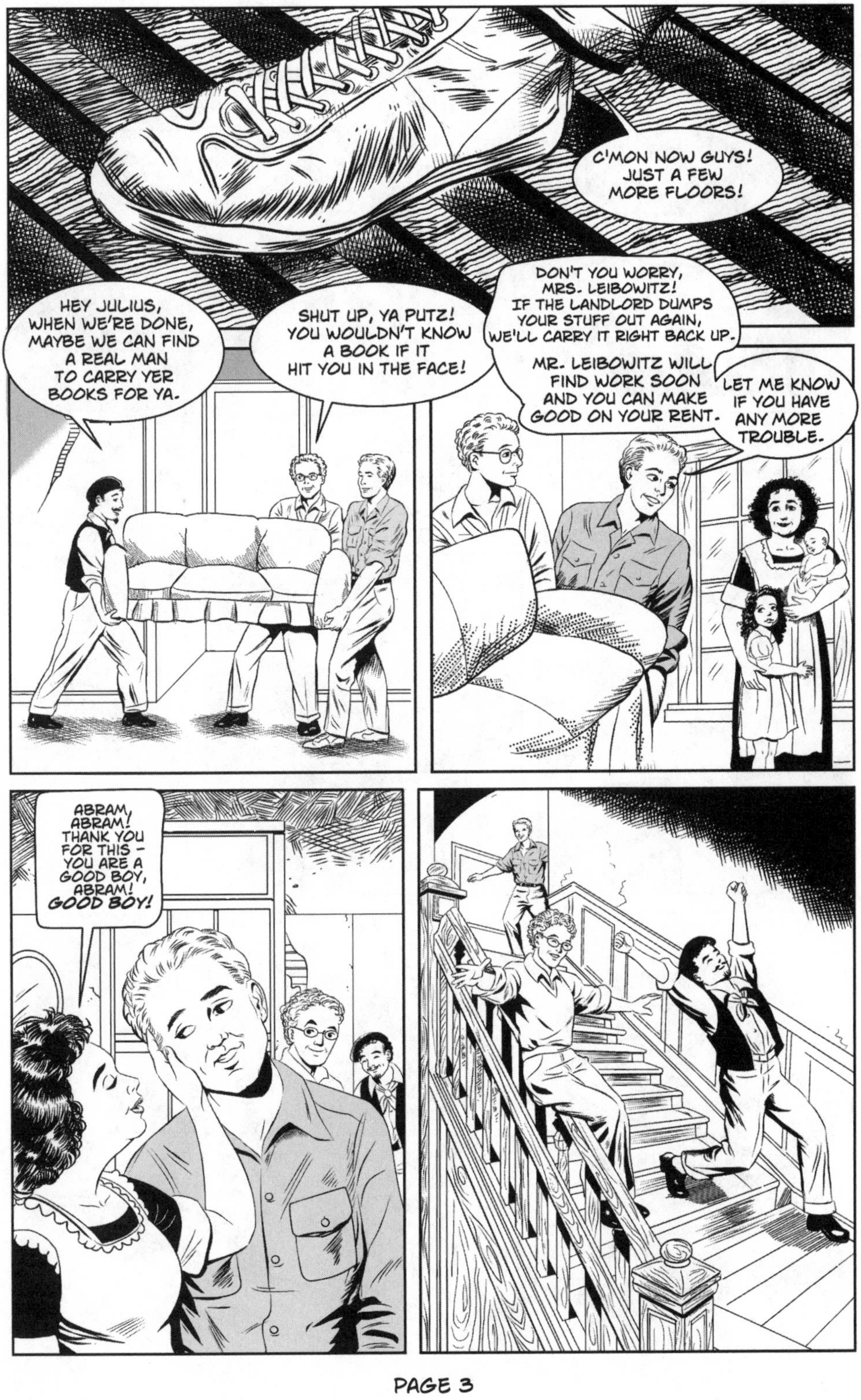
C'MON NOW GUYS! JUST A FEW MORE FLOORS!
HEY JULIUS, WHEN WE'RE DONE, MAYBE WE CAN FIND A REAL MAN TO CARRY YER BOOKS FOR YA.
SHUT UP, YA PUTZ! YOU WOULDN'T KNOW A BOOK IF IT HIT YOU IN THE FACE!
DON'T YOU WORRY, MRS. LEIBOWITZ! IF THE LANDLORD DUMPS YOUR STUFF OUT AGAIN, WE'LL CARRY IT RIGHT BACK UP.
MR. LEIBOWITZ WILL FIND WORK SOON AND YOU CAN MAKE GOOD ON YOUR RENT.
LET ME KNOW IF YOU HAVE ANY MORE TROUBLE.
ABRAM, ABRAM! THANK YOU FOR THIS - YOU ARE A GOOD BOY, ABRAM! GOOD BOY!

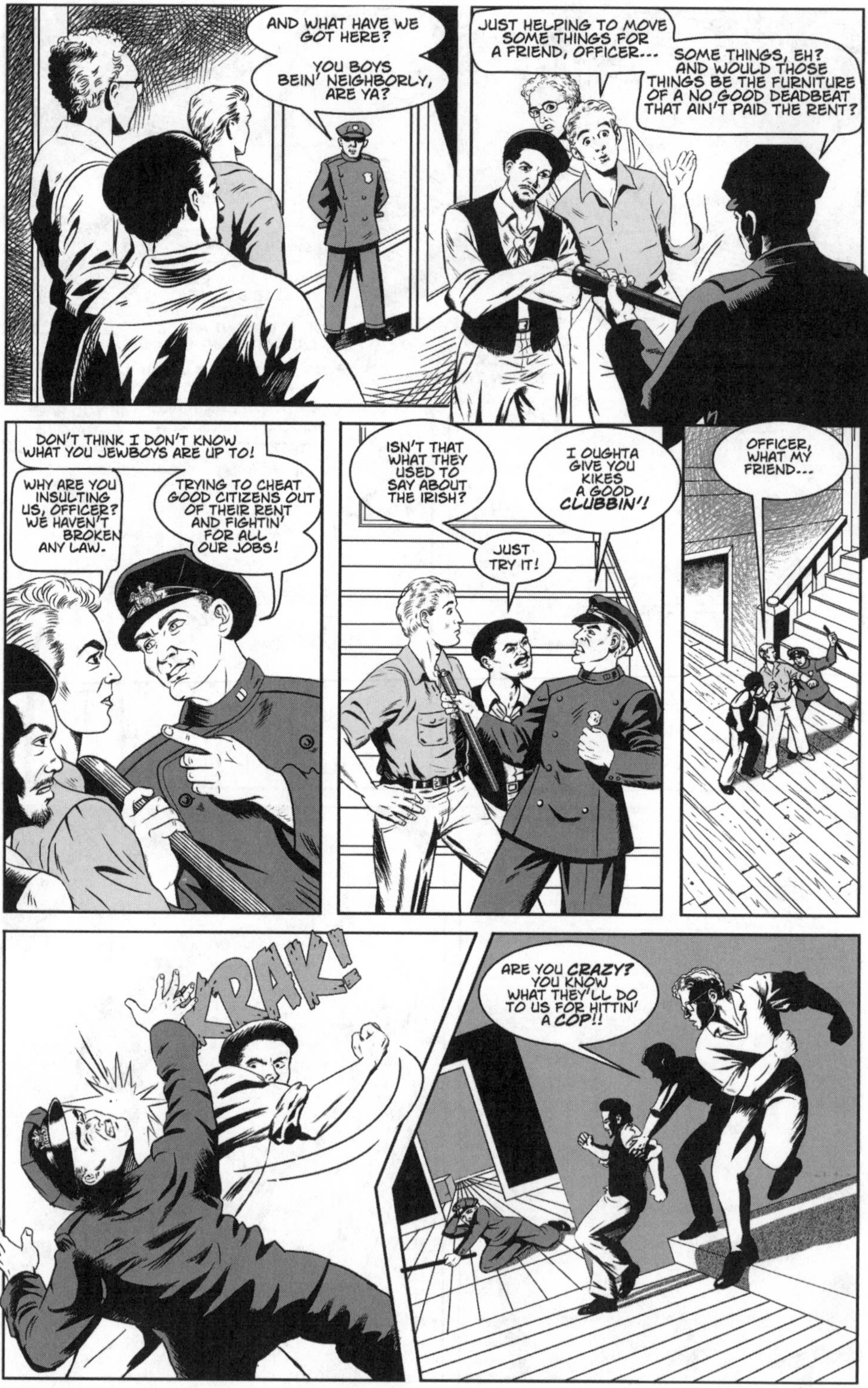
AND WHAT HAVE WE GOT HERE?
YOU BOYS BEIN' NEIGHBORLY, ARE YA?
JUST HELPING TO MOVE SOME THINGS FOR A FRIEND, OFFICER...
SOME THINGS, EH? AND WOULD THOSE THINGS BE THE FURNITURE OF A NO GOOD DEADBEAT THAT AIN'T PAID THE RENT?
DON'T THINK I DON'T KNOW WHAT YOU JEWBOYS ARE UP TO!
WHY ARE YOU INSULTING US, OFFICER? WE HAVEN'T BROKEN ANY LAW.
TRYING TO CHEAT GOOD CITIZENS OUT OF THEIR RENT AND FIGHTIN' FOR ALL OUR JOBS!
ISN'T THAT WHAT THEY USED TO SAY ABOUT THE IRISH?
I OUGHTA GIVE YOU KIKES A GOOD CLUBBIN'!
JUST TRY IT!
OFFICER, WHAT MY FRIEND...
KRAK!
ARE YOU CRAZY? YOU KNOW WHAT THEY'LL DO TO US FOR HITTIN' A COP!!

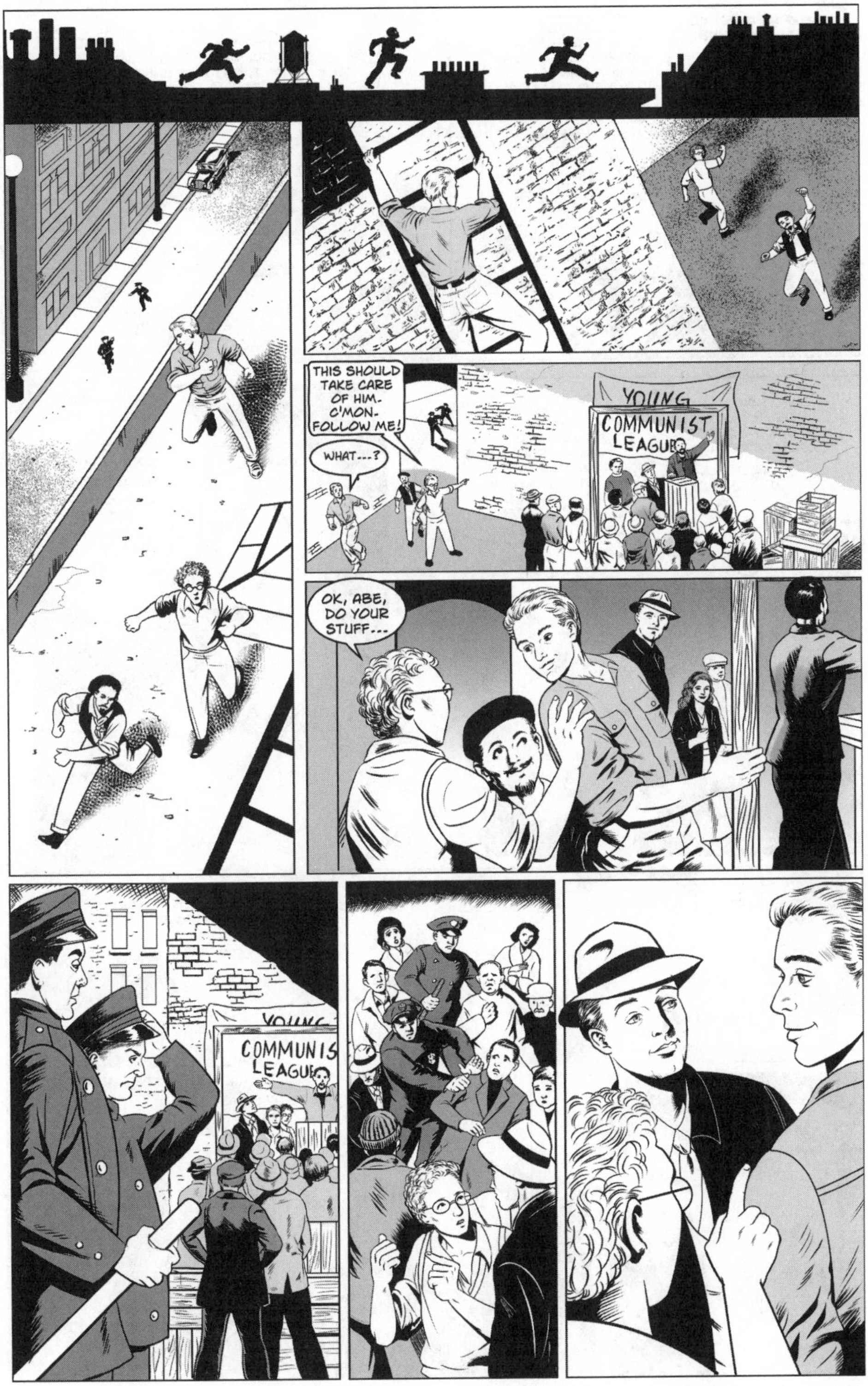
THIS SHOULD TAKE CARE OF HIM. C'MON- FOLLOW ME!
WHAT...?
YOUNG COMMUNIST LEAGUE
OK, ABE, DO YOUR STUFF...
YOUNG COMMUNIST LEAGUE

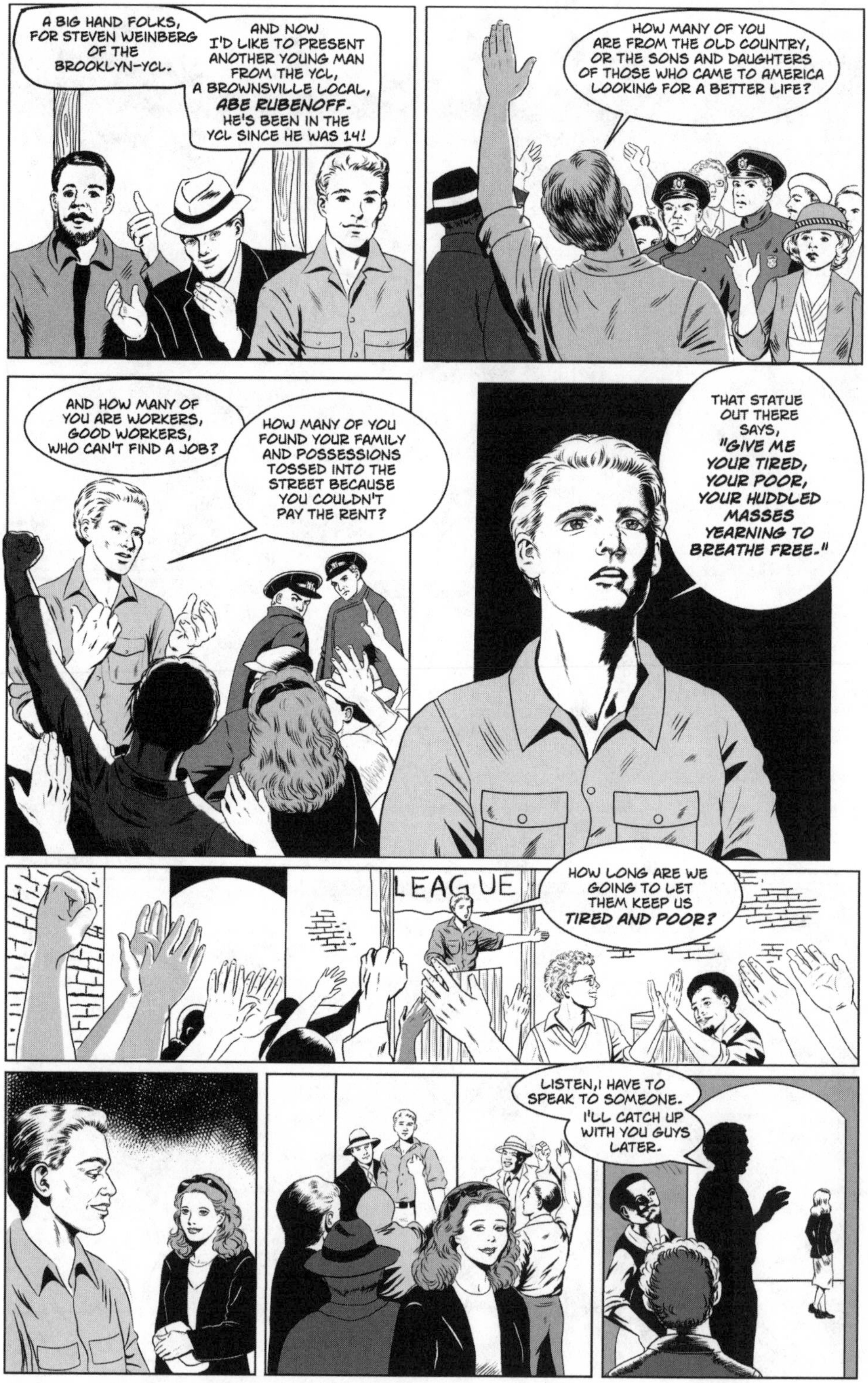
A BIG HAND FOLKS, FOR STEVEN WEINBERG OF THE BROOKLYN-YCL.
AND NOW I'D LIKE TO PRESENT ANOTHER YOUNG MAN FROM THE YCL, A BROWNSVILLE LOCAL, ABE RUBENOFF. HE'S BEEN IN THE YCL SINCE HE WAS 14!
HOW MANY OF YOU ARE FROM THE OLD COUNTRY, OR THE SONS AND DAUGHTERS OF THOSE WHO CAME TO AMERICA LOOKING FOR A BETTER LIFE?
AND HOW MANY OF YOU ARE WORKERS, GOOD WORKERS, WHO CAN'T FIND A JOB?
HOW MANY OF YOU FOUND YOUR FAMILY AND POSSESSIONS TOSSED INTO THE STREET BECAUSE YOU COULDN'T PAY THE RENT?
THAT STATUE OUT THERE SAYS, "GIVE ME YOUR TIRED, YOUR POOR, YOUR HUDDLED MASSES YEARNING TO BREATHE FREE."
LEAGUE
HOW LONG ARE WE GOING TO LET THEM KEEP US TIRED AND POOR?
LISTEN, I HAVE TO SPEAK TO SOMEONE. I'LL CATCH UP WITH YOU GUYS LATER.

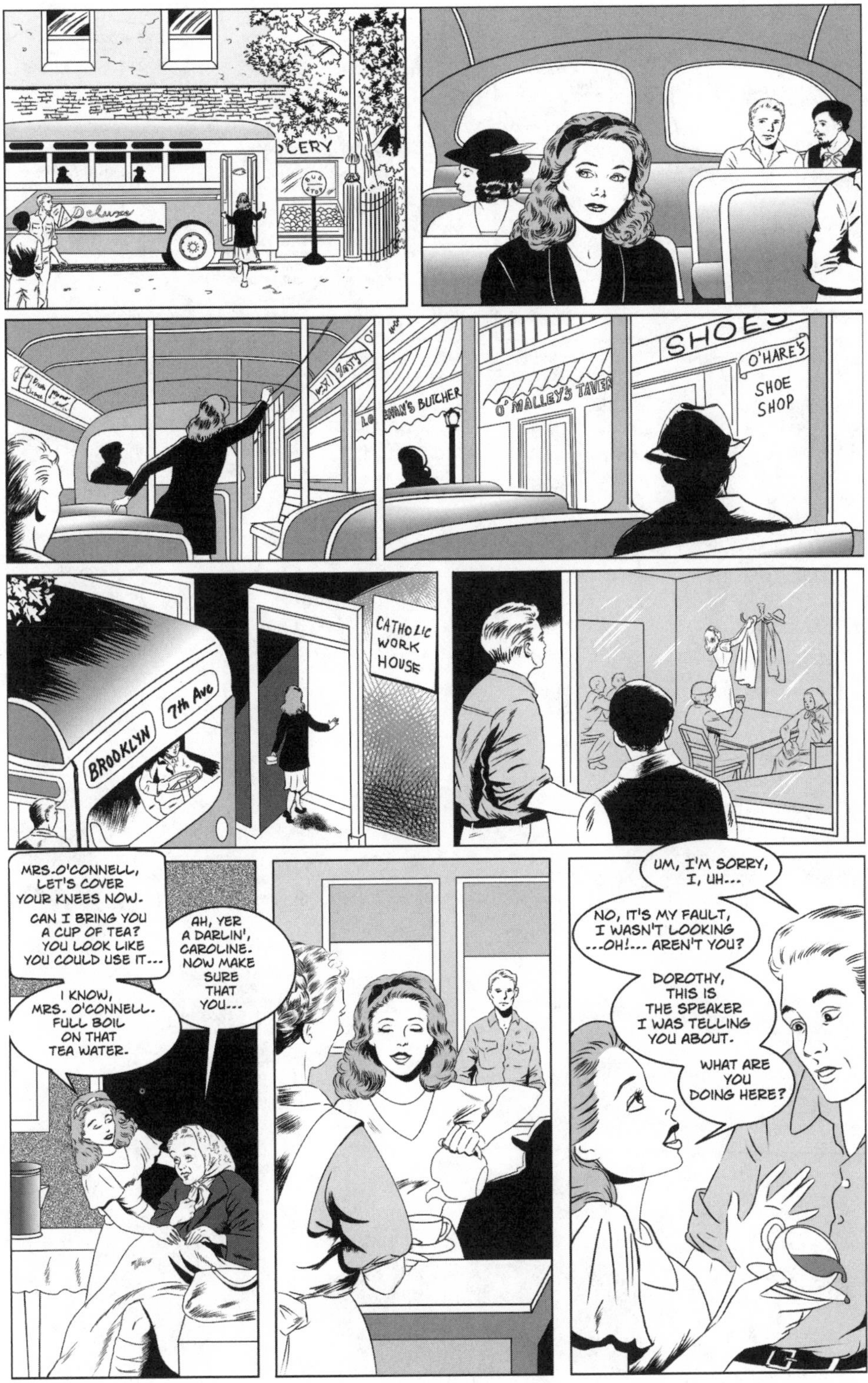
SHOES
O'HARE'S
SHOE SHOP
BROOKLYN
7th Ave
CATHOLIC WORK HOUSE
MRS. O'CONNELL, LET'S COVER YOUR KNEES NOW.
CAN I BRING YOU A CUP OF TEA? YOU LOOK LIKE YOU COULD USE IT...
AH, YER A DARLIN', CAROLINE. NOW MAKE SURE THAT YOU...
I KNOW, MRS. O'CONNELL. FULL BOIL ON THAT TEA WATER.
UM, I'M SORRY, I, UH...
NO, IT'S MY FAULT, I WASN'T LOOKING ...OH!... AREN'T YOU?
DOROTHY, THIS IS THE SPEAKER I WAS TELLING YOU ABOUT.
WHAT ARE YOU DOING HERE?

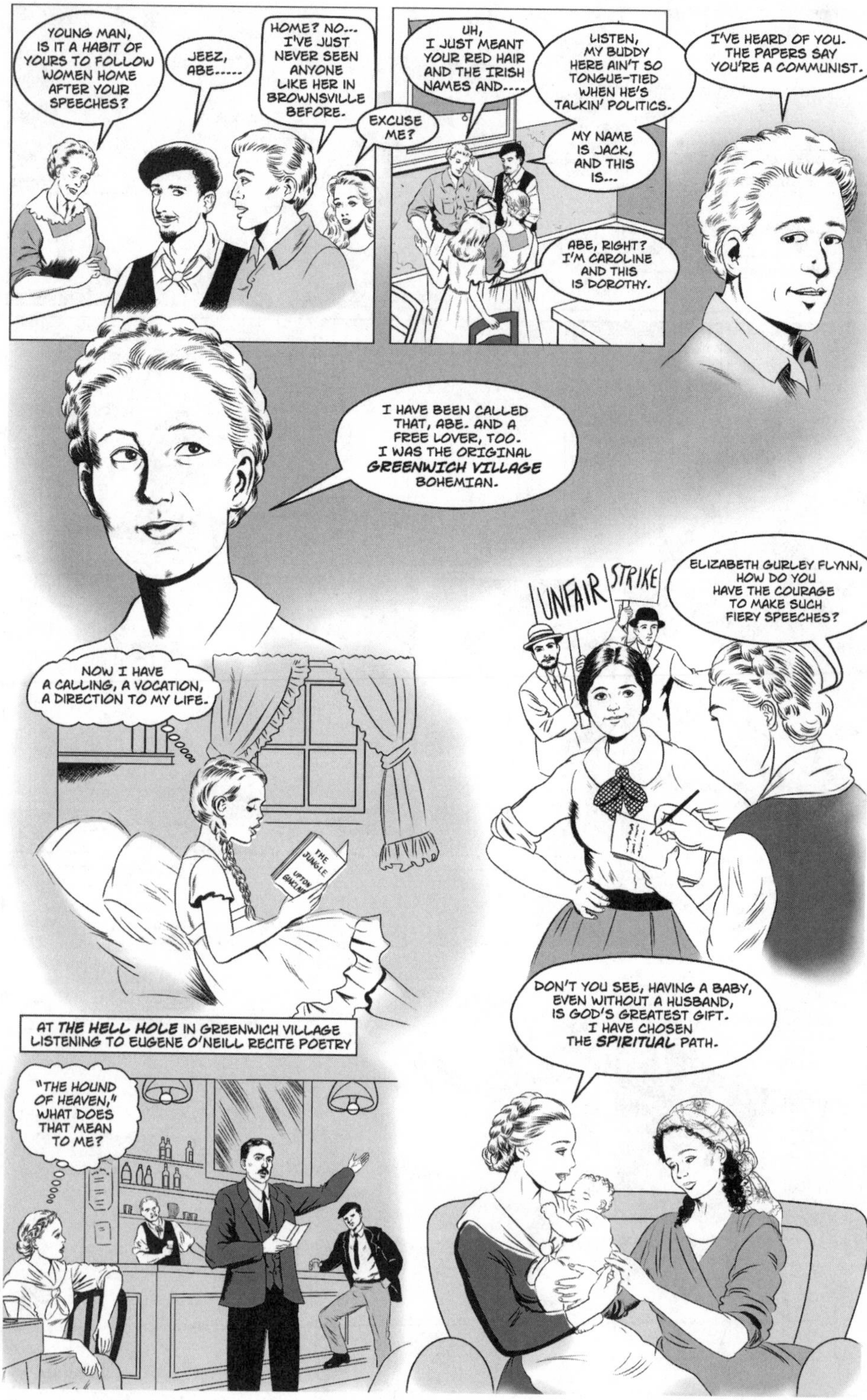
YOUNG MAN, IS IT A HABIT OF YOURS TO FOLLOW WOMEN HOME AFTER YOUR SPEECHES?
JEEZ, ABE.....
HOME? NO... I'VE JUST NEVER SEEN ANYONE LIKE HER IN BROWNSVILLE BEFORE.
EXCUSE ME?
UH, I JUST MEANT YOUR RED HAIR AND THE IRISH NAMES AND....
LISTEN, MY BUDDY HERE AIN'T SO TONGUE-TIED WHEN HE'S TALKIN' POLITICS.
MY NAME IS JACK, AND THIS IS...
ABE, RIGHT? I'M CAROLINE AND THIS IS DOROTHY.
I'VE HEARD OF YOU. THE PAPERS SAY YOU'RE A COMMUNIST.
I HAVE BEEN CALLED THAT, ABE. AND A FREE LOVER, TOO. I WAS THE ORIGINAL GREENWICH VILLAGE BOHEMIAN.
NOW I HAVE A CALLING, A VOCATION, A DIRECTION TO MY LIFE.
THE JUNGLE UPTON SINCLAIR
UNFAIR
STRIKE
ELIZABETH GURLEY FLYNN, HOW DO YOU HAVE THE COURAGE TO MAKE SUCH FIERY SPEECHES?
AT THE HELL HOLE IN GREENWICH VILLAGE LISTENING TO EUGENE O'NEILL RECITE POETRY
"THE HOUND OF HEAVEN," WHAT DOES THAT MEAN TO ME?
DON'T YOU SEE, HAVING A BABY, EVEN WITHOUT A HUSBAND, IS GOD'S GREATEST GIFT. I HAVE CHOSEN THE SPIRITUAL PATH.

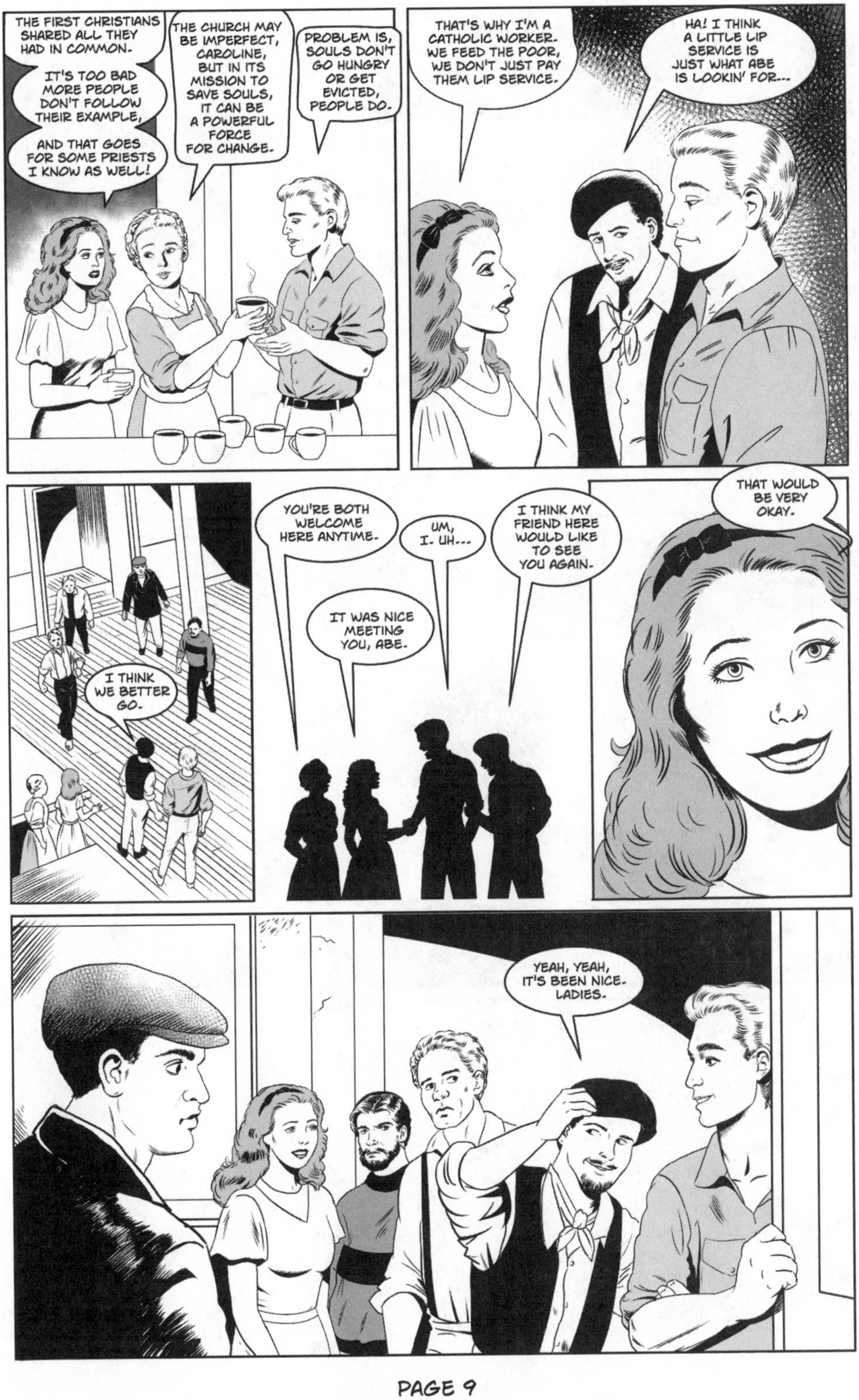

THE FIRST CHRISTIANS SHARED ALL THEY HAD IN COMMON.
IT'S TOO BAD MORE PEOPLE DON'T FOLLOW THEIR EXAMPLE,
AND THAT GOES FOR SOME PRIESTS I KNOW AS WELL!
THE CHURCH MAY BE IMPERFECT, CAROLINE, BUT IN ITS MISSION TO SAVE SOULS, IT CAN BE A POWERFUL FORCE FOR CHANGE.
PROBLEM IS, SOULS DON'T GO HUNGRY OR GET EVICTED, PEOPLE DO.
THAT'S WHY I'M A CATHOLIC WORKER. WE FEED THE POOR, WE DON'T JUST PAY THEM LIP SERVICE.
HA! I THINK A LITTLE LIP SERVICE IS JUST WHAT ABE IS LOOKIN' FOR...
I THINK WE BETTER GO.
YOU'RE BOTH WELCOME HERE ANYTIME.
UM, I. UH...
I THINK MY FRIEND HERE WOULD LIKE TO SEE YOU AGAIN.
IT WAS NICE MEETING YOU, ABE.
THAT WOULD BE VERY OKAY.
YEAH, YEAH, IT'S BEEN NICE. LADIES.

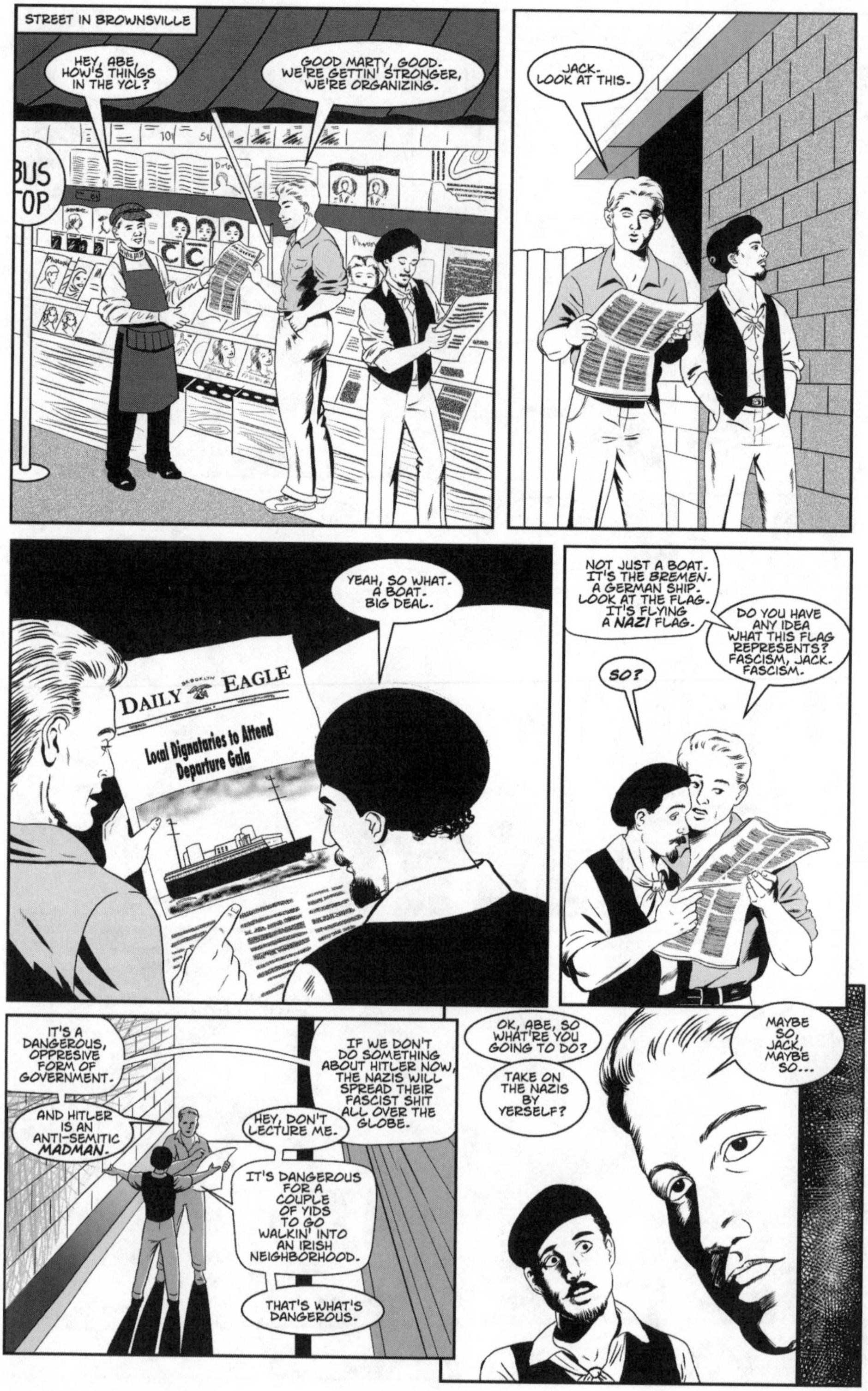
STREET IN BROWNSVILLE
HEY, ABE, HOW'S THINGS IN THE YCL?
GOOD MARTY, GOOD. WE'RE GETTIN' STRONGER, WE'RE ORGANIZING.
BUS STOP
JACK- LOOK AT THIS-
YEAH, SO WHAT. A BOAT. BIG DEAL.
BROOKLYN DAILY EAGLE
Local Dignitaries to Attend Departure Gala
NOT JUST A BOAT. IT'S THE *BREMEN*. A GERMAN SHIP. LOOK AT THE FLAG. IT'S FLYING A ***NAZI*** FLAG.
DO YOU HAVE ANY IDEA WHAT THIS FLAG REPRESENTS? FASCISM, JACK. FASCISM.
SO?
IT'S A DANGEROUS, OPPRESIVE FORM OF GOVERNMENT.
IF WE DON'T DO SOMETHING ABOUT HITLER NOW, THE NAZIS WILL SPREAD THEIR FASCIST SHIT ALL OVER THE GLOBE.
AND HITLER IS AN ANTI-SEMITIC ***MADMAN***.
HEY, DON'T LECTURE ME.
IT'S DANGEROUS FOR A COUPLE OF YIDS TO GO WALKIN' INTO AN IRISH NEIGHBORHOOD.
THAT'S WHAT'S DANGEROUS.
OK, ABE, SO WHAT'RE YOU GOING TO DO?
TAKE ON THE NAZIS BY YERSELF?
MAYBE SO, JACK, MAYBE SO...

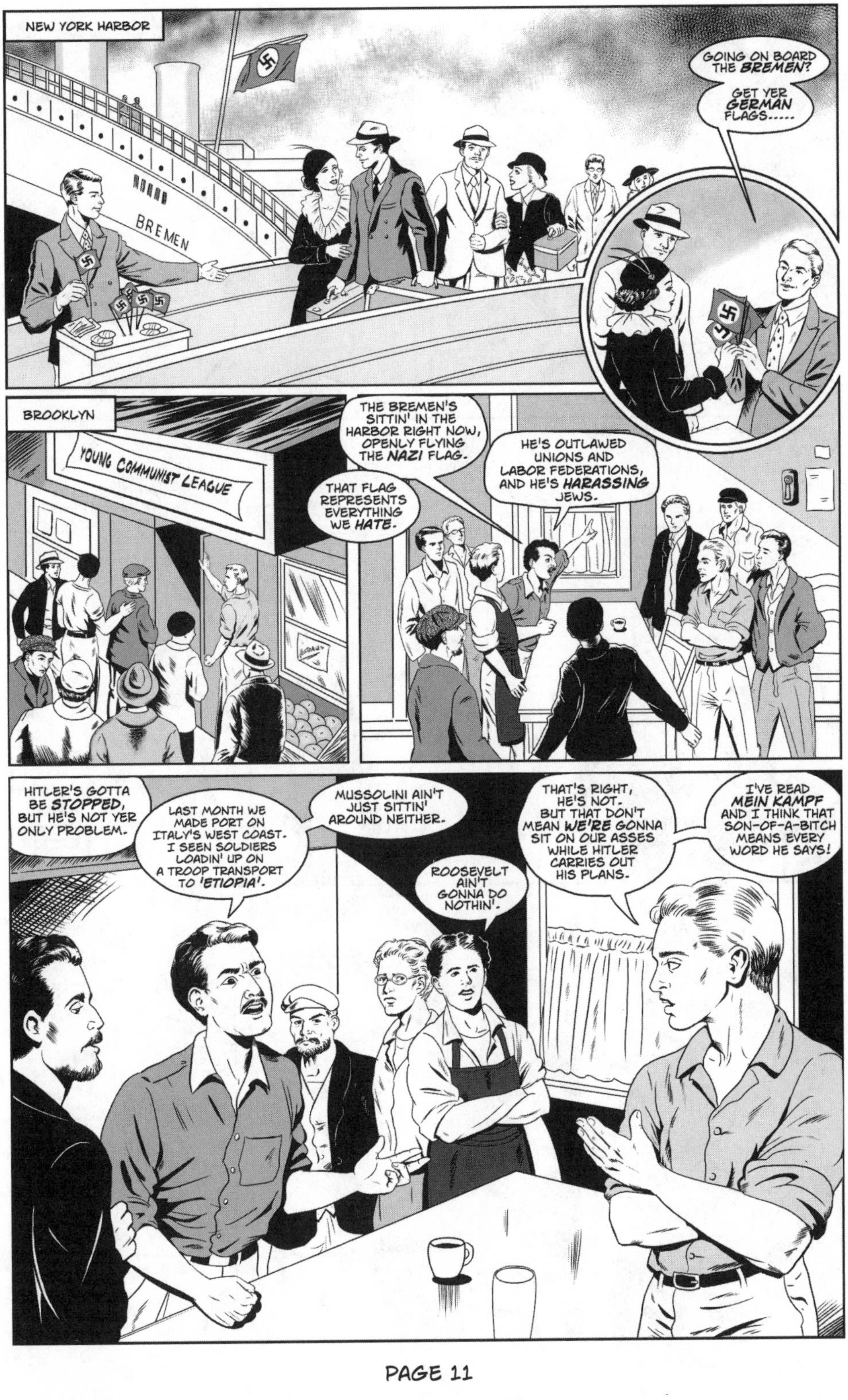
NEW YORK HARBOR
BREMEN
GOING ON BOARD THE BREMEN?
GET YER GERMAN FLAGS......
BROOKLYN
YOUNG COMMUNIST LEAGUE
THE BREMEN'S SITTIN' IN THE HARBOR RIGHT NOW, OPENLY FLYING THE NAZI FLAG.
THAT FLAG REPRESENTS EVERYTHING WE HATE.
HE'S OUTLAWED UNIONS AND LABOR FEDERATIONS, AND HE'S HARASSING JEWS.
HITLER'S GOTTA BE STOPPED, BUT HE'S NOT YER ONLY PROBLEM.
LAST MONTH WE MADE PORT ON ITALY'S WEST COAST. I SEEN SOLDIERS LOADIN' UP ON A TROOP TRANSPORT TO 'ETIOPIA'.
MUSSOLINI AIN'T JUST SITTIN' AROUND NEITHER.
ROOSEVELT AIN'T GONNA DO NOTHIN'.
THAT'S RIGHT, HE'S NOT. BUT THAT DON'T MEAN WE'RE GONNA SIT ON OUR ASSES WHILE HITLER CARRIES OUT HIS PLANS.
I'VE READ MEIN KAMPF AND I THINK THAT SON-OF-A-BITCH MEANS EVERY WORD HE SAYS!

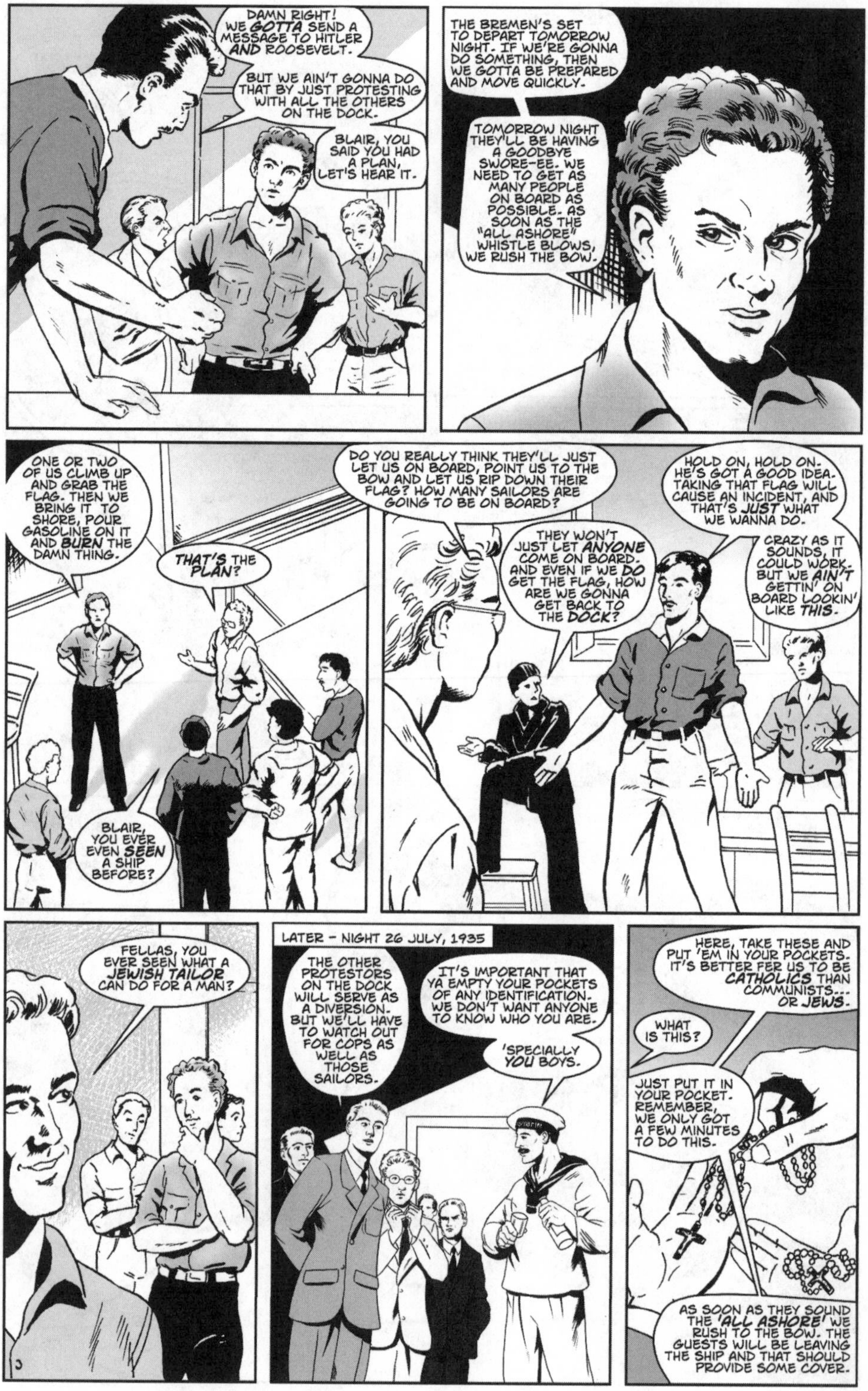
DAMN RIGHT! WE GOTTA SEND A MESSAGE TO HITLER AND ROOSEVELT.
BUT WE AIN'T GONNA DO THAT BY JUST PROTESTING WITH ALL THE OTHERS ON THE DOCK.
BLAIR, YOU SAID YOU HAD A PLAN, LET'S HEAR IT.
THE BREMEN'S SET TO DEPART TOMORROW NIGHT. IF WE'RE GONNA DO SOMETHING, THEN WE GOTTA BE PREPARED AND MOVE QUICKLY.
TOMORROW NIGHT THEY'LL BE HAVING A GOODBYE SWORE-EE. WE NEED TO GET AS MANY PEOPLE ON BOARD AS POSSIBLE. AS SOON AS THE "ALL ASHORE" WHISTLE BLOWS, WE RUSH THE BOW.
ONE OR TWO OF US CLIMB UP AND GRAB THE FLAG. THEN WE BRING IT TO SHORE, POUR GASOLINE ON IT AND BURN THE DAMN THING.
THAT'S THE PLAN?
BLAIR, YOU EVER EVEN SEEN A SHIP BEFORE?
DO YOU REALLY THINK THEY'LL JUST LET US ON BOARD, POINT US TO THE BOW AND LET US RIP DOWN THEIR FLAG? HOW MANY SAILORS ARE GOING TO BE ON BOARD?
THEY WON'T JUST LET ANYONE COME ON BOARD. AND EVEN IF WE DO GET THE FLAG, HOW ARE WE GONNA GET BACK TO THE DOCK?
HOLD ON, HOLD ON. HE'S GOT A GOOD IDEA. TAKING THAT FLAG WILL CAUSE AN INCIDENT, AND THAT'S JUST WHAT WE WANNA DO.
CRAZY AS IT SOUNDS, IT COULD WORK. BUT WE AIN'T GETTIN' ON BOARD LOOKIN' LIKE THIS.
FELLAS, YOU EVER SEEN WHAT A JEWISH TAILOR CAN DO FOR A MAN?
LATER - NIGHT 26 JULY, 1935
THE OTHER PROTESTORS ON THE DOCK WILL SERVE AS A DIVERSION. BUT WE'LL HAVE TO WATCH OUT FOR COPS AS WELL AS THOSE SAILORS.
IT'S IMPORTANT THAT YA EMPTY YOUR POCKETS OF ANY IDENTIFICATION. WE DON'T WANT ANYONE TO KNOW WHO YOU ARE.
'SPECIALLY YOU BOYS.
HERE, TAKE THESE AND PUT 'EM IN YOUR POCKETS. IT'S BETTER FER US TO BE CATHOLICS THAN COMMUNISTS... OR JEWS.
WHAT IS THIS?
JUST PUT IT IN YOUR POCKET. REMEMBER, WE ONLY GOT A FEW MINUTES TO DO THIS.
AS SOON AS THEY SOUND THE 'ALL ASHORE' WE RUSH TO THE BOW. THE GUESTS WILL BE LEAVING THE SHIP AND THAT SHOULD PROVIDE SOME COVER.

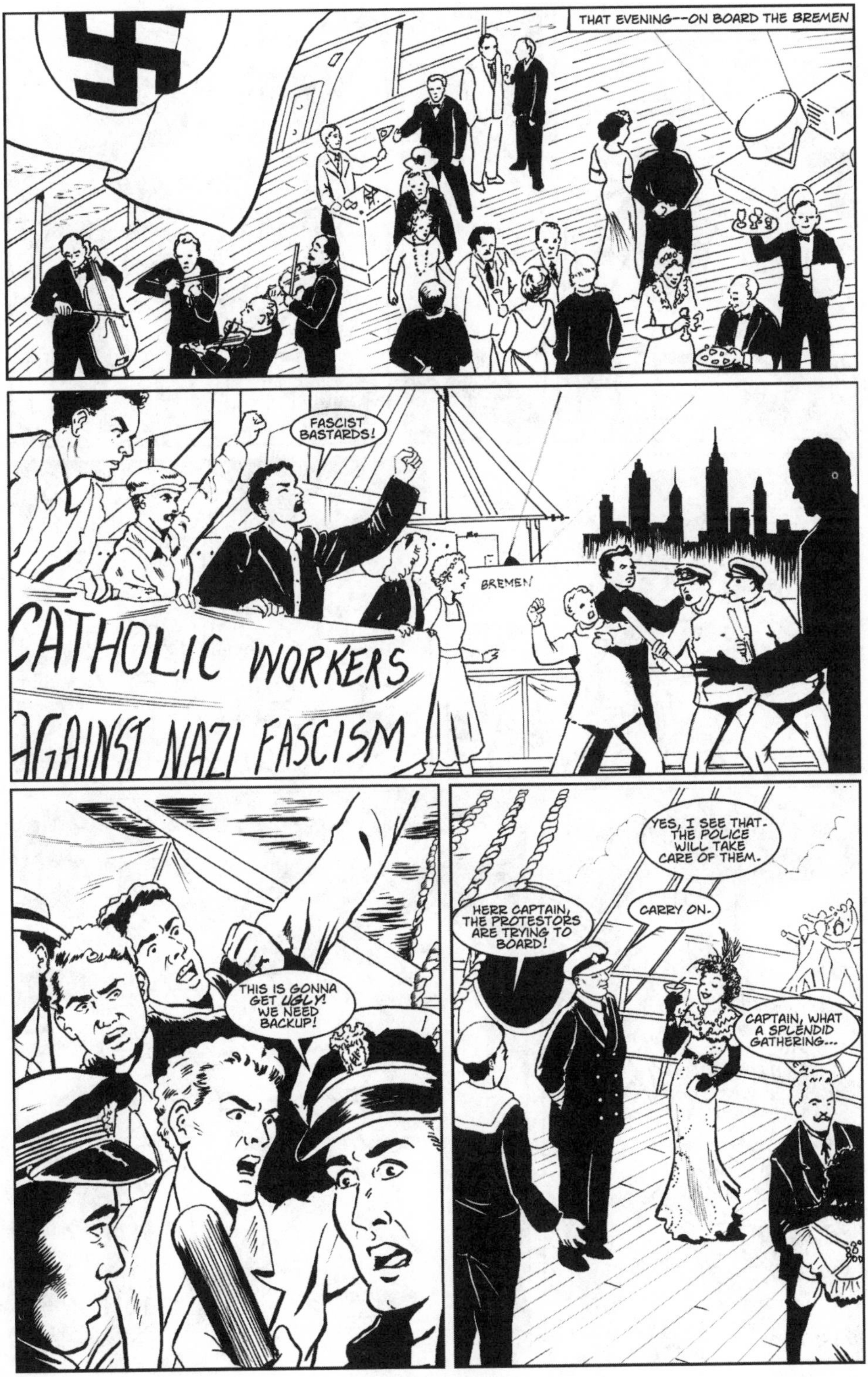
THAT EVENING--ON BOARD THE BREMEN
FASCIST BASTARDS!
BREMEN
CATHOLIC WORKERS AGAINST NAZI FASCISM
THIS IS GONNA GET UGLY! WE NEED BACKUP!
HERR CAPTAIN, THE PROTESTORS ARE TRYING TO BOARD!
YES, I SEE THAT. THE POLICE WILL TAKE CARE OF THEM.
CARRY ON.
CAPTAIN, WHAT A SPLENDID GATHERING...

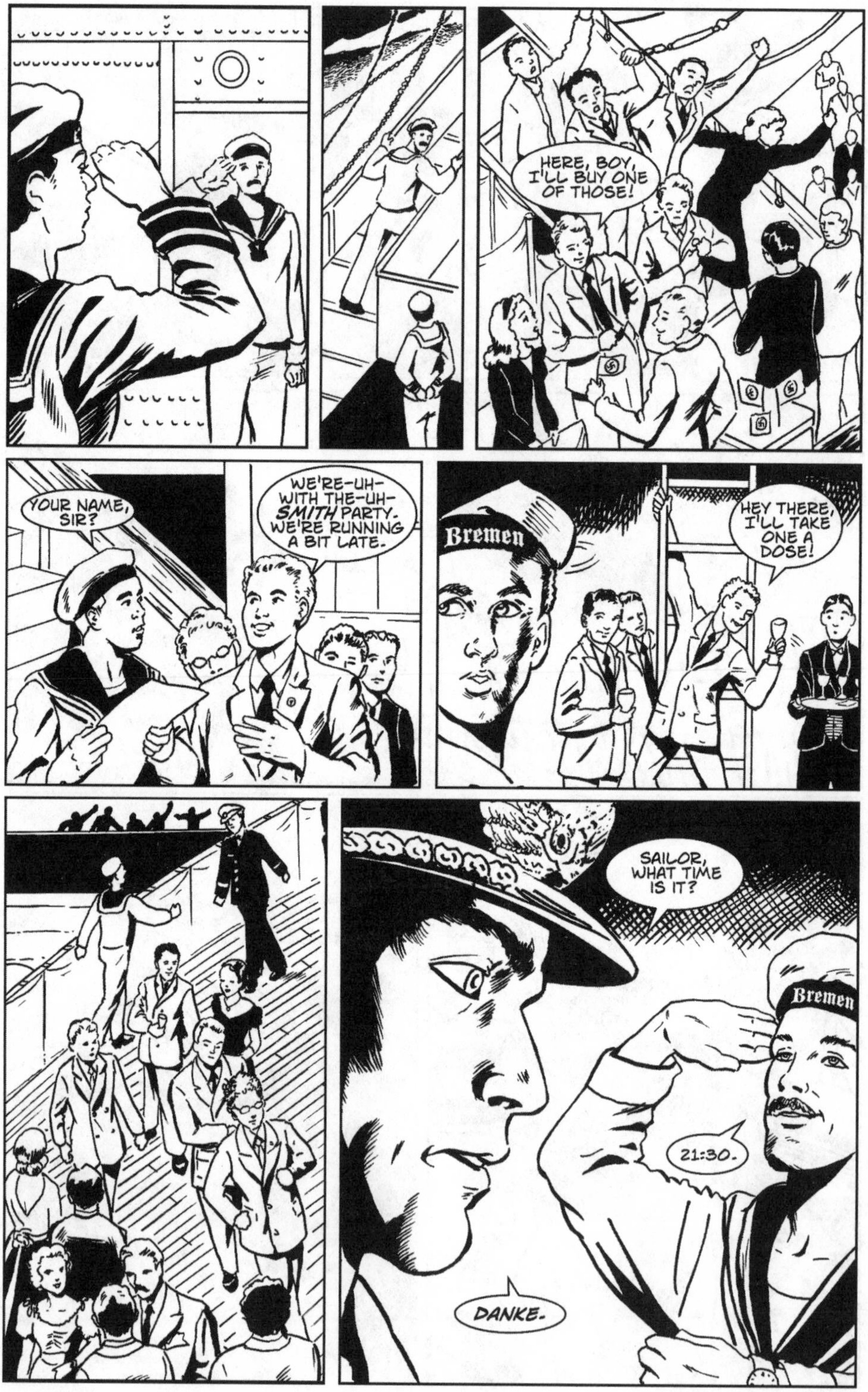
HERE, BOY, I'LL BUY ONE OF THOSE!
YOUR NAME, SIR?
WE'RE-UH-WITH THE-UH-SMITH PARTY. WE'RE RUNNING A BIT LATE.
Bremen
HEY THERE, I'LL TAKE ONE A DOSE!
SAILOR, WHAT TIME IS IT?
Bremen
21:30.
DANKE.

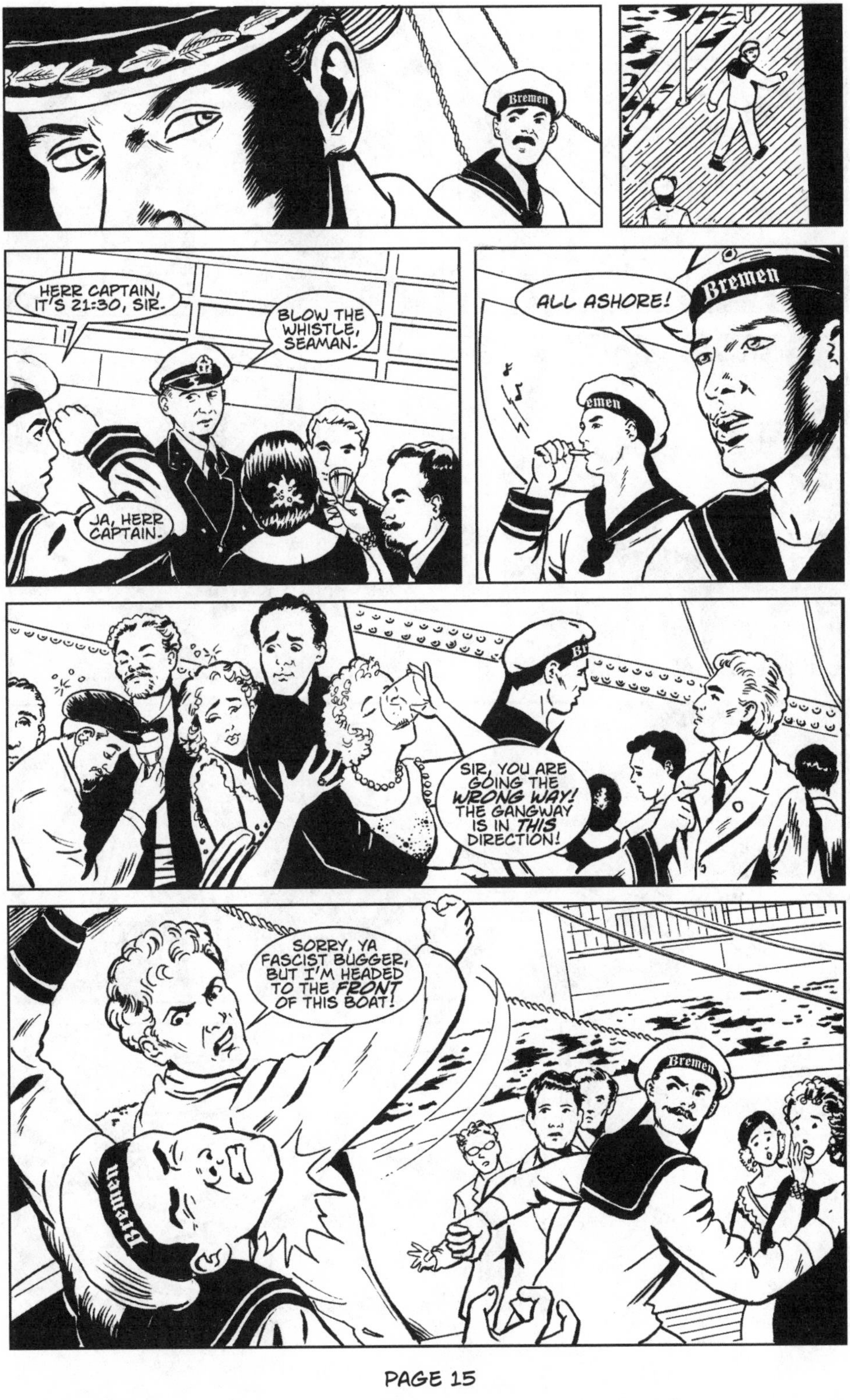
HERR CAPTAIN, IT'S 21:30, SIR.
BLOW THE WHISTLE, SEAMAN.
JA, HERR CAPTAIN.
Bremen
ALL ASHORE!
SIR, YOU ARE GOING THE WRONG WAY! THE GANGWAY IS IN THIS DIRECTION!
SORRY, YA FASCIST BUGGER, BUT I'M HEADED TO THE FRONT OF THIS BOAT!
Bremen

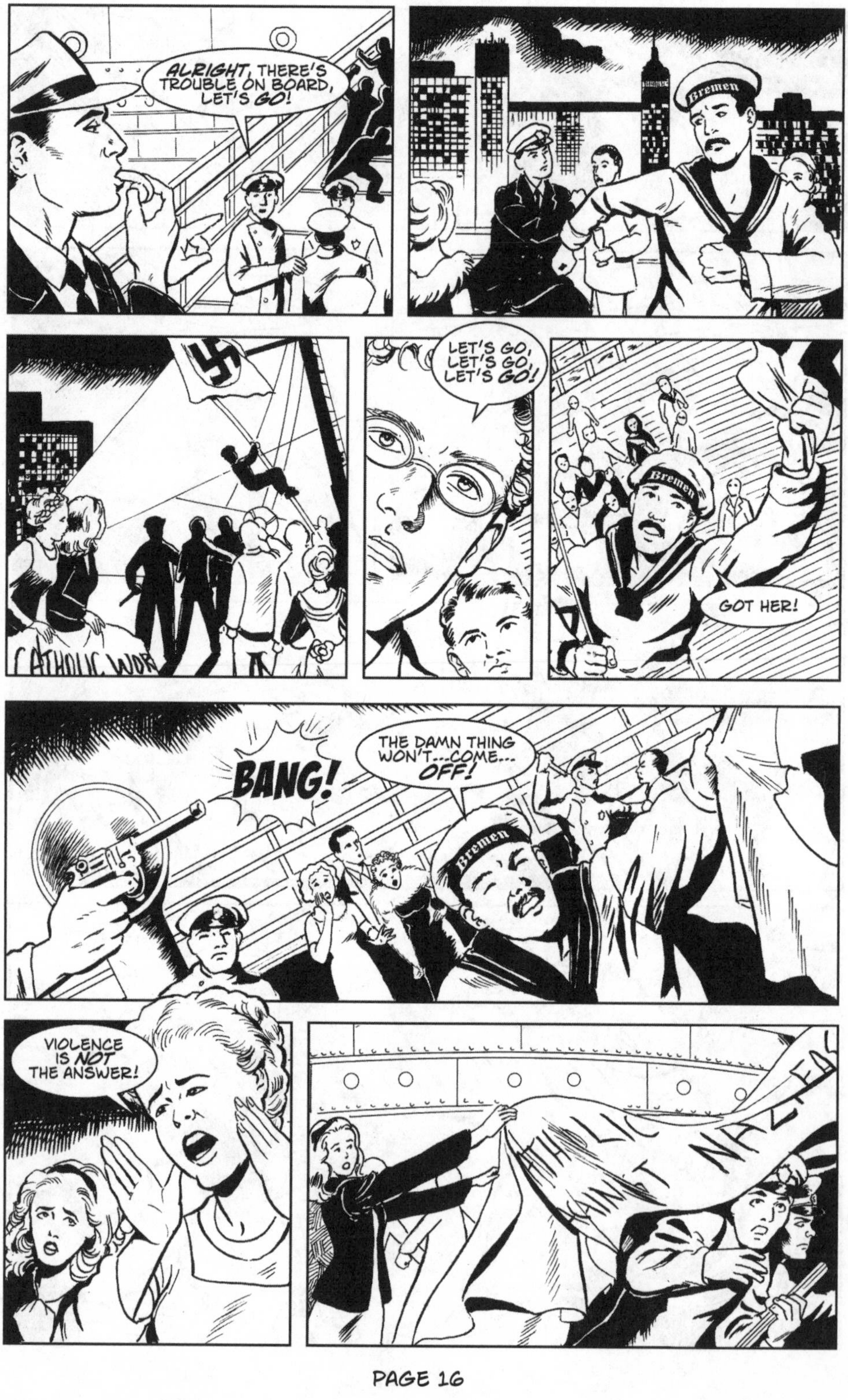
ALRIGHT, THERE'S TROUBLE ON BOARD, LET'S GO!
Bremen
CATHOLIC WOR
LET'S GO, LET'S GO, LET'S GO!
Bremen
GOT HER!
BANG!
THE DAMN THING WON'T...COME... OFF!
Bremen
VIOLENCE IS NOT THE ANSWER!

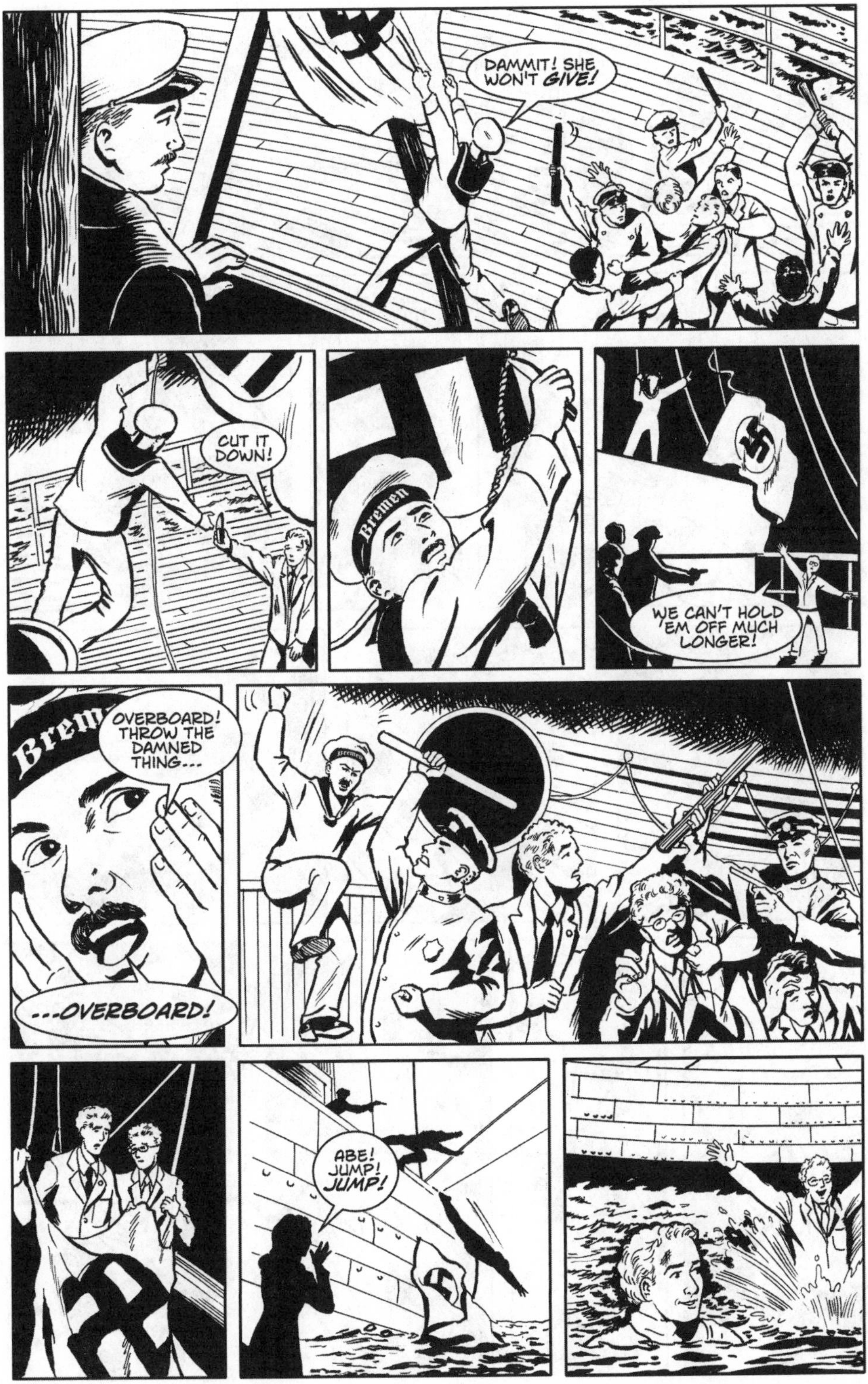
DAMMIT! SHE WON'T GIVE!
CUT IT DOWN!
WE CAN'T HOLD 'EM OFF MUCH LONGER!
OVERBOARD! THROW THE DAMNED THING...
...OVERBOARD!
ABE! JUMP! JUMP!

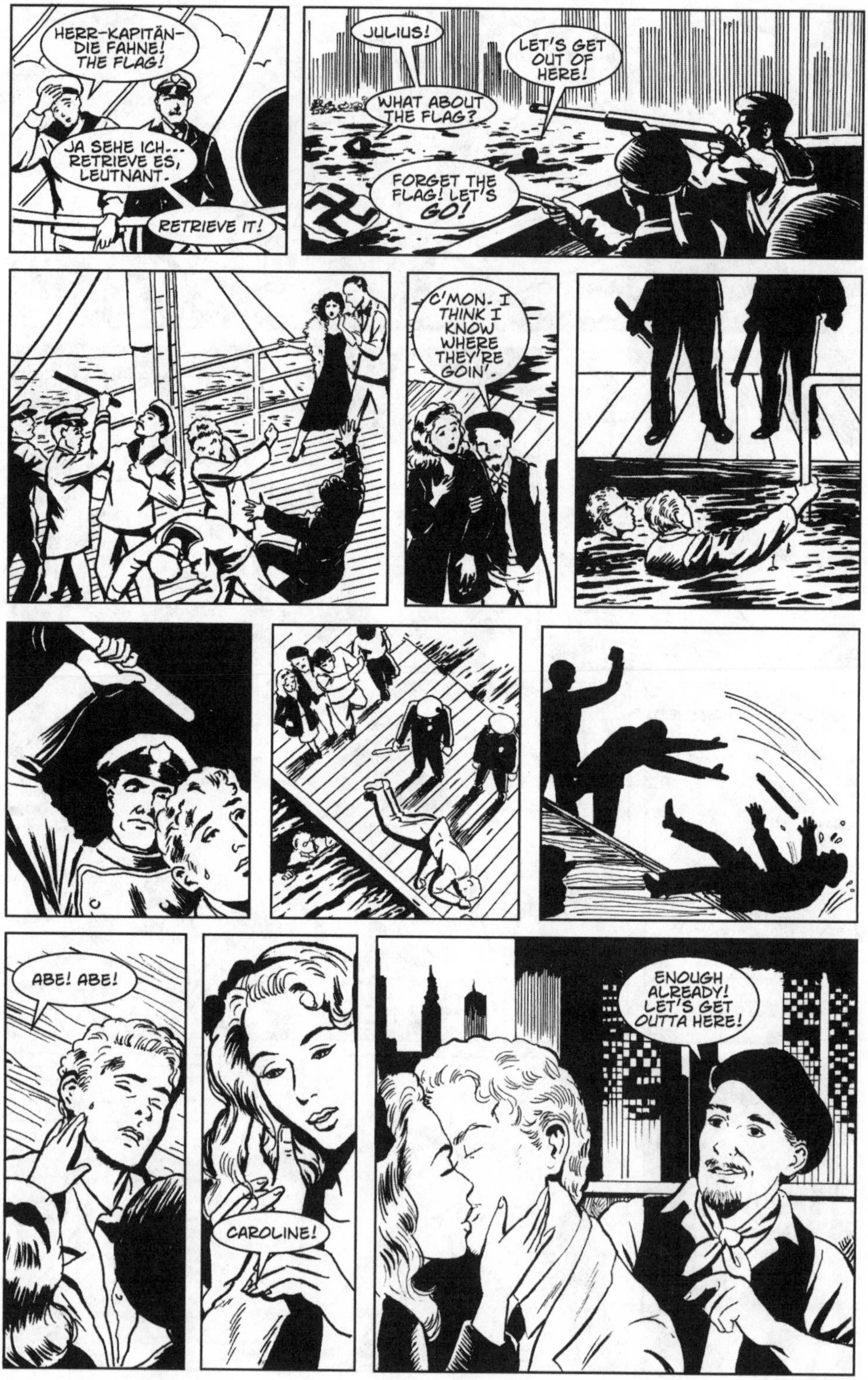
HERR-KAPITÄN-DIE FAHNE! THE FLAG!
JA SEHE ICH... RETRIEVE ES, LEUTNANT.
RETRIEVE IT!
JULIUS!
WHAT ABOUT THE FLAG?
LET'S GET OUT OF HERE!
FORGET THE FLAG! LET'S GO!
C'MON. I THINK I KNOW WHERE THEY'RE GOIN'.
ABE! ABE!
CAROLINE!
ENOUGH ALREADY! LET'S GET OUTTA HERE!

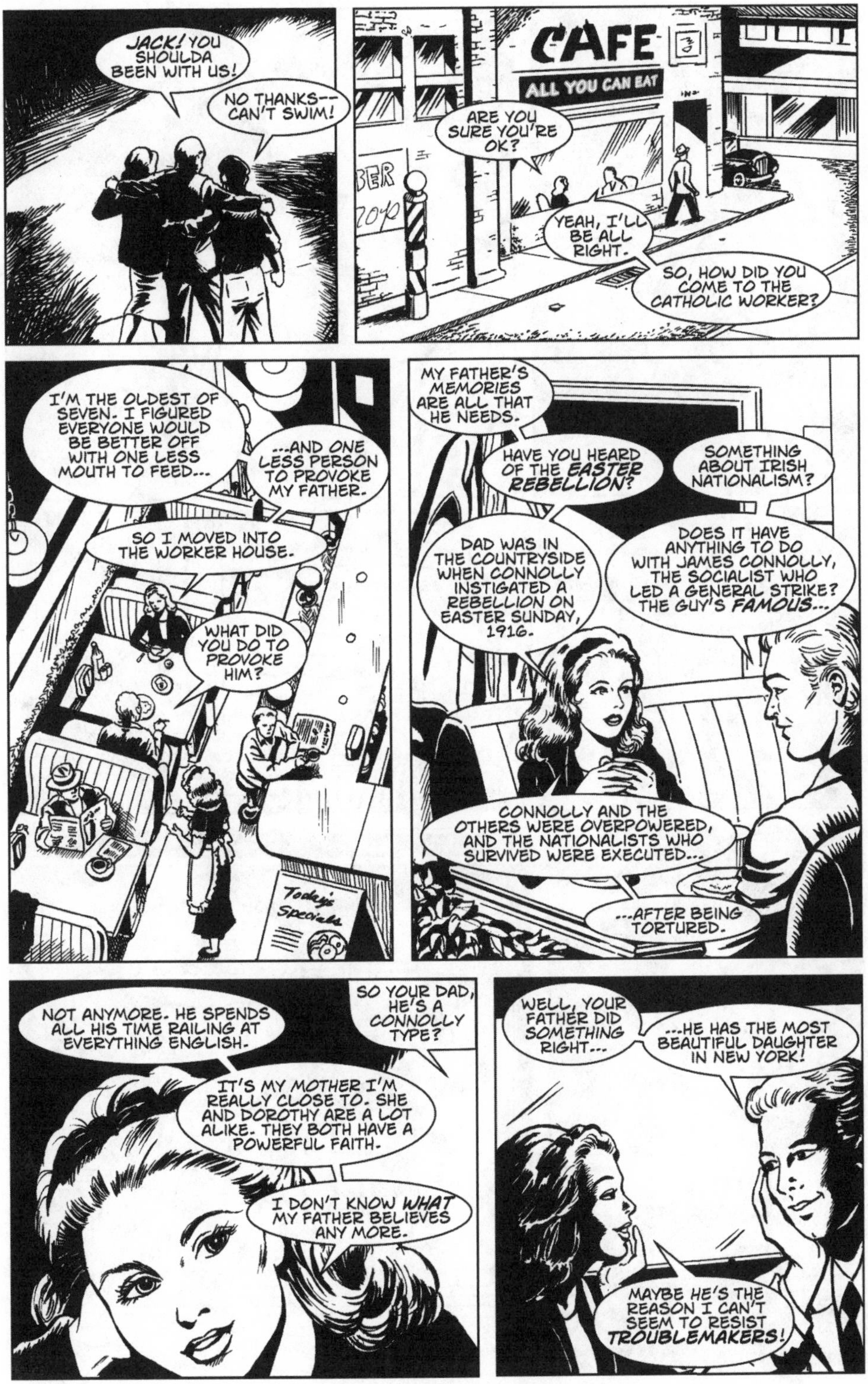
JACK! YOU SHOULDA BEEN WITH US!
NO THANKS-- CAN'T SWIM!
CAFE
ALL YOU CAN EAT
ARE YOU SURE YOU'RE OK?
YEAH, I'LL BE ALL RIGHT.
SO, HOW DID YOU COME TO THE CATHOLIC WORKER?
I'M THE OLDEST OF SEVEN. I FIGURED EVERYONE WOULD BE BETTER OFF WITH ONE LESS MOUTH TO FEED...
...AND ONE LESS PERSON TO PROVOKE MY FATHER.
SO I MOVED INTO THE WORKER HOUSE.
WHAT DID YOU DO TO PROVOKE HIM?
Today's Specials
MY FATHER'S MEMORIES ARE ALL THAT HE NEEDS.
HAVE YOU HEARD OF THE EASTER REBELLION?
SOMETHING ABOUT IRISH NATIONALISM?
DAD WAS IN THE COUNTRYSIDE WHEN CONNOLLY INSTIGATED A REBELLION ON EASTER SUNDAY, 1916.
DOES IT HAVE ANYTHING TO DO WITH JAMES CONNOLLY, THE SOCIALIST WHO LED A GENERAL STRIKE? THE GUY'S FAMOUS...
CONNOLLY AND THE OTHERS WERE OVERPOWERED, AND THE NATIONALISTS WHO SURVIVED WERE EXECUTED...
...AFTER BEING TORTURED.
NOT ANYMORE. HE SPENDS ALL HIS TIME RAILING AT EVERYTHING ENGLISH.
SO YOUR DAD, HE'S A CONNOLLY TYPE?
IT'S MY MOTHER I'M REALLY CLOSE TO. SHE AND DOROTHY ARE A LOT ALIKE. THEY BOTH HAVE A POWERFUL FAITH.
I DON'T KNOW WHAT MY FATHER BELIEVES ANY MORE.
WELL, YOUR FATHER DID SOMETHING RIGHT...
...HE HAS THE MOST BEAUTIFUL DAUGHTER IN NEW YORK!
MAYBE HE'S THE REASON I CAN'T SEEM TO RESIST TROUBLEMAKERS!

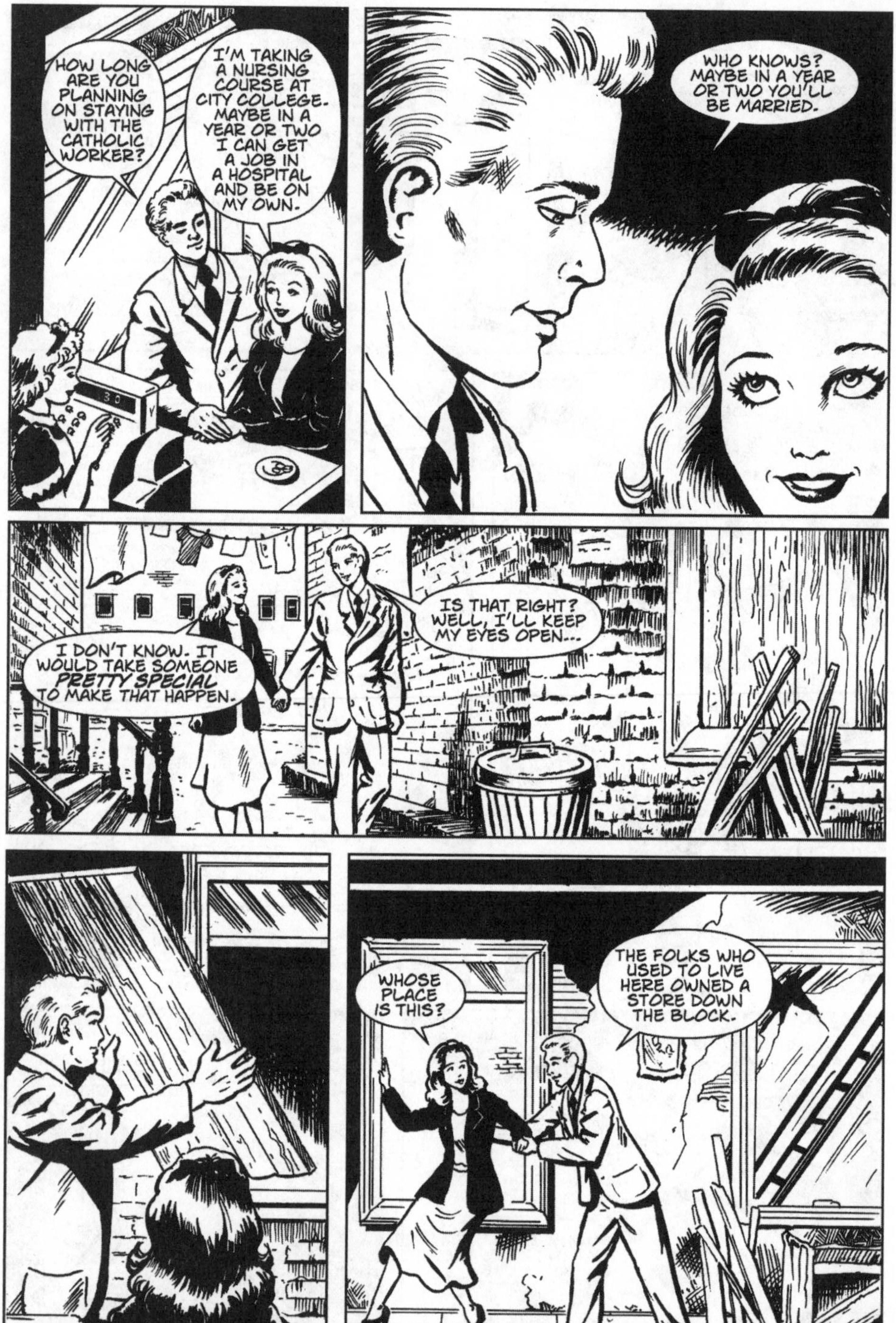

HOW LONG ARE YOU PLANNING ON STAYING WITH THE CATHOLIC WORKER?
I'M TAKING A NURSING COURSE AT CITY COLLEGE. MAYBE IN A YEAR OR TWO I CAN GET A JOB IN A HOSPITAL AND BE ON MY OWN.
WHO KNOWS? MAYBE IN A YEAR OR TWO YOU'LL BE MARRIED.
I DON'T KNOW. IT WOULD TAKE SOMEONE PRETTY SPECIAL TO MAKE THAT HAPPEN.
IS THAT RIGHT? WELL, I'LL KEEP MY EYES OPEN...
WHOSE PLACE IS THIS?
THE FOLKS WHO USED TO LIVE HERE OWNED A STORE DOWN THE BLOCK.

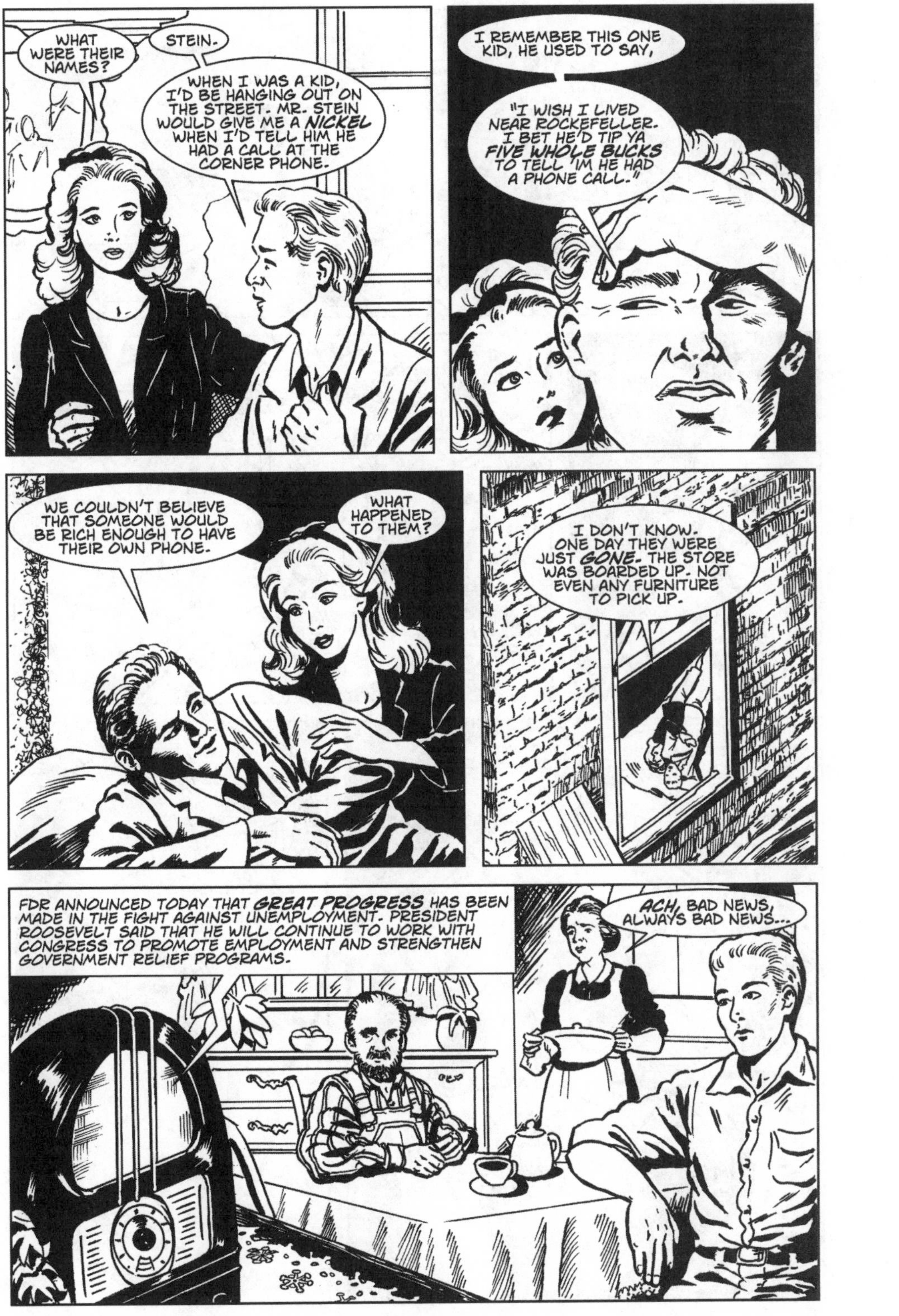
WHAT WERE THEIR NAMES?
STEIN.
WHEN I WAS A KID, I'D BE HANGING OUT ON THE STREET. MR. STEIN WOULD GIVE ME A NICKEL WHEN I'D TELL HIM HE HAD A CALL AT THE CORNER PHONE.
I REMEMBER THIS ONE KID, HE USED TO SAY,
"I WISH I LIVED NEAR ROCKEFELLER. I BET HE'D TIP YA FIVE WHOLE BUCKS TO TELL 'IM HE HAD A PHONE CALL."
WE COULDN'T BELIEVE THAT SOMEONE WOULD BE RICH ENOUGH TO HAVE THEIR OWN PHONE.
WHAT HAPPENED TO THEM?
I DON'T KNOW. ONE DAY THEY WERE JUST GONE. THE STORE WAS BOARDED UP. NOT EVEN ANY FURNITURE TO PICK UP.
FDR ANNOUNCED TODAY THAT GREAT PROGRESS HAS BEEN MADE IN THE FIGHT AGAINST UNEMPLOYMENT. PRESIDENT ROOSEVELT SAID THAT HE WILL CONTINUE TO WORK WITH CONGRESS TO PROMOTE EMPLOYMENT AND STRENGTHEN GOVERNMENT RELIEF PROGRAMS.
ACH, BAD NEWS, ALWAYS BAD NEWS...

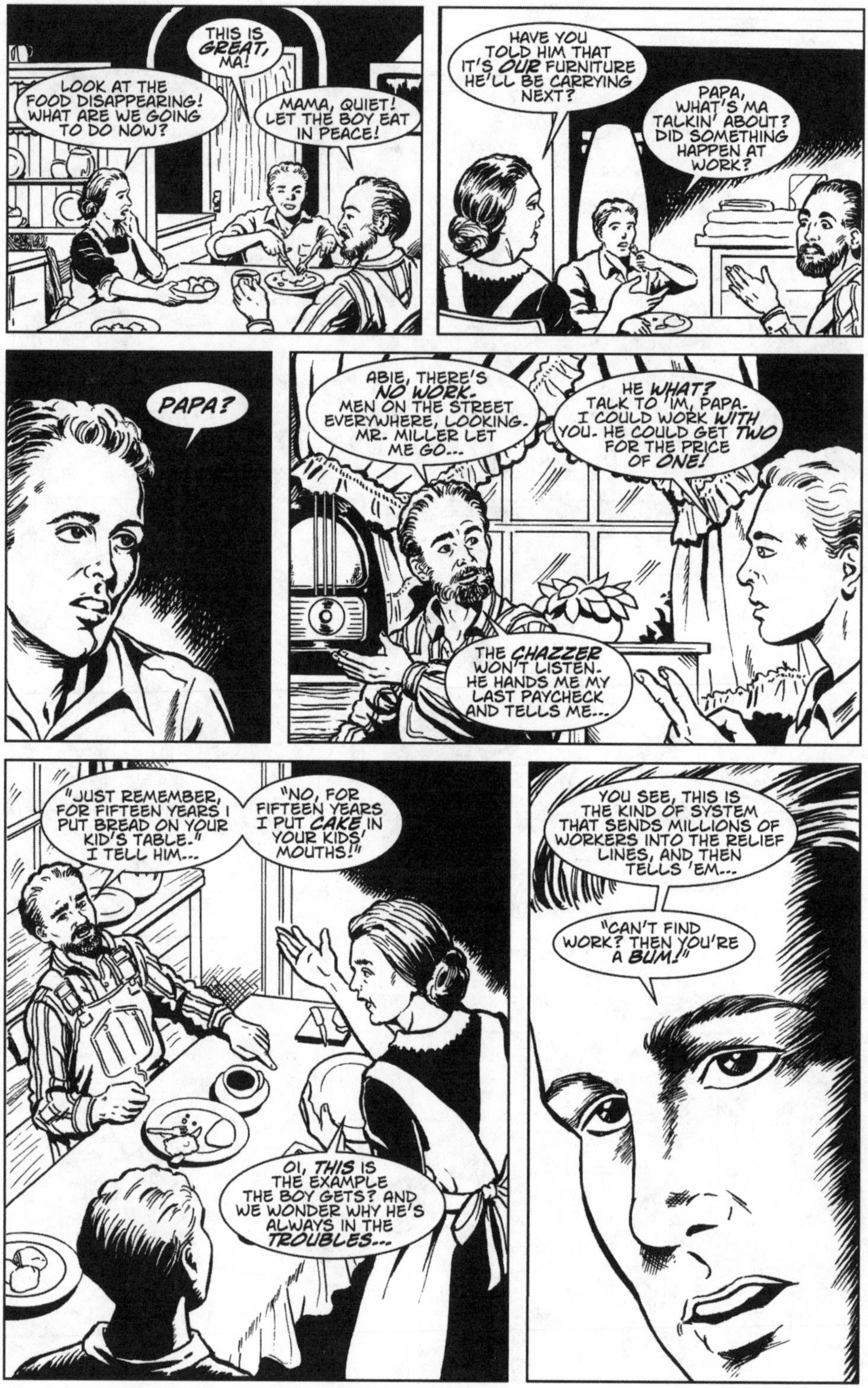
LOOK AT THE FOOD DISAPPEARING! WHAT ARE WE GOING TO DO NOW?
THIS IS *GREAT*, MA!
MAMA, QUIET! LET THE BOY EAT IN PEACE!
HAVE YOU TOLD HIM THAT IT'S *OUR* FURNITURE HE'LL BE CARRYING NEXT?
PAPA, WHAT'S MA TALKIN' ABOUT? DID SOMETHING HAPPEN AT WORK?
PAPA?
ABIE, THERE'S *NO WORK*. MEN ON THE STREET EVERYWHERE, LOOKING. MR. MILLER LET ME GO...
HE *WHAT?* TALK TO 'IM, PAPA. I COULD WORK *WITH* YOU. HE COULD GET *TWO* FOR THE PRICE OF *ONE!*
THE *CHAZZER* WON'T LISTEN. HE HANDS ME MY LAST PAYCHECK AND TELLS ME...
"JUST REMEMBER, FOR FIFTEEN YEARS I PUT BREAD ON YOUR KID'S TABLE." I TELL HIM...
"NO, FOR FIFTEEN YEARS I PUT *CAKE* IN YOUR KIDS' MOUTHS!"
OI, *THIS* IS THE EXAMPLE THE BOY GETS? AND WE WONDER WHY HE'S ALWAYS IN THE *TROUBLES...*
YOU SEE, THIS IS THE KIND OF SYSTEM THAT SENDS MILLIONS OF WORKERS INTO THE RELIEF LINES, AND THEN TELLS 'EM...
"CAN'T FIND WORK? THEN YOU'RE A *BUM!*"

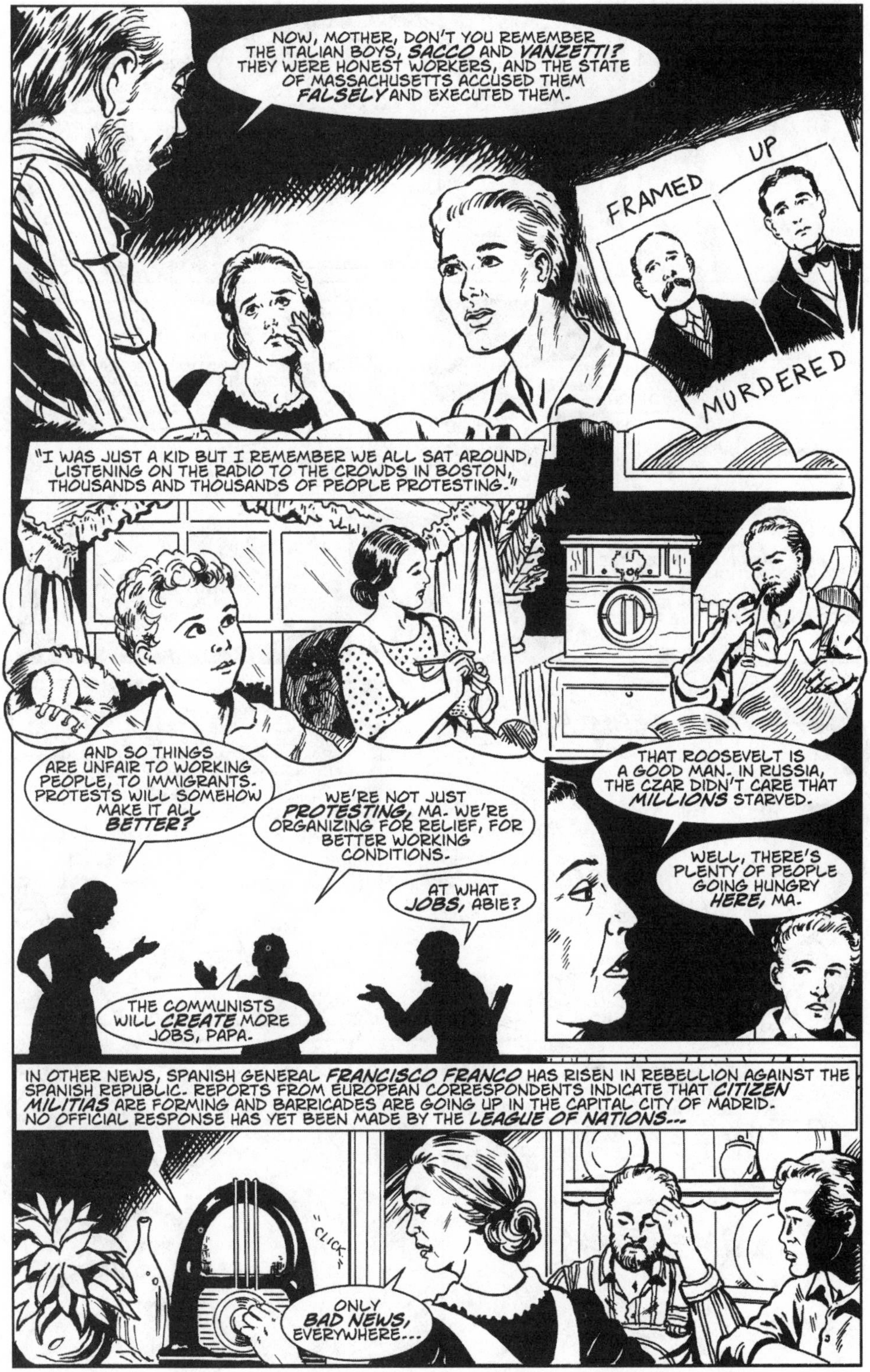
NOW, MOTHER, DON'T YOU REMEMBER THE ITALIAN BOYS, SACCO AND VANZETTI? THEY WERE HONEST WORKERS, AND THE STATE OF MASSACHUSETTS ACCUSED THEM FALSELY AND EXECUTED THEM.
FRAMED
UP
MURDERED
"I WAS JUST A KID BUT I REMEMBER WE ALL SAT AROUND, LISTENING ON THE RADIO TO THE CROWDS IN BOSTON, THOUSANDS AND THOUSANDS OF PEOPLE PROTESTING."
AND SO THINGS ARE UNFAIR TO WORKING PEOPLE, TO IMMIGRANTS. PROTESTS WILL SOMEHOW MAKE IT ALL BETTER?
WE'RE NOT JUST PROTESTING, MA. WE'RE ORGANIZING FOR RELIEF, FOR BETTER WORKING CONDITIONS.
AT WHAT JOBS, ABIE?
THE COMMUNISTS WILL CREATE MORE JOBS, PAPA.
THAT ROOSEVELT IS A GOOD MAN. IN RUSSIA, THE CZAR DIDN'T CARE THAT MILLIONS STARVED.
WELL, THERE'S PLENTY OF PEOPLE GOING HUNGRY HERE, MA.
IN OTHER NEWS, SPANISH GENERAL FRANCISCO FRANCO HAS RISEN IN REBELLION AGAINST THE SPANISH REPUBLIC. REPORTS FROM EUROPEAN CORRESPONDENTS INDICATE THAT CITIZEN MILITIAS ARE FORMING AND BARRICADES ARE GOING UP IN THE CAPITAL CITY OF MADRID. NO OFFICIAL RESPONSE HAS YET BEEN MADE BY THE LEAGUE OF NATIONS...
"CLICK"
ONLY BAD NEWS, EVERYWHERE...

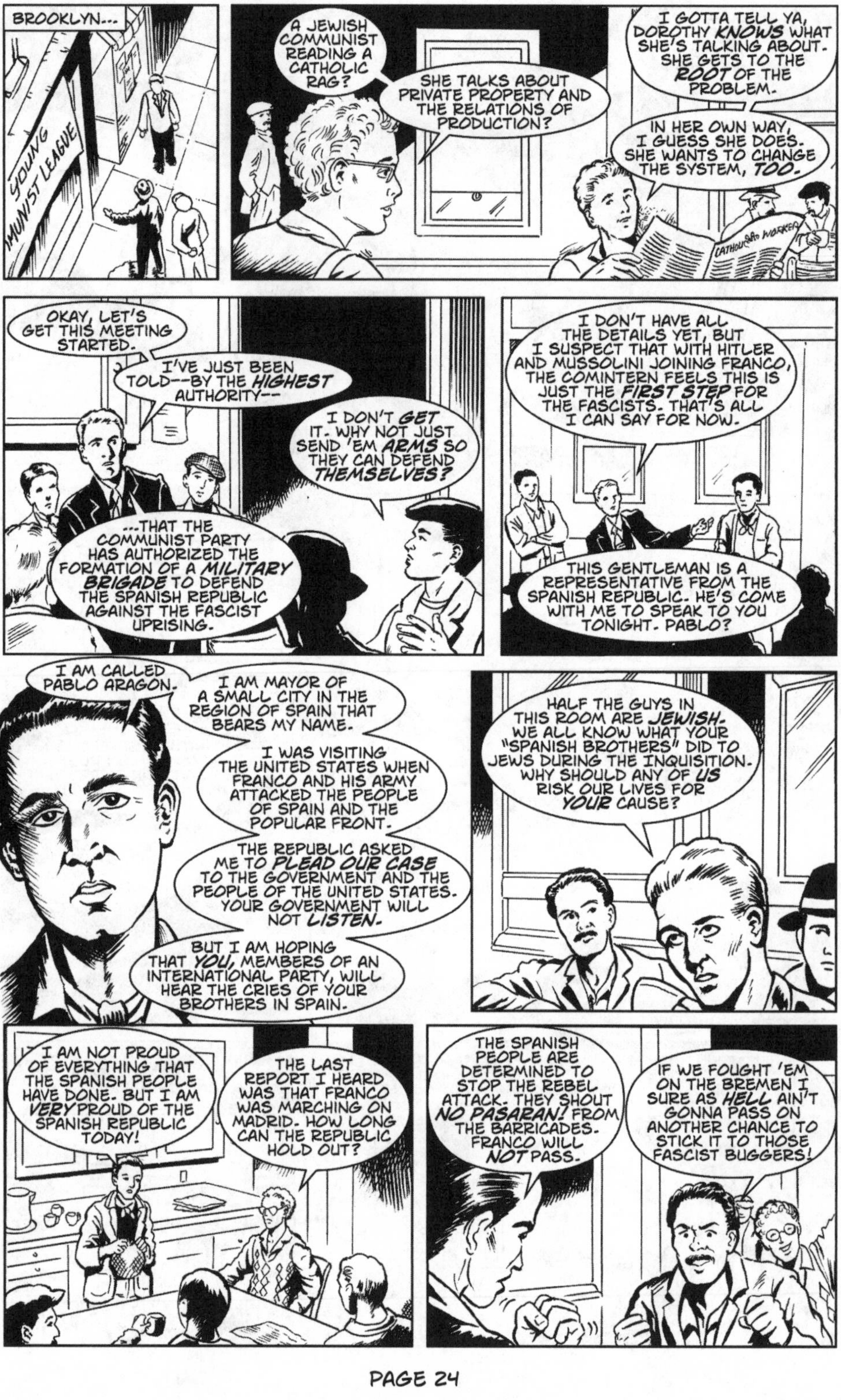
BROOKLYN...
YOUNG ...MUNIST LEAGUE
A JEWISH COMMUNIST READING A CATHOLIC RAG?
SHE TALKS ABOUT PRIVATE PROPERTY AND THE RELATIONS OF PRODUCTION?
I GOTTA TELL YA, DOROTHY KNOWS WHAT SHE'S TALKING ABOUT. SHE GETS TO THE ROOT OF THE PROBLEM.
IN HER OWN WAY, I GUESS SHE DOES. SHE WANTS TO CHANGE THE SYSTEM, TOO.
CATHOLIC WORKER
OKAY, LET'S GET THIS MEETING STARTED.
I'VE JUST BEEN TOLD--BY THE HIGHEST AUTHORITY--
--THAT THE COMMUNIST PARTY HAS AUTHORIZED THE FORMATION OF A MILITARY BRIGADE TO DEFEND THE SPANISH REPUBLIC AGAINST THE FASCIST UPRISING.
I DON'T GET IT. WHY NOT JUST SEND 'EM ARMS SO THEY CAN DEFEND THEMSELVES?
I DON'T HAVE ALL THE DETAILS YET, BUT I SUSPECT THAT WITH HITLER AND MUSSOLINI JOINING FRANCO, THE COMINTERN FEELS THIS IS JUST THE FIRST STEP FOR THE FASCISTS. THAT'S ALL I CAN SAY FOR NOW.
THIS GENTLEMAN IS A REPRESENTATIVE FROM THE SPANISH REPUBLIC. HE'S COME WITH ME TO SPEAK TO YOU TONIGHT. PABLO?
I AM CALLED PABLO ARAGON.
I AM MAYOR OF A SMALL CITY IN THE REGION OF SPAIN THAT BEARS MY NAME.
I WAS VISITING THE UNITED STATES WHEN FRANCO AND HIS ARMY ATTACKED THE PEOPLE OF SPAIN AND THE POPULAR FRONT.
THE REPUBLIC ASKED ME TO PLEAD OUR CASE TO THE GOVERNMENT AND THE PEOPLE OF THE UNITED STATES. YOUR GOVERNMENT WILL NOT LISTEN.
BUT I AM HOPING THAT YOU, MEMBERS OF AN INTERNATIONAL PARTY, WILL HEAR THE CRIES OF YOUR BROTHERS IN SPAIN.
HALF THE GUYS IN THIS ROOM ARE JEWISH. WE ALL KNOW WHAT YOUR "SPANISH BROTHERS" DID TO JEWS DURING THE INQUISITION. WHY SHOULD ANY OF US RISK OUR LIVES FOR YOUR CAUSE?
I AM NOT PROUD OF EVERYTHING THAT THE SPANISH PEOPLE HAVE DONE. BUT I AM VERY PROUD OF THE SPANISH REPUBLIC TODAY!
THE LAST REPORT I HEARD WAS THAT FRANCO WAS MARCHING ON MADRID. HOW LONG CAN THE REPUBLIC HOLD OUT?
THE SPANISH PEOPLE ARE DETERMINED TO STOP THE REBEL ATTACK. THEY SHOUT NO PASARAN! FROM THE BARRICADES. FRANCO WILL NOT PASS.
IF WE FOUGHT 'EM ON THE BREMEN I SURE AS HELL AIN'T GONNA PASS ON ANOTHER CHANCE TO STICK IT TO THOSE FASCIST BUGGERS!

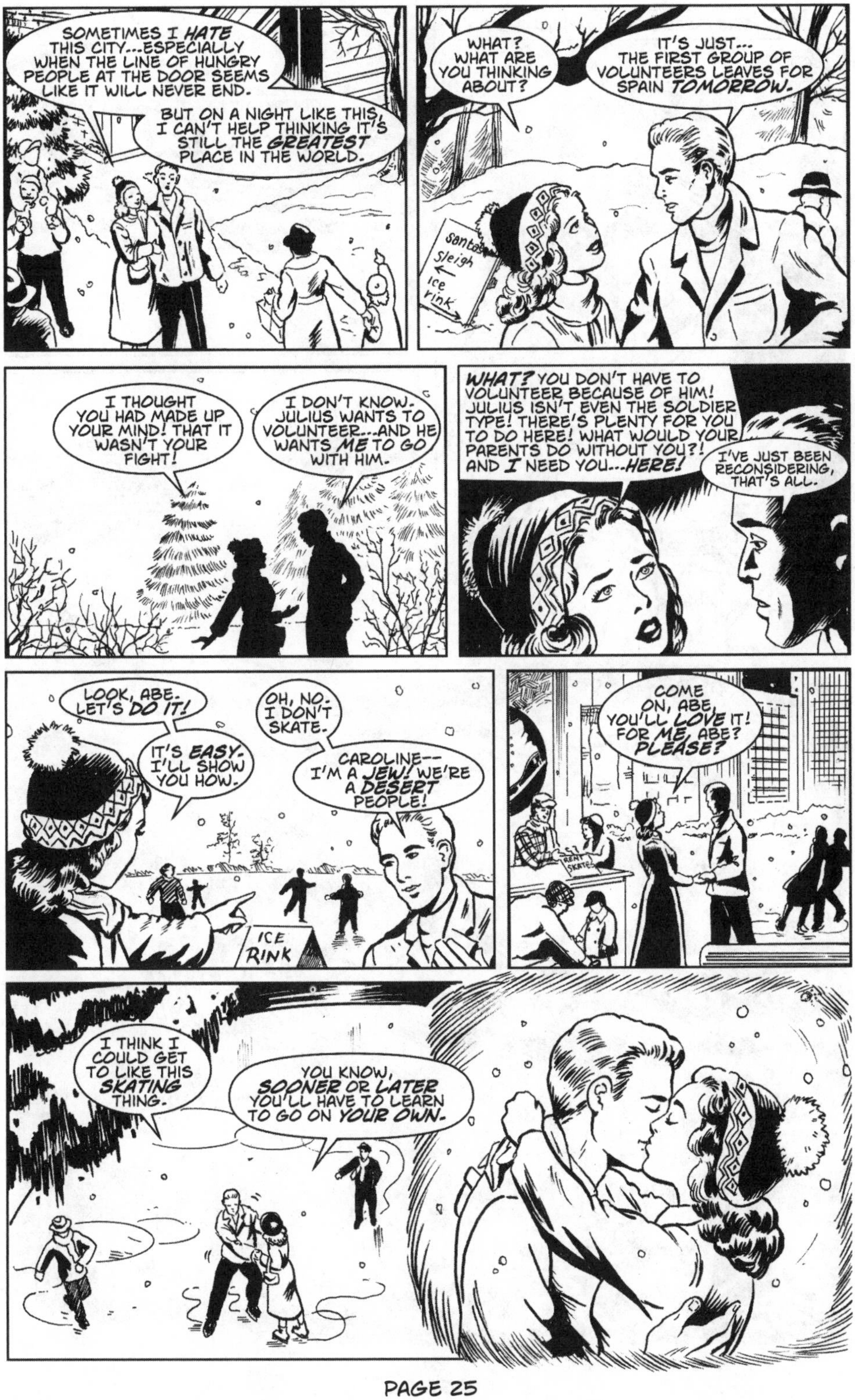
SOMETIMES I HATE THIS CITY...ESPECIALLY WHEN THE LINE OF HUNGRY PEOPLE AT THE DOOR SEEMS LIKE IT WILL NEVER END.
BUT ON A NIGHT LIKE THIS, I CAN'T HELP THINKING IT'S STILL THE GREATEST PLACE IN THE WORLD.
WHAT? WHAT ARE YOU THINKING ABOUT?
IT'S JUST... THE FIRST GROUP OF VOLUNTEERS LEAVES FOR SPAIN TOMORROW.
Santa's Sleigh
ice rink
I THOUGHT YOU HAD MADE UP YOUR MIND! THAT IT WASN'T YOUR FIGHT!
I DON'T KNOW. JULIUS WANTS TO VOLUNTEER...AND HE WANTS ME TO GO WITH HIM.
WHAT? YOU DON'T HAVE TO VOLUNTEER BECAUSE OF HIM! JULIUS ISN'T EVEN THE SOLDIER TYPE! THERE'S PLENTY FOR YOU TO DO HERE! WHAT WOULD YOUR PARENTS DO WITHOUT YOU?! AND I NEED YOU...HERE!
I'VE JUST BEEN RECONSIDERING, THAT'S ALL.
LOOK, ABE. LET'S DO IT!
IT'S EASY. I'LL SHOW YOU HOW.
OH, NO. I DON'T SKATE.
CAROLINE-- I'M A JEW! WE'RE A DESERT PEOPLE!
ICE RINK
COME ON, ABE, YOU'LL LOVE IT! FOR ME, ABE? PLEASE?
RENT SKATES
I THINK I COULD GET TO LIKE THIS SKATING THING.
YOU KNOW, SOONER OR LATER YOU'LL HAVE TO LEARN TO GO ON YOUR OWN.

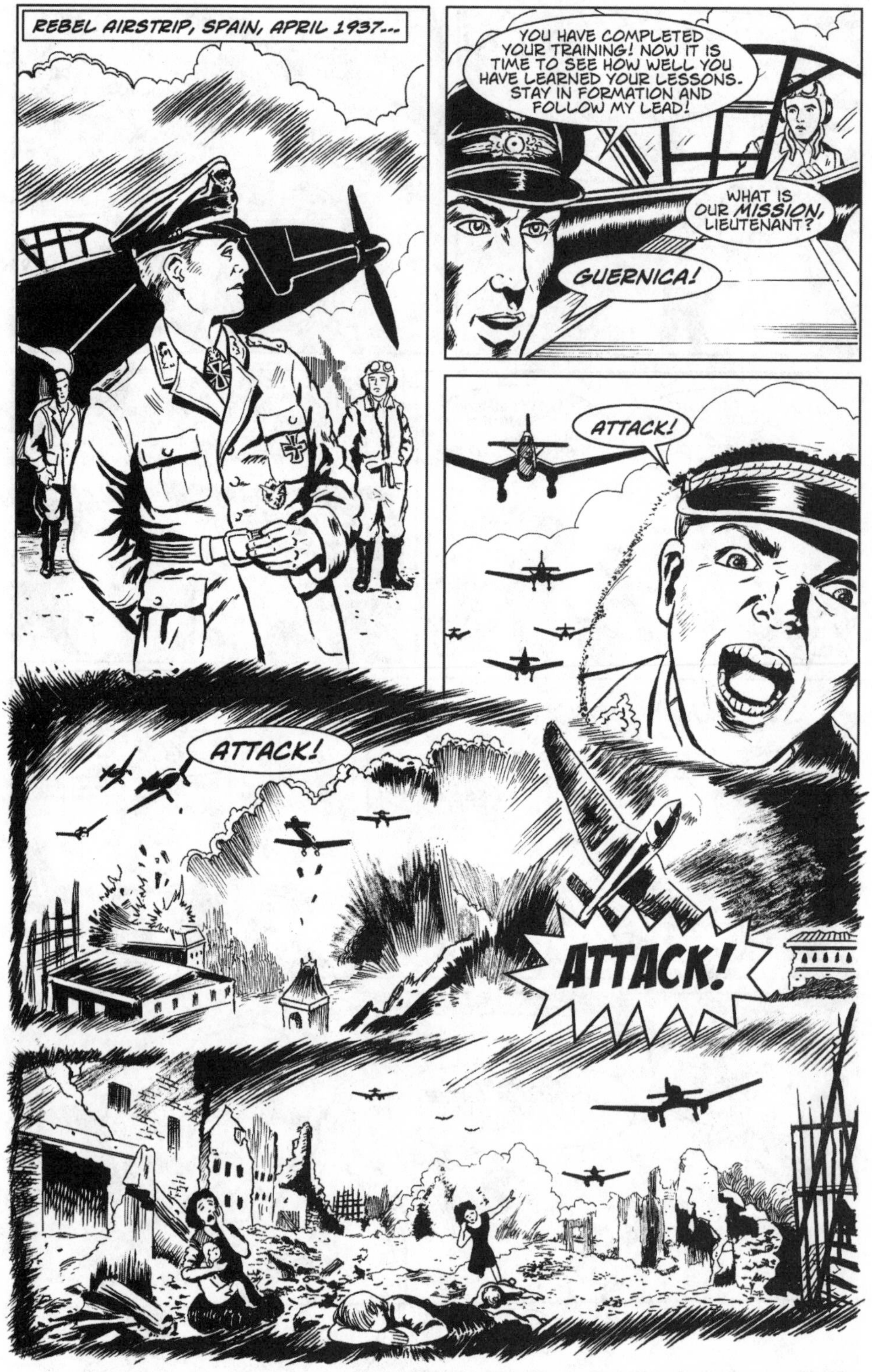
REBEL AIRSTRIP, SPAIN, APRIL 1937...
YOU HAVE COMPLETED YOUR TRAINING! NOW IT IS TIME TO SEE HOW WELL YOU HAVE LEARNED YOUR LESSONS. STAY IN FORMATION AND FOLLOW MY LEAD!
WHAT IS OUR MISSION, LIEUTENANT?
GUERNICA!
ATTACK!
ATTACK!
ATTACK!

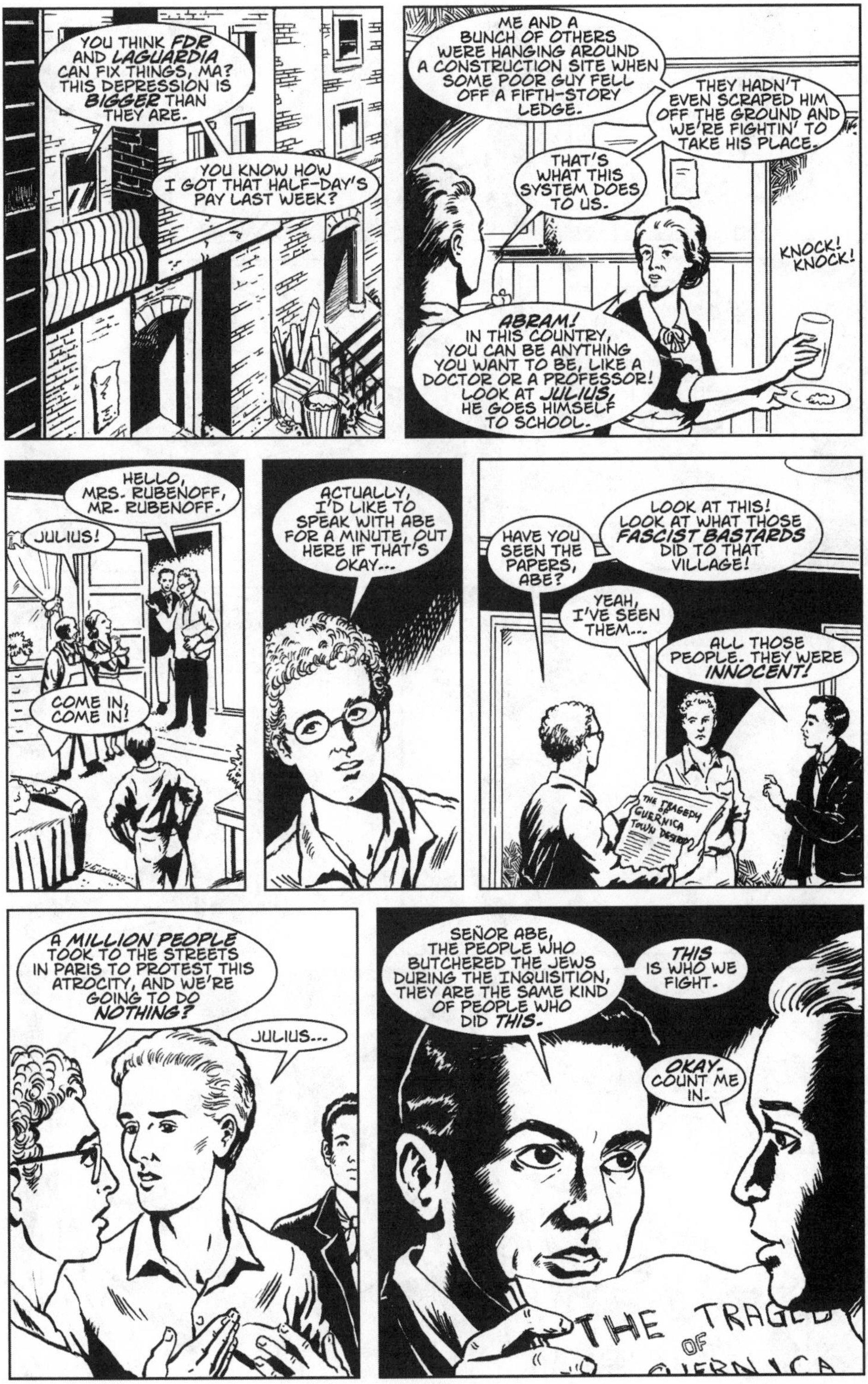
YOU THINK FDR AND LAGUARDIA CAN FIX THINGS, MA? THIS DEPRESSION IS BIGGER THAN THEY ARE.
YOU KNOW HOW I GOT THAT HALF-DAY'S PAY LAST WEEK?
ME AND A BUNCH OF OTHERS WERE HANGING AROUND A CONSTRUCTION SITE WHEN SOME POOR GUY FELL OFF A FIFTH-STORY LEDGE.
THEY HADN'T EVEN SCRAPED HIM OFF THE GROUND AND WE'RE FIGHTIN' TO TAKE HIS PLACE.
THAT'S WHAT THIS SYSTEM DOES TO US.
ABRAM! IN THIS COUNTRY, YOU CAN BE ANYTHING YOU WANT TO BE, LIKE A DOCTOR OR A PROFESSOR! LOOK AT JULIUS, HE GOES HIMSELF TO SCHOOL.
KNOCK! KNOCK!
HELLO, MRS. RUBENOFF, MR. RUBENOFF.
JULIUS!
COME IN, COME IN!
ACTUALLY, I'D LIKE TO SPEAK WITH ABE FOR A MINUTE, OUT HERE IF THAT'S OKAY...
HAVE YOU SEEN THE PAPERS, ABE?
LOOK AT THIS! LOOK AT WHAT THOSE FASCIST BASTARDS DID TO THAT VILLAGE!
YEAH, I'VE SEEN THEM...
ALL THOSE PEOPLE. THEY WERE INNOCENT!
THE TRAGEDY OF GUERNICA TOWN DESTRO
A MILLION PEOPLE TOOK TO THE STREETS IN PARIS TO PROTEST THIS ATROCITY, AND WE'RE GOING TO DO NOTHING?
JULIUS...
SEÑOR ABE, THE PEOPLE WHO BUTCHERED THE JEWS DURING THE INQUISITION, THEY ARE THE SAME KIND OF PEOPLE WHO DID THIS.
THIS IS WHO WE FIGHT.
OKAY. COUNT ME IN.
THE TRAGED OF GUERNICA

CATHOLIC
WORKER
HOUSE

CAROLINE, WHY ARE YOU ACTING LIKE THIS?

CAROLINE, GOD FORGIVE ME, I'M A WOMAN OF PEACE, BUT ABE IS VOLUNTEERING FOR A *JUST CAUSE!*

GETTING HIMSELF KILLED IN SOMEONE ELSE'S FIGHT? *THAT'S* WHAT YOU SUPPORT?

CAROLINE, THE WAY THINGS ARE GOING, IT WILL BE OUR FIGHT SOON ENOUGH.

THIS IS SOMETHING HE *HAS* TO DO.

AREN'T THINGS BAD ENOUGH HERE? WHY WOULD ANYONE NEED TO FIND A *WORSE* SITUATION?

IT'S NOT WHAT A PERSON WHO SAYS HE *LOVES* SOMEONE DOES!

I DON'T KNOW WHAT'S IN HIS HEART, CAROLINE. BUT I DO KNOW...

...IF HE DOESN'T VOLUNTEER, OR IF YOU STAND IN HIS WAY, HE WOULD NEVER FORGIVE HIMSELF, *OR YOU.*

AND HE WOULDN'T BE THE COURAGEOUS YOUNG MAN THAT YOU *LOVE* SO MUCH!

COME ON.

NOW GO, ENJOY THE TIME THAT YOU HAVE LEFT. I'LL PRAY FOR YOU BOTH.

THANKS, DOROTHY.

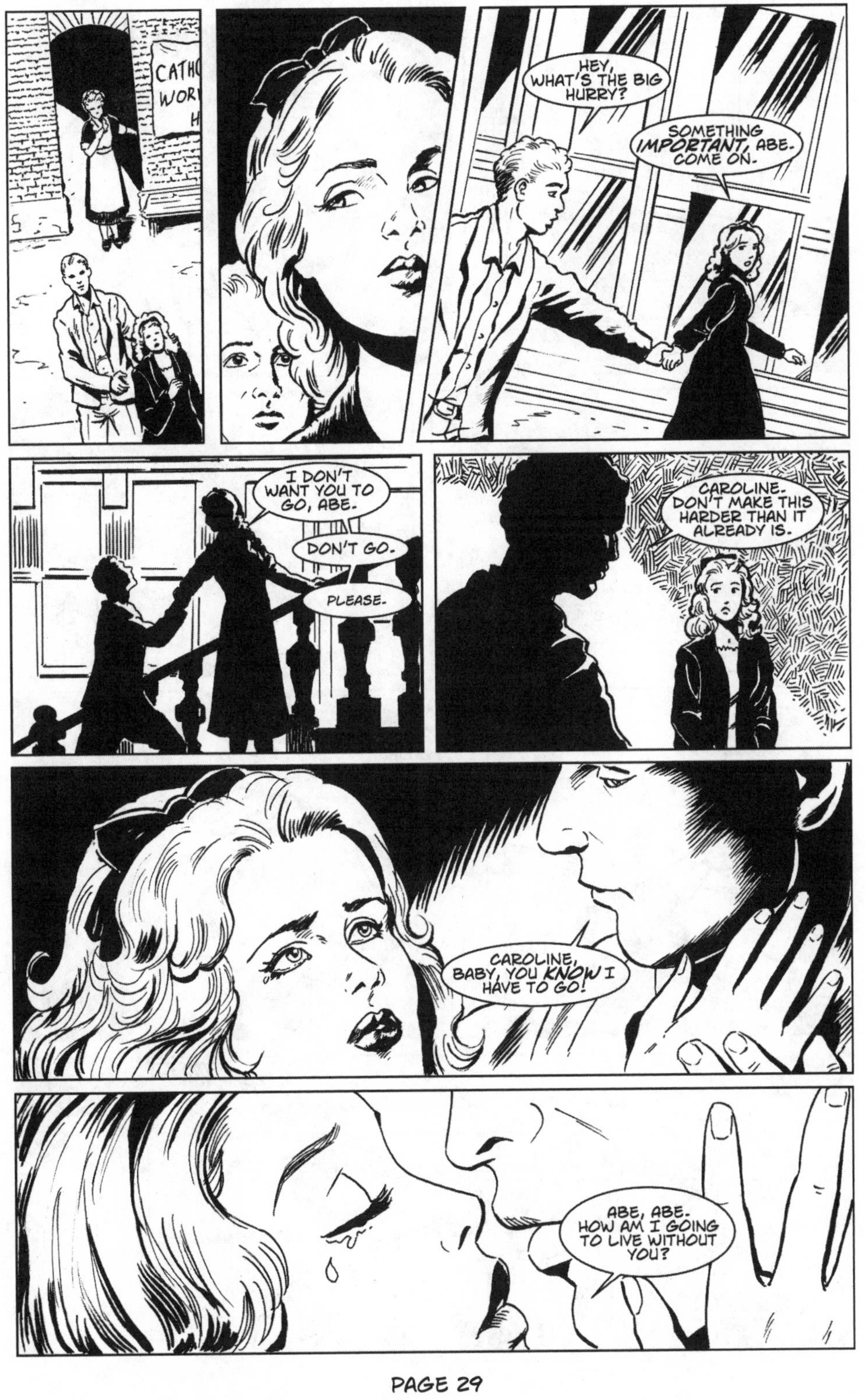
HEY, WHAT'S THE BIG HURRY?
SOMETHING *IMPORTANT*, ABE. COME ON.
I DON'T WANT YOU TO GO, ABE.
DON'T GO.
PLEASE.
CAROLINE. DON'T MAKE THIS HARDER THAN IT ALREADY IS.
CAROLINE, BABY, YOU *KNOW* I HAVE TO GO!
ABE, ABE. HOW AM I GOING TO LIVE WITHOUT YOU?

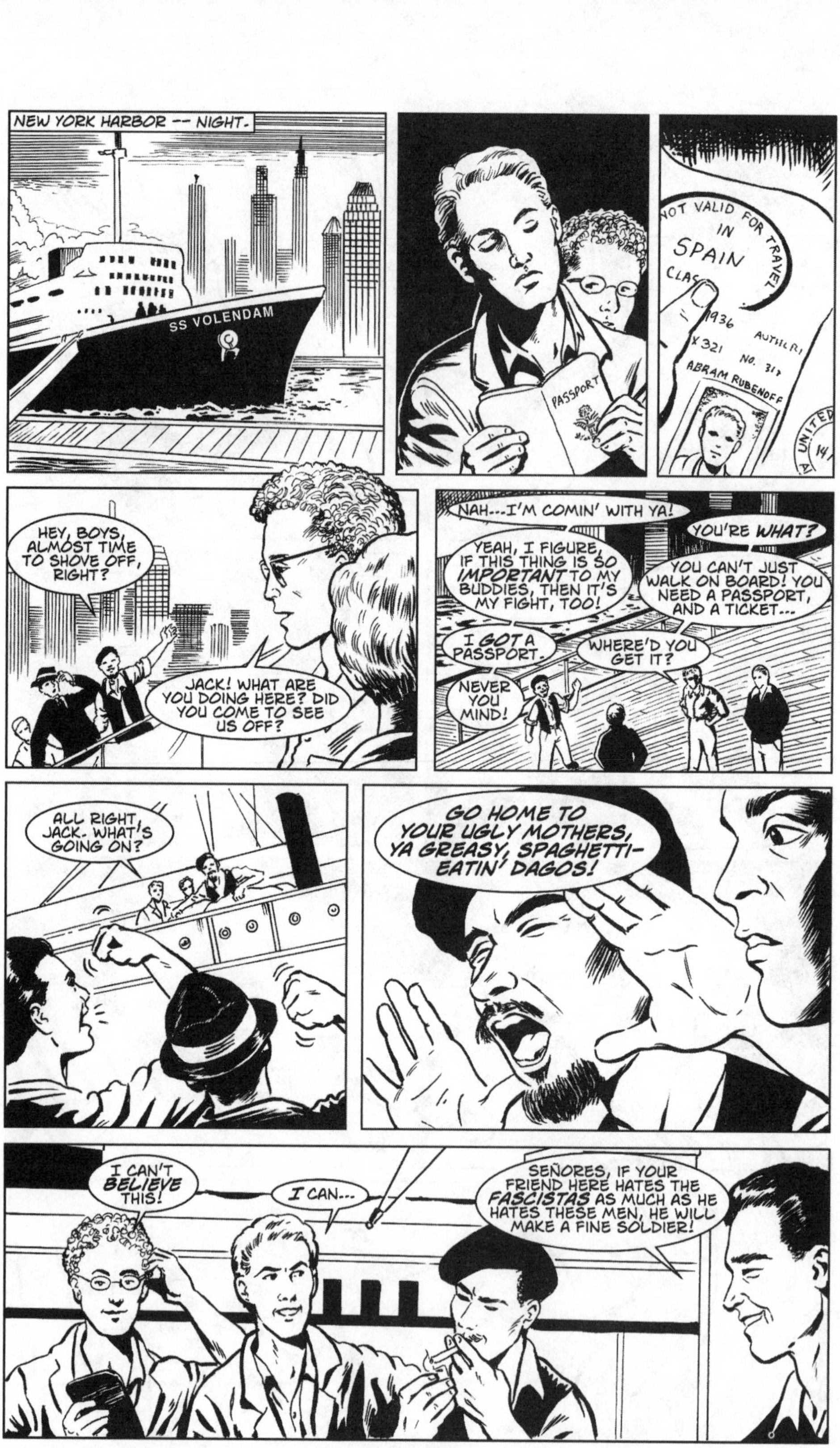
NEW YORK HARBOR -- NIGHT.
SS VOLENDAM
PASSPORT
NOT VALID FOR TRAVEL IN SPAIN
1936
X 321
NO. 317
ABRAM RUBENOFF
HEY, BOYS, ALMOST TIME TO SHOVE OFF, RIGHT?
JACK! WHAT ARE YOU DOING HERE? DID YOU COME TO SEE US OFF?
NAH---I'M COMIN' WITH YA!
YEAH, I FIGURE, IF THIS THING IS SO *IMPORTANT* TO MY BUDDIES, THEN IT'S MY FIGHT, TOO!
YOU'RE *WHAT?*
YOU CAN'T JUST WALK ON BOARD! YOU NEED A PASSPORT, AND A TICKET...
I *GOT* A PASSPORT.
WHERE'D YOU GET IT?
NEVER YOU MIND!
ALL RIGHT, JACK. WHAT'S GOING ON?
GO HOME TO YOUR UGLY MOTHERS, YA GREASY, SPAGHETTI-EATIN' DAGOS!
I CAN'T *BELIEVE* THIS!
I CAN...
SEÑORES, IF YOUR FRIEND HERE HATES THE *FASCISTAS* AS MUCH AS HE HATES THESE MEN, HE WILL MAKE A FINE SOLDIER!

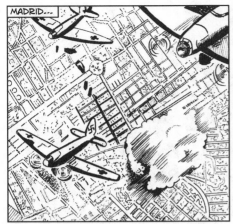

MADRID...

WE'VE BEEN HIT!

CONTINUE THE ASSAULT. REPEAT: CONTINUE THE ASSAULT! THE MISSION *MUST* BE COMPLETED!

HELP ME, HERR LEUTNANT! I THINK MY LEG IS BROKEN!

YES, JOHANN, SO IT APPEARS.

GENERAL MOLA'S ADVANCE LINES ARE ABOUT 50 KILO-METERS NORTH OF HERE.

BUT I'M AFRAID YOU WOULD ONLY SLOW ME DOWN.

HERR LEUTNANT?

YOUR HEART WAS NEVER IN THIS, WAS IT, JOHANN?

HERR LEUTNANT! I WOULD GIVE MY *LIFE* FOR THE CAUSE!

YES, JOHANN, I BELIEVE YOU *WILL*.

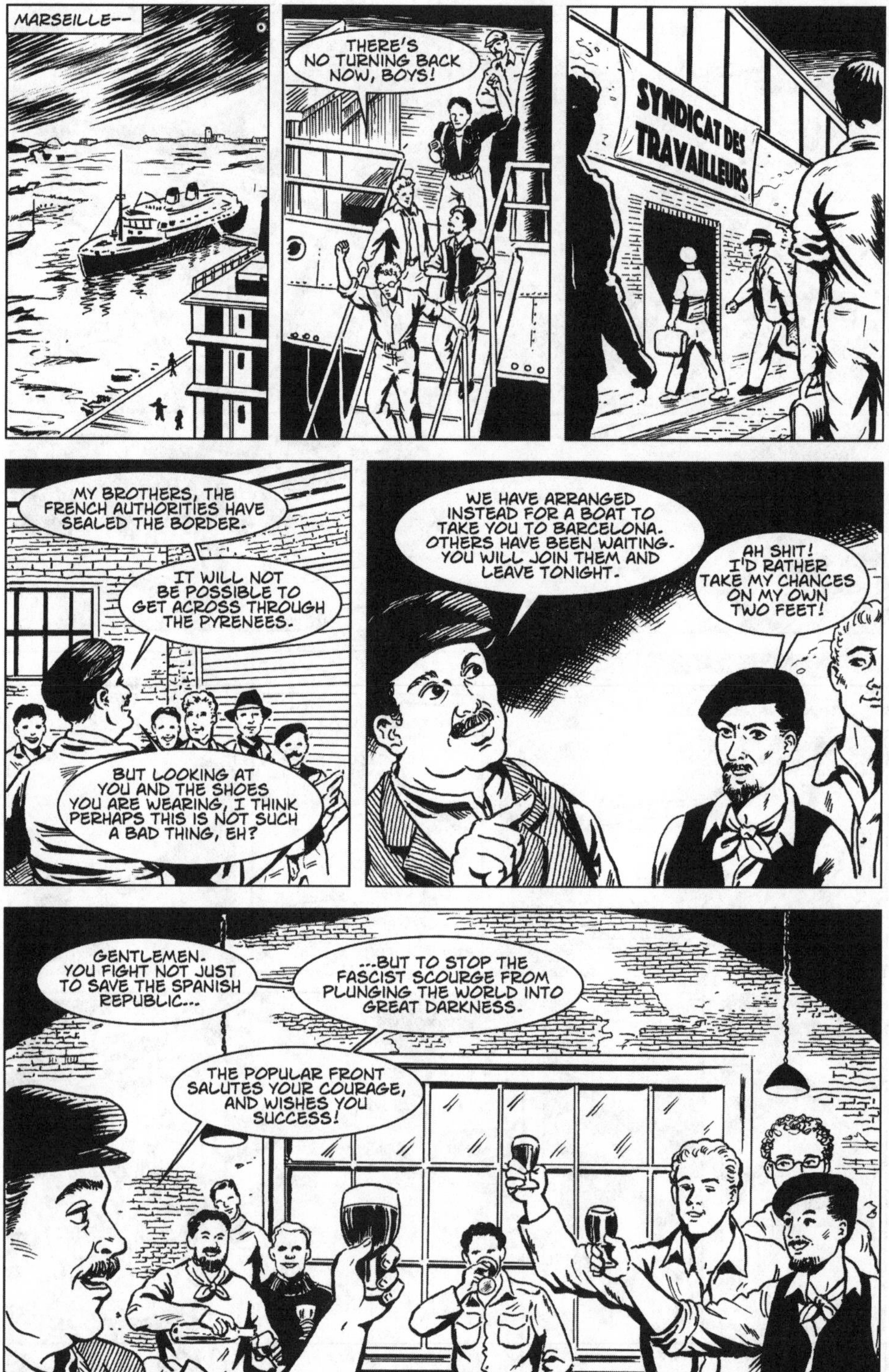
MARSEILLE--
THERE'S NO TURNING BACK NOW, BOYS!
SYNDICAT DES TRAVAILLEURS
MY BROTHERS, THE FRENCH AUTHORITIES HAVE SEALED THE BORDER.
IT WILL NOT BE POSSIBLE TO GET ACROSS THROUGH THE PYRENEES.
BUT LOOKING AT YOU AND THE SHOES YOU ARE WEARING, I THINK PERHAPS THIS IS NOT SUCH A BAD THING, EH?
WE HAVE ARRANGED INSTEAD FOR A BOAT TO TAKE YOU TO BARCELONA. OTHERS HAVE BEEN WAITING. YOU WILL JOIN THEM AND LEAVE TONIGHT.
AH SHIT! I'D RATHER TAKE MY CHANCES ON MY OWN TWO FEET!
GENTLEMEN. YOU FIGHT NOT JUST TO SAVE THE SPANISH REPUBLIC...
...BUT TO STOP THE FASCIST SCOURGE FROM PLUNGING THE WORLD INTO GREAT DARKNESS.
THE POPULAR FRONT SALUTES YOUR COURAGE, AND WISHES YOU SUCCESS!

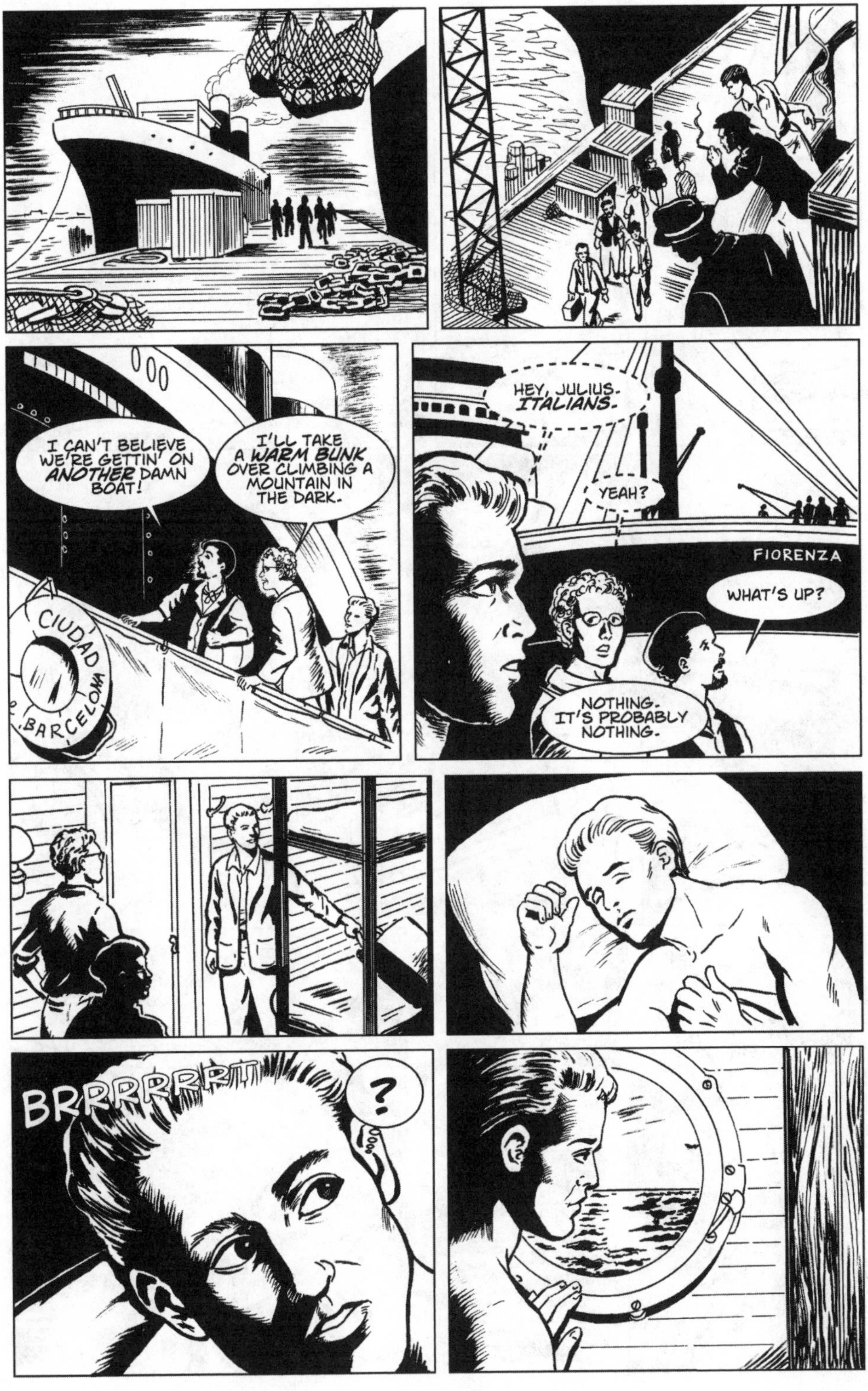
I CAN'T BELIEVE WE'RE GETTIN' ON ANOTHER DAMN BOAT!
I'LL TAKE A WARM BUNK OVER CLIMBING A MOUNTAIN IN THE DARK.
CIUDAD
BARCELONA
HEY, JULIUS. ITALIANS.
YEAH?
FIORENZA
WHAT'S UP?
NOTHING. IT'S PROBABLY NOTHING.
BRRRRRRTT
?

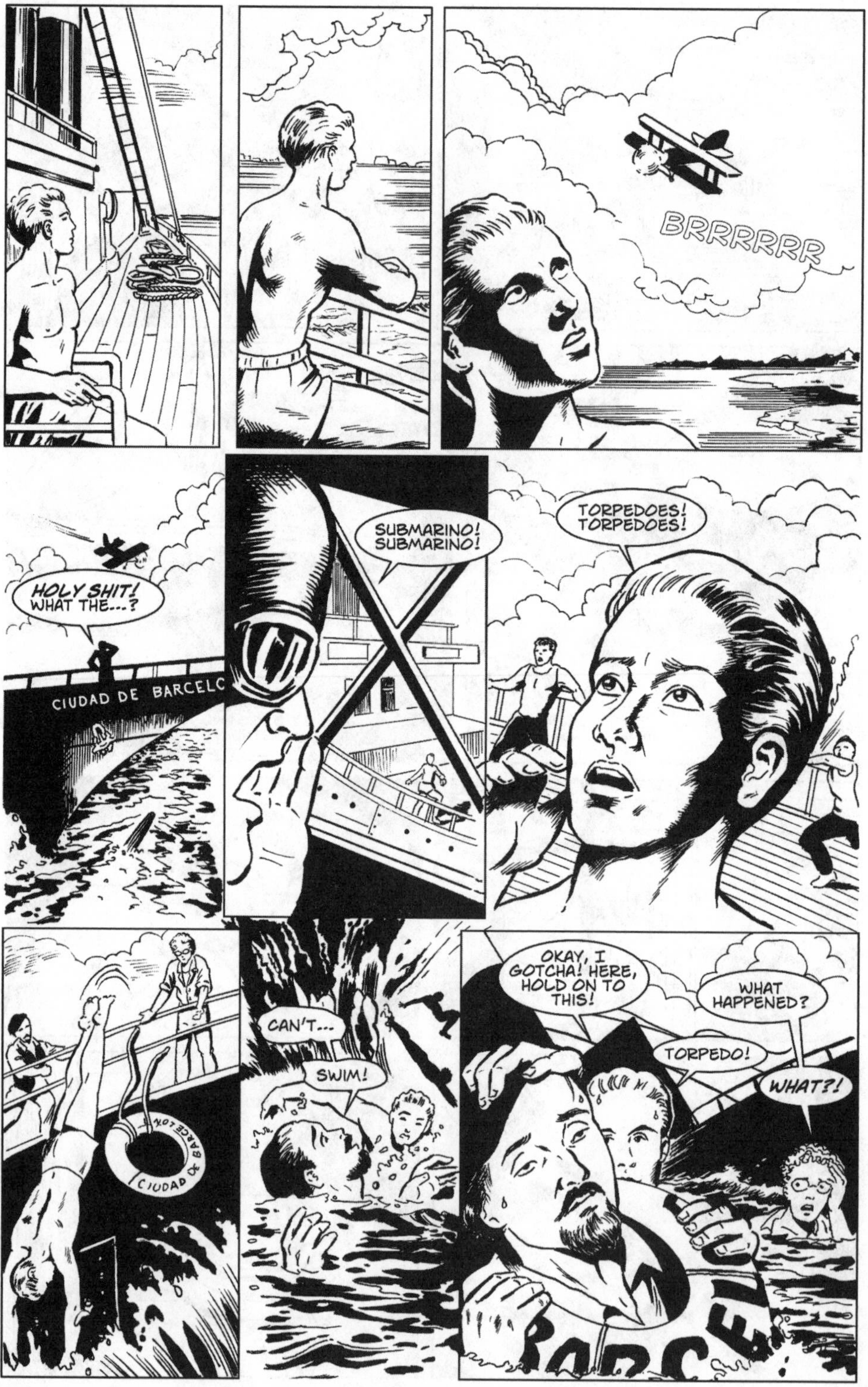
BRRRRRRR
HOLY SHIT! WHAT THE...?
CIUDAD DE BARCELO
SUBMARINO! SUBMARINO!
TORPEDOES! TORPEDOES!
CIUDAD DE BARCELONA
CAN'T...
SWIM!
OKAY, I GOTCHA! HERE, HOLD ON TO THIS!
WHAT HAPPENED?
TORPEDO!
WHAT?!

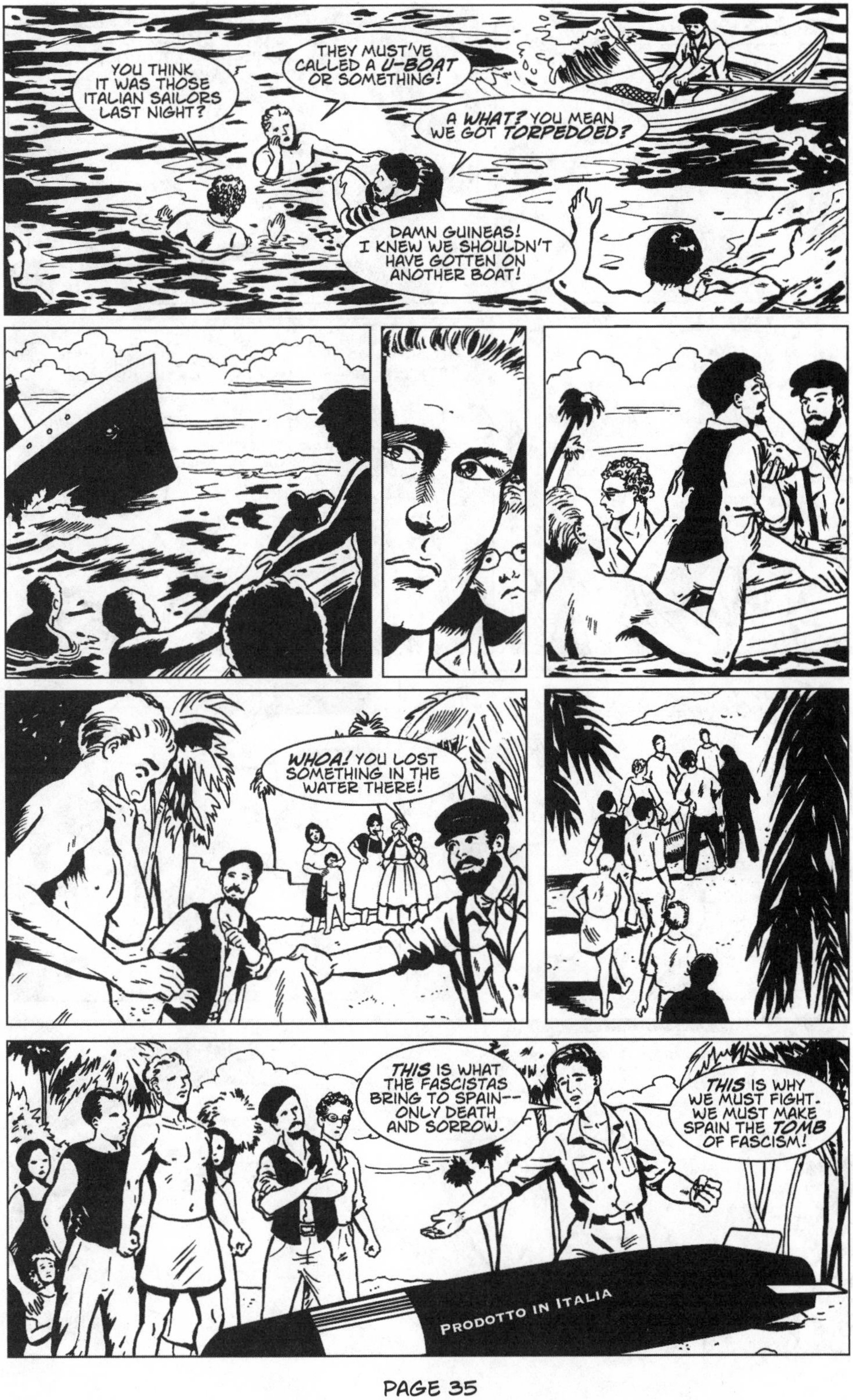
YOU THINK IT WAS THOSE ITALIAN SAILORS LAST NIGHT?
THEY MUST'VE CALLED A U-BOAT OR SOMETHING!
A WHAT? YOU MEAN WE GOT TORPEDOED?
DAMN GUINEAS! I KNEW WE SHOULDN'T HAVE GOTTEN ON ANOTHER BOAT!
WHOA! YOU LOST SOMETHING IN THE WATER THERE!
THIS IS WHAT THE FASCISTAS BRING TO SPAIN--ONLY DEATH AND SORROW.
THIS IS WHY WE MUST FIGHT. WE MUST MAKE SPAIN THE TOMB OF FASCISM!
PRODOTTO IN ITALIA

MILITARY CAMP, ALBACETE, TERRAZONA DE LA MANCHA

ABE! JULIUS!

HEY, JOEY. HOW YA DOIN'? I HEARD YOU WERE ONE OF THE FIRST TO LEAVE.

WHAT TOOK YOU SO LONG TO GET HERE?

OUR BOAT HAD A LITTLE *RUN IN* WITH THE ITALIANS.

DID YOU BRING ANY SUPPLIES?

WELL IF WE DID, THEY'RE AT THE BOTTOM OF THE SEA NOW.

YOU WERE ON THE *CIUDAD*, EH? GLAD YOU MADE IT OUT.

WE WERE EXPECTING A SHIPMENT OF GUNS FROM *RUSSIA* BUT IT AIN'T COME YET.

GUNS? YOU AIN'T GOT ANY *GUNS*?

HEY JOEY, YOU KNOW JACK?

YEAH, I THINK SO. YOU THE BROTHER OF MAXIE TIGHER, USED TO RUN WITH *BUGSY SIEGEL*?

YEAH, HE'S MY OLDER BROTHER.

YOU RUN WITH HIS GANG?

DID MY PART.

EXCEPT FOR A FEW *BIG WAR* VETS, YOU'LL BE ONE OF THE FEW WHO HAS EVER EVEN *SEEN* A GUN!

C'MON, I'LL SHOW YOU GUYS THE CAMP.

PAGE 36

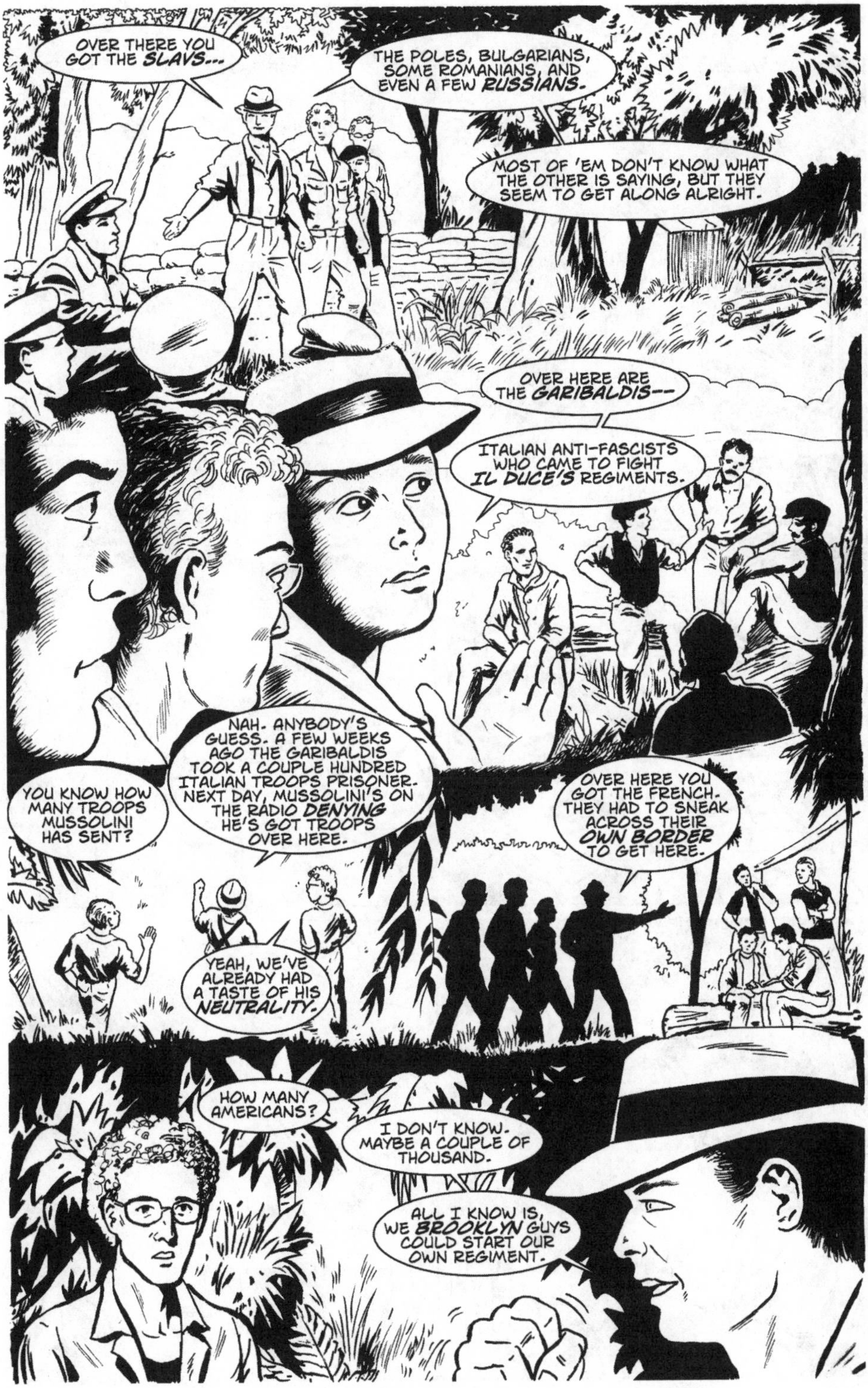
OVER THERE YOU GOT THE SLAVS...
THE POLES, BULGARIANS, SOME ROMANIANS, AND EVEN A FEW RUSSIANS.
MOST OF 'EM DON'T KNOW WHAT THE OTHER IS SAYING, BUT THEY SEEM TO GET ALONG ALRIGHT.
OVER HERE ARE THE GARIBALDIS--
ITALIAN ANTI-FASCISTS WHO CAME TO FIGHT IL DUCE'S REGIMENTS.
YOU KNOW HOW MANY TROOPS MUSSOLINI HAS SENT?
NAH. ANYBODY'S GUESS. A FEW WEEKS AGO THE GARIBALDIS TOOK A COUPLE HUNDRED ITALIAN TROOPS PRISONER. NEXT DAY, MUSSOLINI'S ON THE RADIO DENYING HE'S GOT TROOPS OVER HERE.
YEAH, WE'VE ALREADY HAD A TASTE OF HIS NEUTRALITY.
OVER HERE YOU GOT THE FRENCH. THEY HAD TO SNEAK ACROSS THEIR OWN BORDER TO GET HERE.
HOW MANY AMERICANS?
I DON'T KNOW. MAYBE A COUPLE OF THOUSAND.
ALL I KNOW IS, WE BROOKLYN GUYS COULD START OUR OWN REGIMENT.

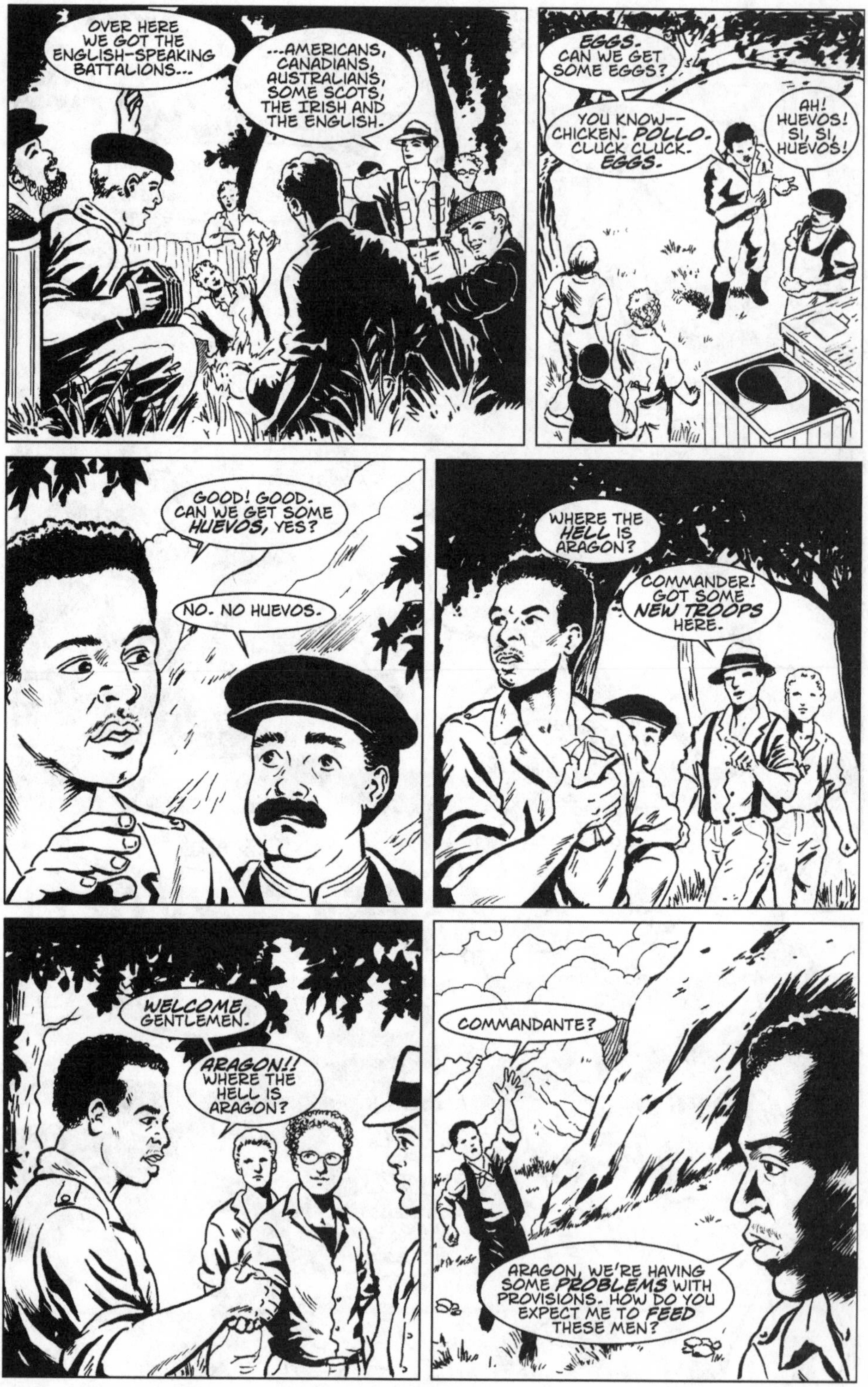
OVER HERE WE GOT THE ENGLISH-SPEAKING BATTALIONS...
...AMERICANS, CANADIANS, AUSTRALIANS, SOME SCOTS, THE IRISH AND THE ENGLISH.
EGGS. CAN WE GET SOME EGGS?
YOU KNOW-- CHICKEN. POLLO. CLUCK CLUCK. EGGS.
AH! HUEVOS! SI, SI, HUEVOS!
GOOD! GOOD. CAN WE GET SOME HUEVOS, YES?
NO. NO HUEVOS.
WHERE THE HELL IS ARAGON?
COMMANDER! GOT SOME NEW TROOPS HERE.
WELCOME, GENTLEMEN.
ARAGON!! WHERE THE HELL IS ARAGON?
COMMANDANTE?
ARAGON, WE'RE HAVING SOME PROBLEMS WITH PROVISIONS. HOW DO YOU EXPECT ME TO FEED THESE MEN?

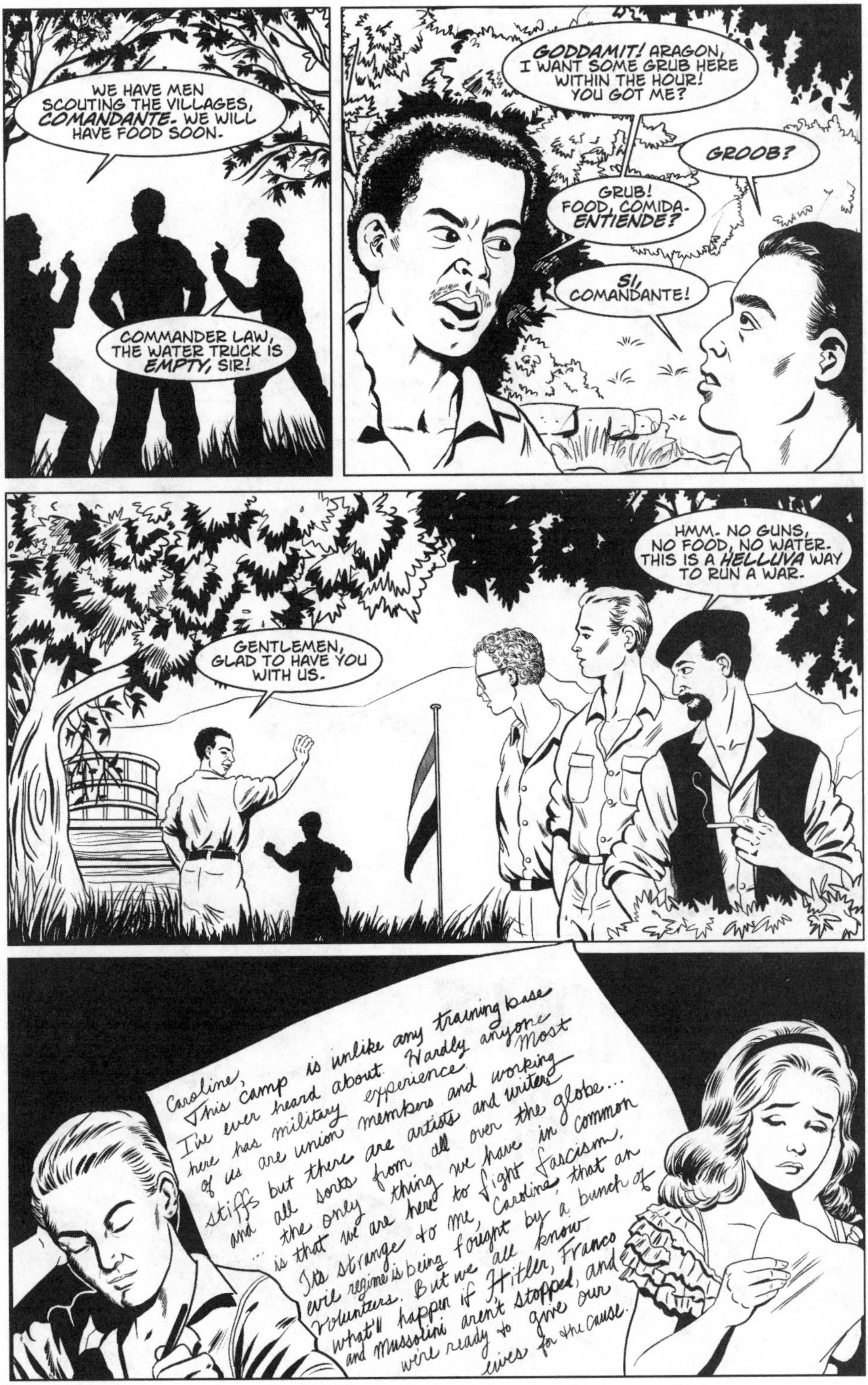
WE HAVE MEN SCOUTING THE VILLAGES, *COMANDANTE*. WE WILL HAVE FOOD SOON.
COMMANDER LAW, THE WATER TRUCK IS *EMPTY*, SIR!
GODDAMIT! ARAGON, I WANT SOME GRUB HERE WITHIN THE HOUR! YOU GOT ME?
GROOB?
GRUB! FOOD, COMIDA. *ENTIENDE?*
SI, COMANDANTE!
HMM. NO GUNS, NO FOOD, NO WATER. THIS IS A *HELLUVA* WAY TO RUN A WAR.
GENTLEMEN, GLAD TO HAVE YOU WITH US.
Caroline,
This camp is unlike any training base
I've ever heard about. Hardly anyone
here has military experience. Most
of us are union members and working
stiffs but there are artists and writers
and all sorts from all over the globe...
... the only thing we have in common
is that we are here to fight fascism.
It's strange to me, Caroline, that an
evil regime is being fought by a bunch of
volunteers. But we all know
what'll happen if Hitler, Franco
and Mussolini aren't stopped, and
we're ready to give our
lives for the cause.

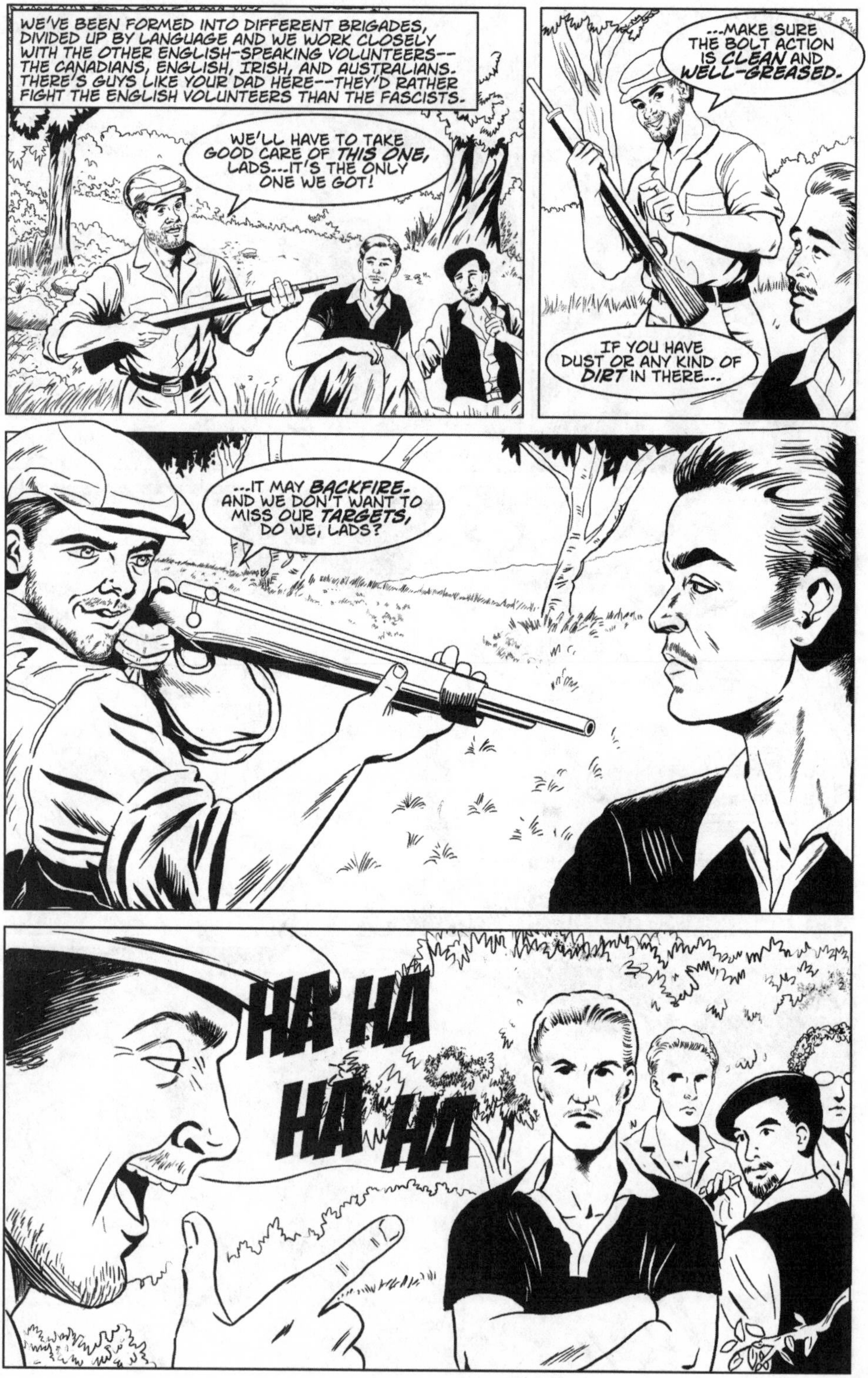
WE'VE BEEN FORMED INTO DIFFERENT BRIGADES, DIVIDED UP BY LANGUAGE AND WE WORK CLOSELY WITH THE OTHER ENGLISH-SPEAKING VOLUNTEERS--THE CANADIANS, ENGLISH, IRISH, AND AUSTRALIANS. THERE'S GUYS LIKE YOUR DAD HERE--THEY'D RATHER FIGHT THE ENGLISH VOLUNTEERS THAN THE FASCISTS.
WE'LL HAVE TO TAKE GOOD CARE OF THIS ONE, LADS...IT'S THE ONLY ONE WE GOT!
...MAKE SURE THE BOLT ACTION IS CLEAN AND WELL-GREASED.
IF YOU HAVE DUST OR ANY KIND OF DIRT IN THERE...
...IT MAY BACKFIRE. AND WE DON'T WANT TO MISS OUR TARGETS, DO WE, LADS?
HA HA HA HA

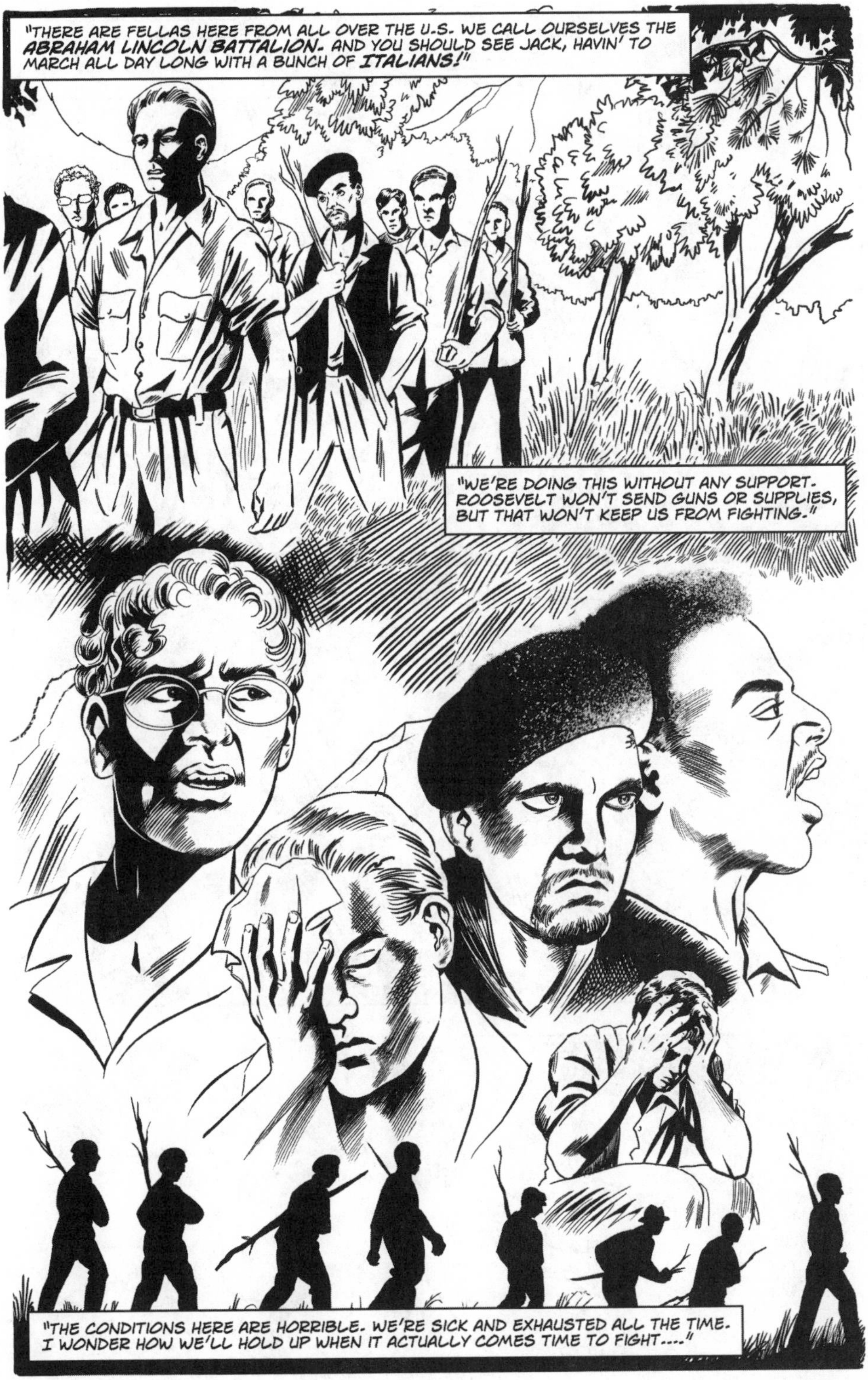
"THERE ARE FELLAS HERE FROM ALL OVER THE U.S. WE CALL OURSELVES THE ABRAHAM LINCOLN BATTALION. AND YOU SHOULD SEE JACK, HAVIN' TO MARCH ALL DAY LONG WITH A BUNCH OF ITALIANS!"
"WE'RE DOING THIS WITHOUT ANY SUPPORT. ROOSEVELT WON'T SEND GUNS OR SUPPLIES, BUT THAT WON'T KEEP US FROM FIGHTING."
"THE CONDITIONS HERE ARE HORRIBLE. WE'RE SICK AND EXHAUSTED ALL THE TIME. I WONDER HOW WE'LL HOLD UP WHEN IT ACTUALLY COMES TIME TO FIGHT...."

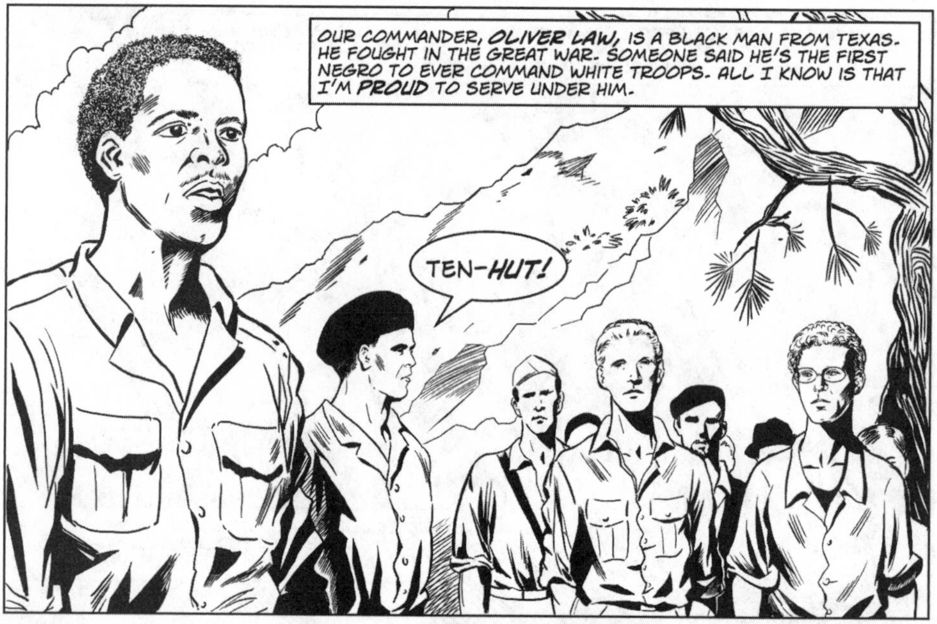
OUR COMMANDER, OLIVER LAW, IS A BLACK MAN FROM TEXAS. HE FOUGHT IN THE GREAT WAR. SOMEONE SAID HE'S THE FIRST NEGRO TO EVER COMMAND WHITE TROOPS. ALL I KNOW IS THAT I'M PROUD TO SERVE UNDER HIM.
TEN-HUT!

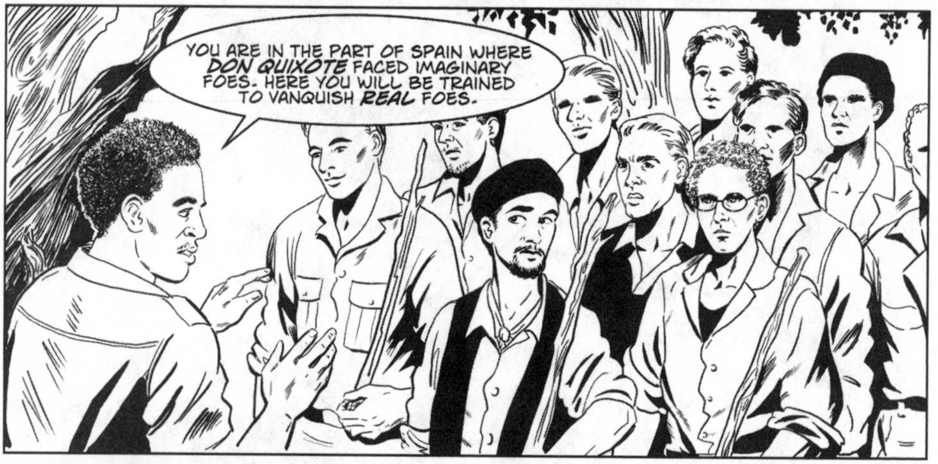
YOU ARE IN THE PART OF SPAIN WHERE DON QUIXOTE FACED IMAGINARY FOES. HERE YOU WILL BE TRAINED TO VANQUISH REAL FOES.

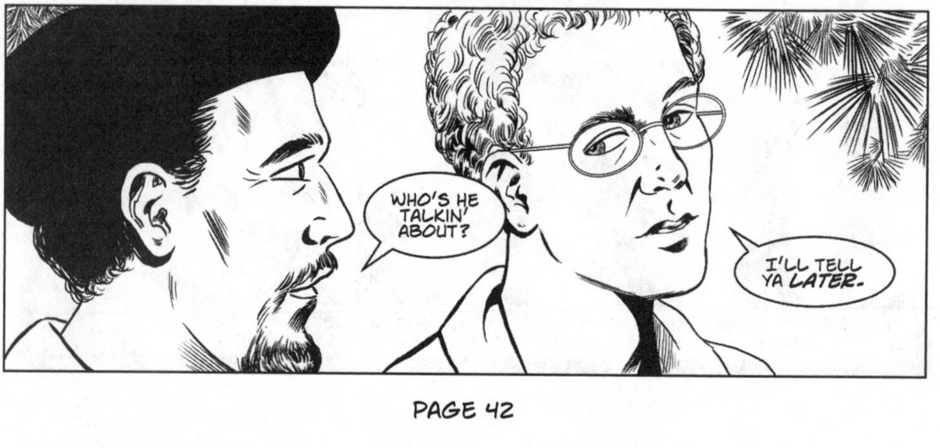
WHO'S HE TALKIN' ABOUT?
I'LL TELL YA LATER.

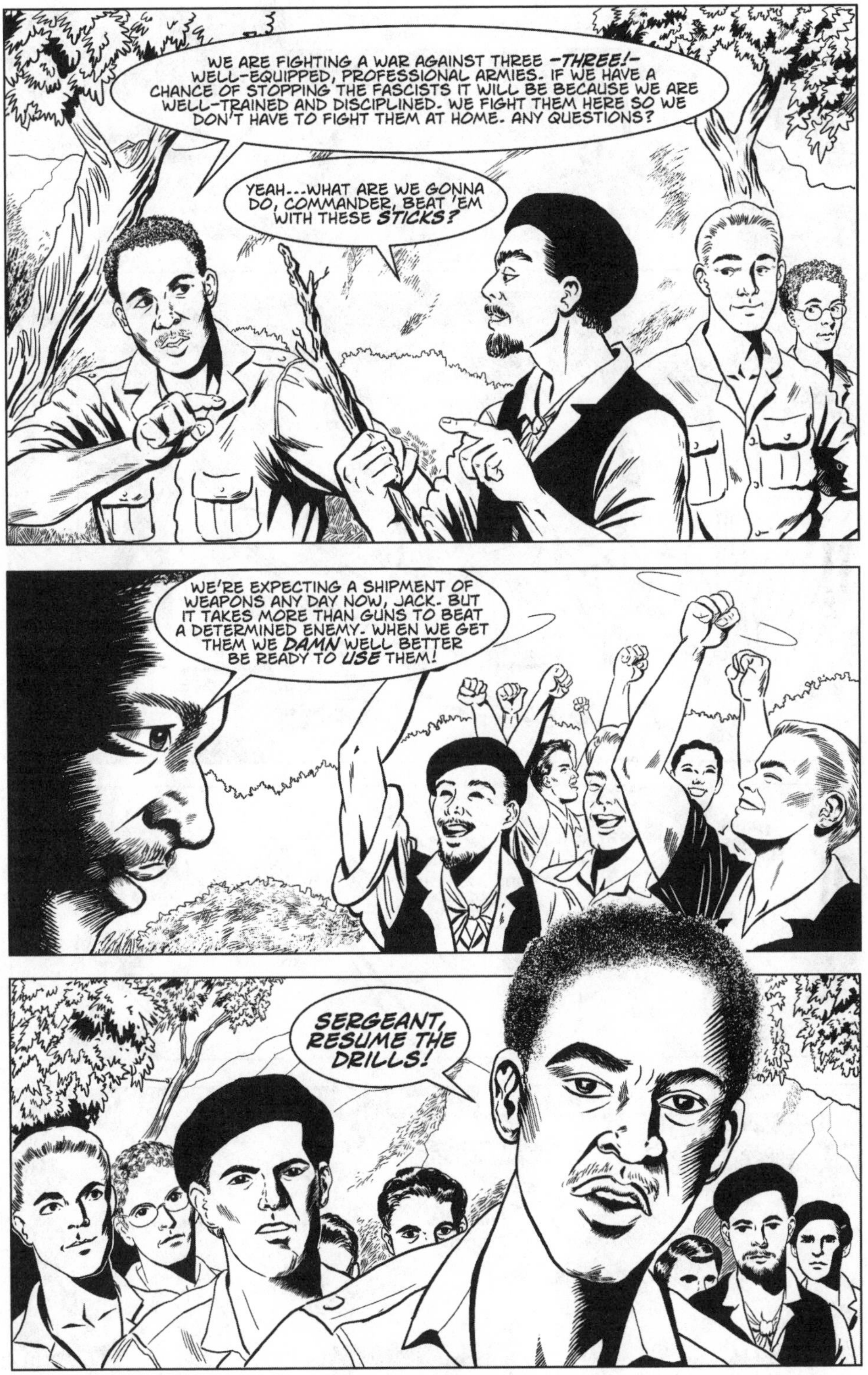
WE ARE FIGHTING A WAR AGAINST THREE -THREE!- WELL-EQUIPPED, PROFESSIONAL ARMIES. IF WE HAVE A CHANCE OF STOPPING THE FASCISTS IT WILL BE BECAUSE WE ARE WELL-TRAINED AND DISCIPLINED. WE FIGHT THEM HERE SO WE DON'T HAVE TO FIGHT THEM AT HOME. ANY QUESTIONS?
YEAH...WHAT ARE WE GONNA DO, COMMANDER, BEAT 'EM WITH THESE STICKS?
WE'RE EXPECTING A SHIPMENT OF WEAPONS ANY DAY NOW, JACK. BUT IT TAKES MORE THAN GUNS TO BEAT A DETERMINED ENEMY. WHEN WE GET THEM WE DAMN WELL BETTER BE READY TO USE THEM!
SERGEANT, RESUME THE DRILLS!

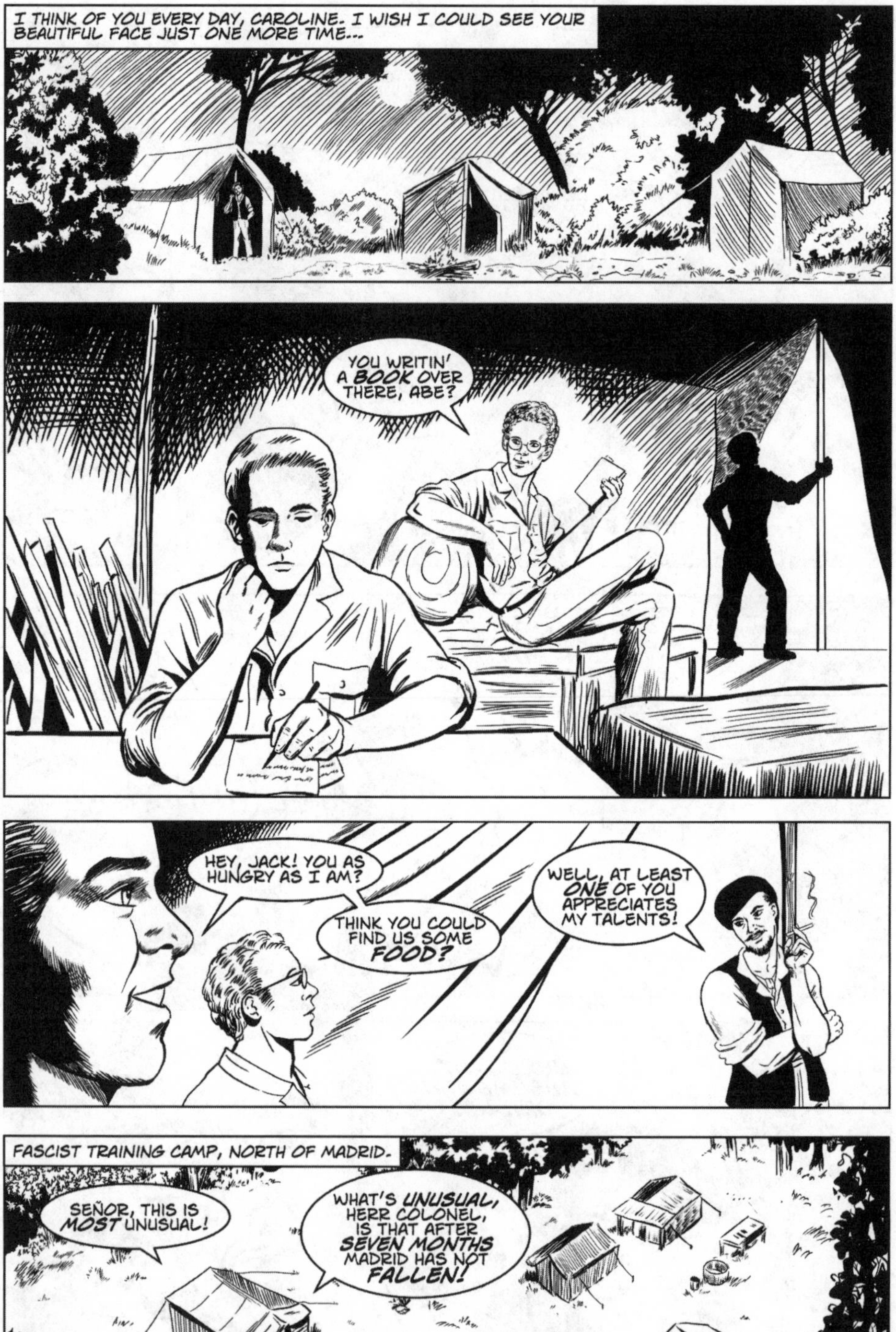
I THINK OF YOU EVERY DAY, CAROLINE. I WISH I COULD SEE YOUR BEAUTIFUL FACE JUST ONE MORE TIME...
YOU WRITIN' A BOOK OVER THERE, ABE?
HEY, JACK! YOU AS HUNGRY AS I AM?
THINK YOU COULD FIND US SOME FOOD?
WELL, AT LEAST ONE OF YOU APPRECIATES MY TALENTS!
FASCIST TRAINING CAMP, NORTH OF MADRID.
SEÑOR, THIS IS MOST UNUSUAL!
WHAT'S UNUSUAL, HERR COLONEL, IS THAT AFTER SEVEN MONTHS MADRID HAS NOT FALLEN!

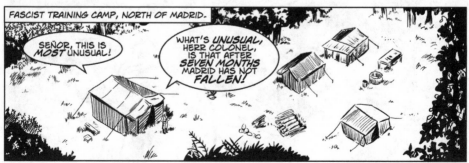

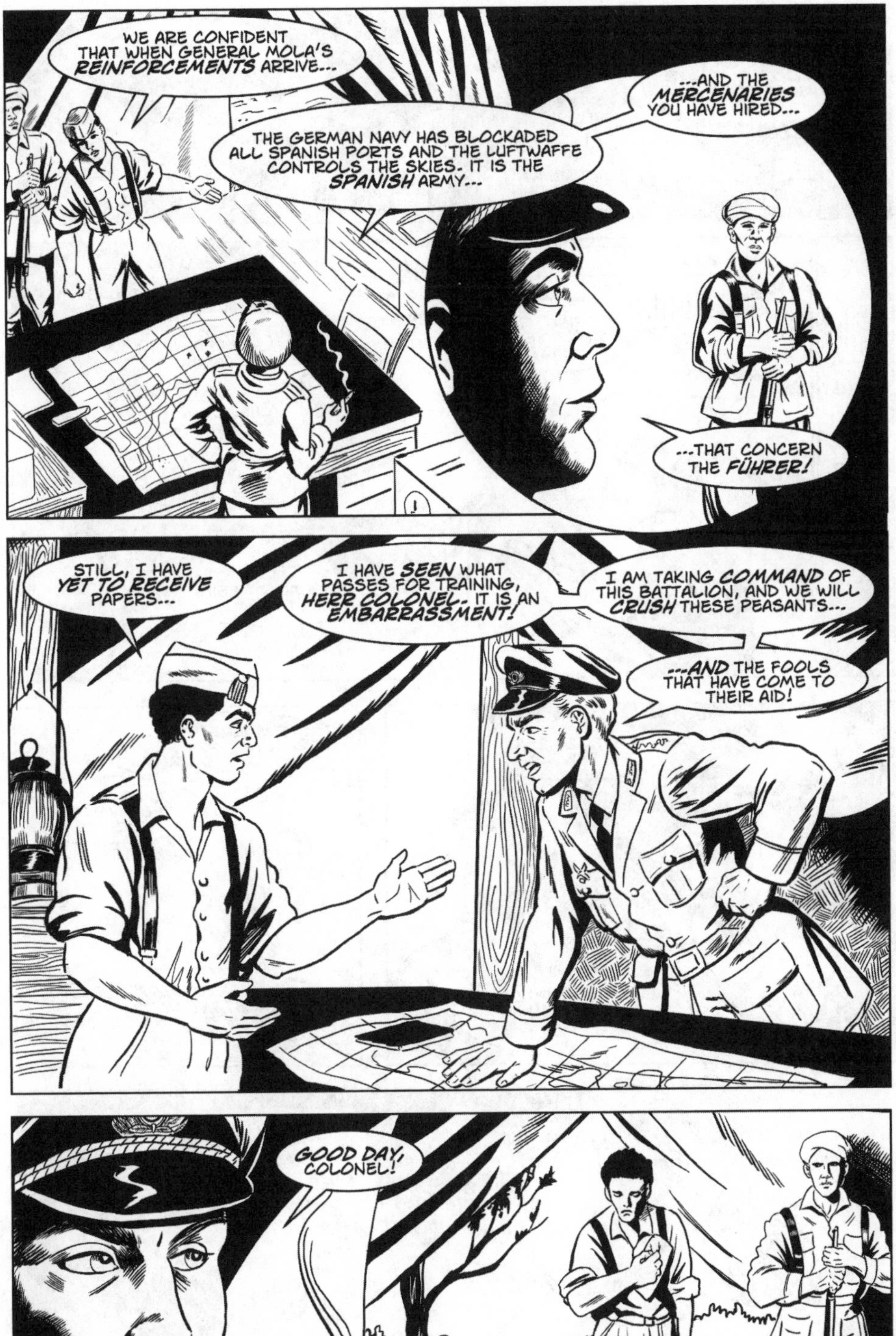
WE ARE CONFIDENT THAT WHEN GENERAL MOLA'S *REINFORCEMENTS* ARRIVE...
THE GERMAN NAVY HAS BLOCKADED ALL SPANISH PORTS AND THE LUFTWAFFE CONTROLS THE SKIES. IT IS THE *SPANISH* ARMY...
...AND THE *MERCENARIES* YOU HAVE HIRED...
...THAT CONCERN THE *FÜHRER!*
STILL, I HAVE *YET TO RECEIVE* PAPERS...
I HAVE *SEEN* WHAT PASSES FOR TRAINING, *HERR COLONEL*. IT IS AN *EMBARRASSMENT!*
I AM TAKING *COMMAND* OF THIS BATTALION, AND WE WILL *CRUSH* THESE PEASANTS...
...AND THE FOOLS THAT HAVE COME TO THEIR AID!
GOOD DAY, COLONEL!

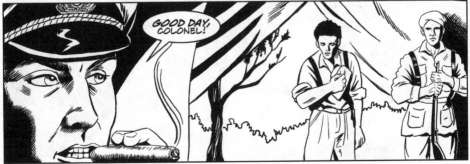

JACK. ABE. THE *COMANDANTE* WISHES TO SPEAK TO YOU.
OK, JACK, WHAT DID YOU DO *NOW?*
WHAT? I AIN'T DONE NOTHIN'!
C'MON, JACK, LET'S SEE WHAT'S UP.
BROOKLYN...
CATHOLIC WORKERS HOUSE
MORE SOUP?
IS THAT *TEA* READY YET, DEAR?
YES, SIR, I'LL GET THAT FOR YOU IN JUST A MINUTE.
THE WATER IS ALMOST READY, MRS. O'CONNELL.
WHERE CAN I WASH MY SOCKS?
THE LAUNDRY SINK IS OUT IN BACK...
CAN I GET SOME MORE SOUP NOW?
IS THE TEA READY YET, CAROLINE?
WHY DON'T YOU GET YOUR *OWN* DAMN TEA, MRS. O'CONNELL?
I'M SO SORRY, DOROTHY! I DON'T KNOW WHAT CAME OVER ME!
YOU HAVEN'T BEEN THE SAME SINCE *ABE* LEFT.
I'M JUST SO *WORRIED*. I CAN'T *STAND* NOT KNOWING WHERE HE IS, IF HE'S BEEN SHOT, OR WOUNDED, OR...OR...
NURSES WANTED
BE A PART OF THE AMERICAN
MEDICAL BUREAU TO AID SPANISH DEMOCRACY
THEN MAYBE YOU SHOULD *DO* SOMETHING ABOUT IT!

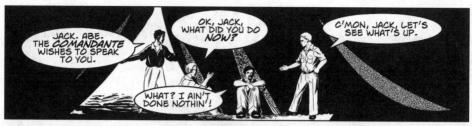

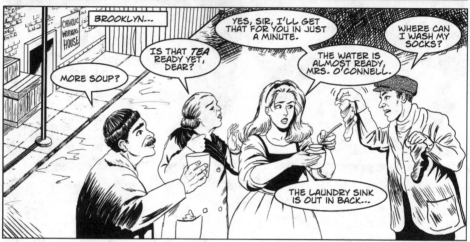

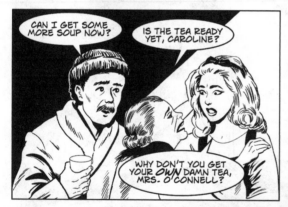

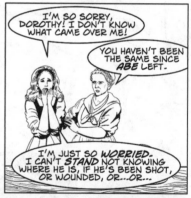

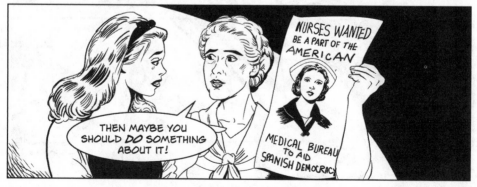

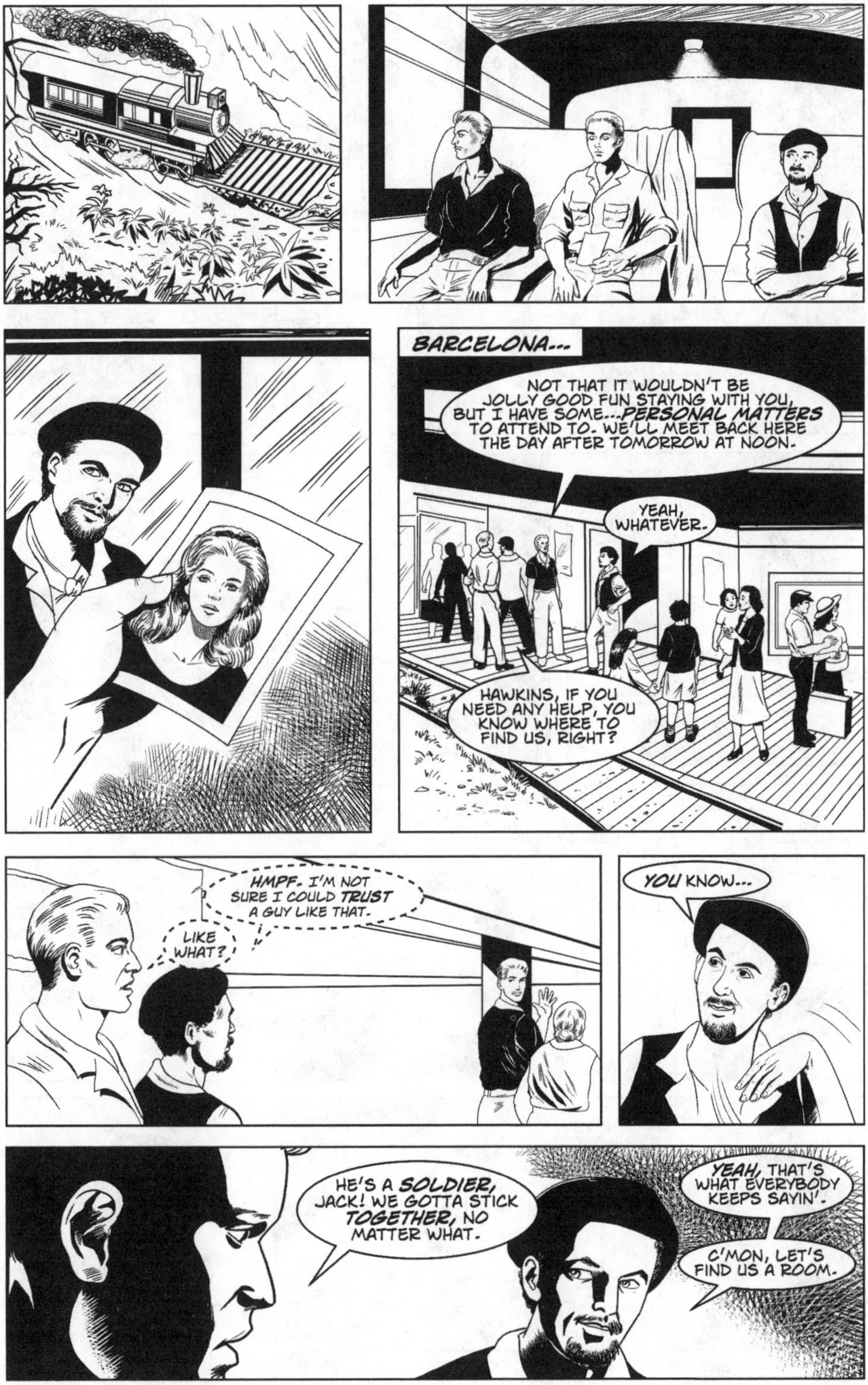
BARCELONA...
NOT THAT IT WOULDN'T BE JOLLY GOOD FUN STAYING WITH YOU, BUT I HAVE SOME...PERSONAL MATTERS TO ATTEND TO. WE'LL MEET BACK HERE THE DAY AFTER TOMORROW AT NOON.
YEAH, WHATEVER.
HAWKINS, IF YOU NEED ANY HELP, YOU KNOW WHERE TO FIND US, RIGHT?
HMPF. I'M NOT SURE I COULD TRUST A GUY LIKE THAT.
LIKE WHAT?
YOU KNOW...
HE'S A SOLDIER, JACK! WE GOTTA STICK TOGETHER, NO MATTER WHAT.
YEAH, THAT'S WHAT EVERYBODY KEEPS SAYIN'.
C'MON, LET'S FIND US A ROOM.

HOTEL DEL SOL
WE'D LIKE A ROOM.
LO SIENTO, SENORES, PERO AHORA MISMO, NO TENGO NADA.
UN CUARTO, POR FAVOR.
WHAT'D HE SAY?
NO ROOMS.
SÍ, SEÑOR. "NO ROOM."
AIN'T THIS WHERE THE COMMANDER TOLD US TO GO?
YEAH.
LISTEN, WE'RE REALLY TIRED. YOU *SURE* YOU AIN'T GOT NO ROOMS?
SI, SENORES, DISCULPAME, TENEMOS UN CUARTO EN EL ULTIMO PISO.*
MARIBEL, NUMERO CUATROCIENTOS.
* FORGIVE ME, BUT WE DO HAVE A ROOM ON THE TOP FLOOR.

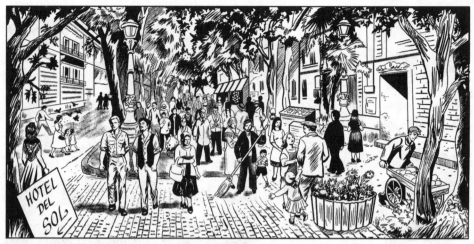

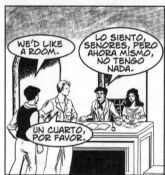

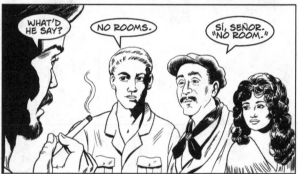

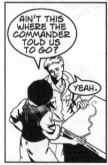

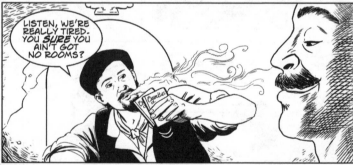

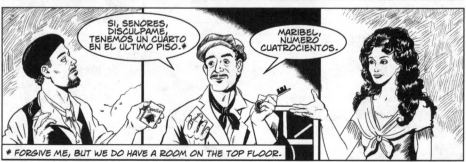

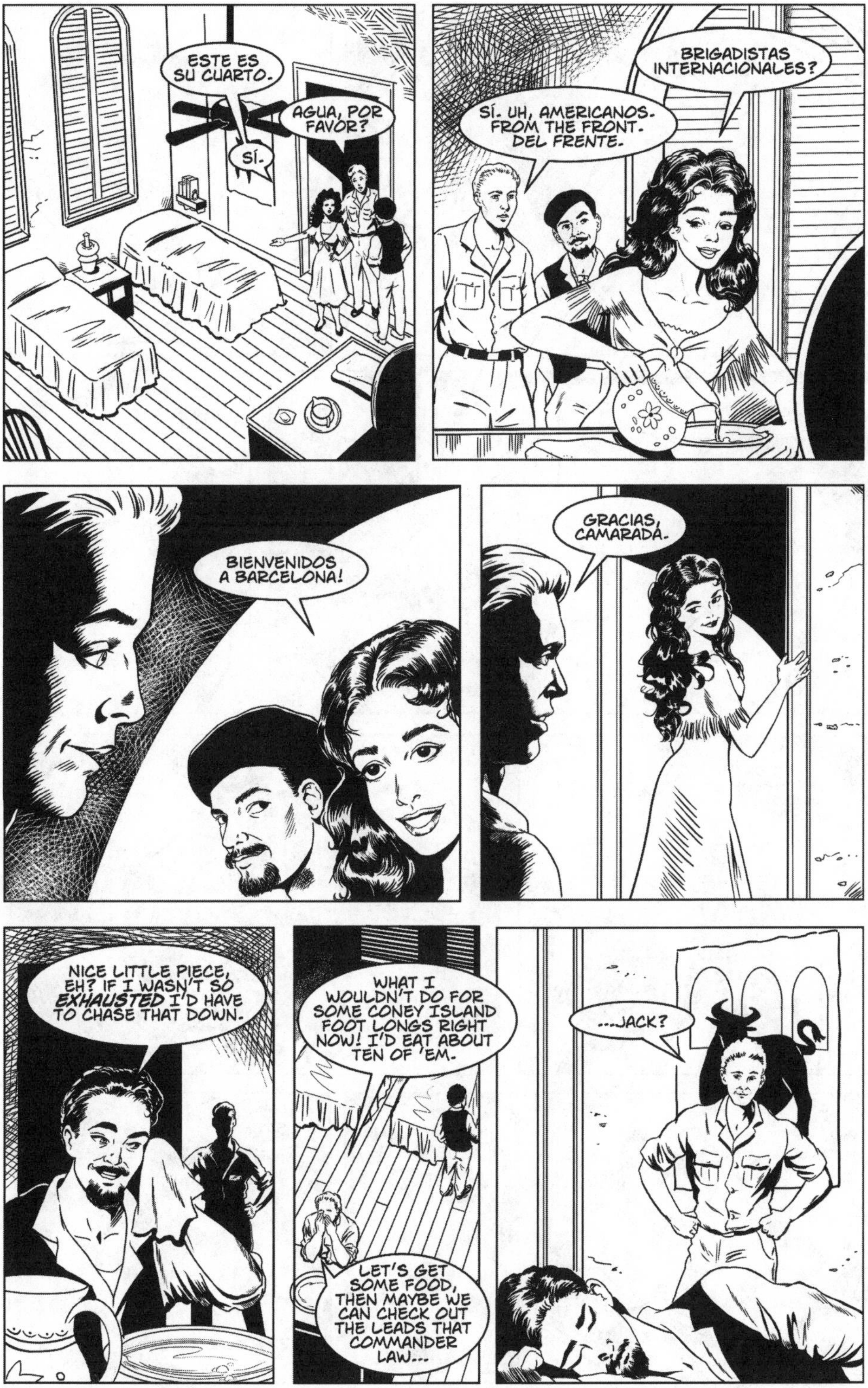
ESTE ES SU CUARTO.
AGUA, POR FAVOR?
SÍ.
BRIGADISTAS INTERNACIONALES?
SÍ. UH, AMERICANOS. FROM THE FRONT. DEL FRENTE.
BIENVENIDOS A BARCELONA!
GRACIAS, CAMARADA.
NICE LITTLE PIECE, EH? IF I WASN'T SO ***EXHAUSTED*** I'D HAVE TO CHASE THAT DOWN.
WHAT I WOULDN'T DO FOR SOME CONEY ISLAND FOOT LONGS RIGHT NOW! I'D EAT ABOUT TEN OF 'EM.
LET'S GET SOME FOOD, THEN MAYBE WE CAN CHECK OUT THE LEADS THAT COMMANDER LAW...
...JACK?

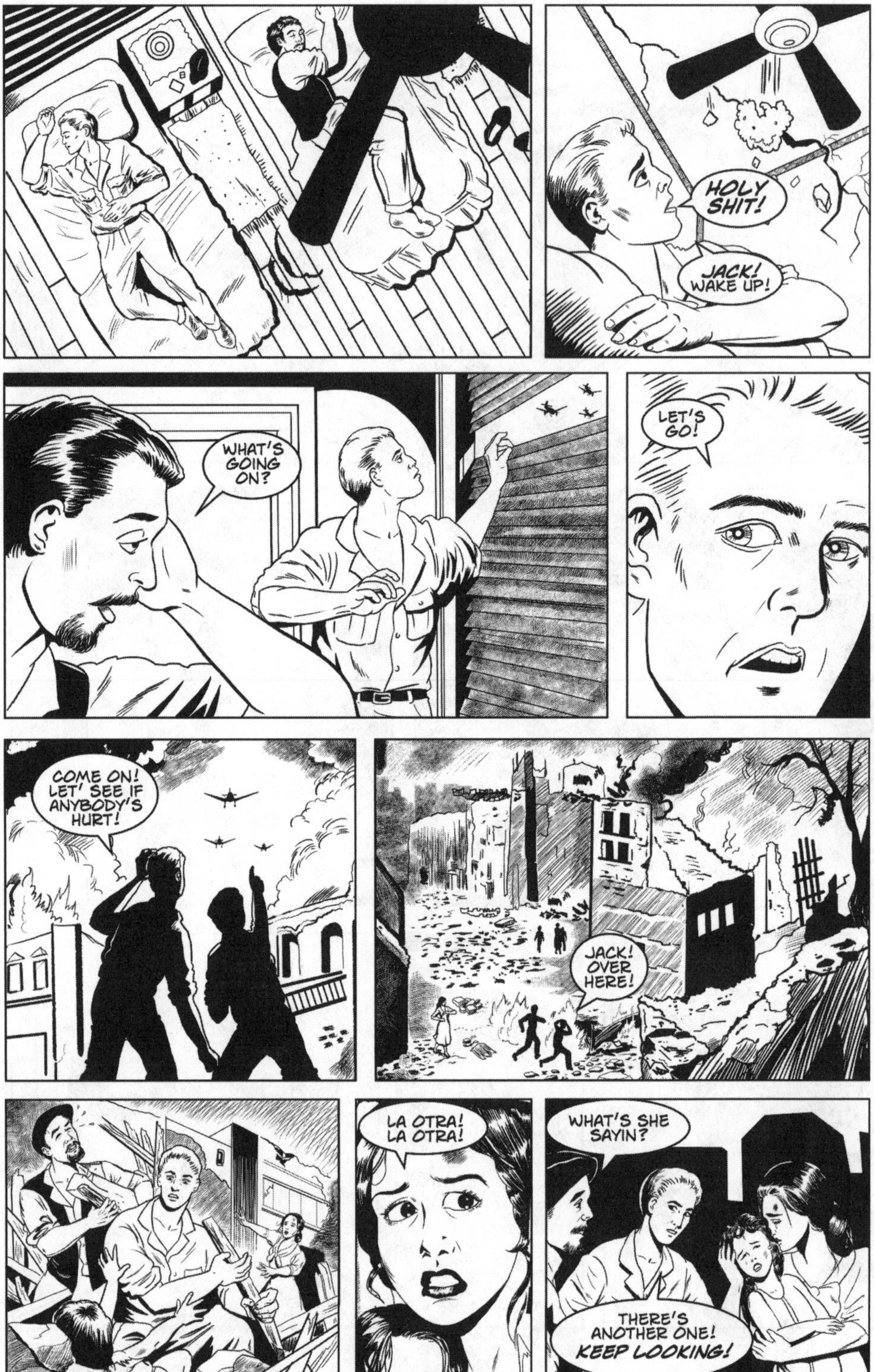
HOLY SHIT!
JACK! WAKE UP!
WHAT'S GOING ON?
LET'S GO!
COME ON! LET' SEE IF ANYBODY'S HURT!
JACK! OVER HERE!
LA OTRA! LA OTRA!
WHAT'S SHE SAYIN?
THERE'S ANOTHER ONE! KEEP LOOKING!

I THOUGHT WARS WERE SUPPOSED TO BE FOUGHT ON *BATTLEFIELDS*...

GUYS IN TRENCHES...

WHAT THE HELL ARE THEY DOIN' BOMBING *KIDS*?

FASCISTS DON'T DISCRIMINATE, JACK.

C'MON, LET'S GET OUR STUFF AND FIND SOMETHING TO EAT.

JACK! THERE'S NOTHING YOU CAN DO. THIS IS WHAT IT'S LIKE.

WAR STINKS, AND IT DOESN'T CARE IF YOU'RE THIRTY YEARS OLD, OR *THREE.*

THESE FASCIST BASTARDS DON'T CARE, JACK! THAT'S WHY WE'RE HERE...THEY DON'T CARE.

NOW C'MON.

YEAH. OKAY.

I'M OKAY.

PAGE 51

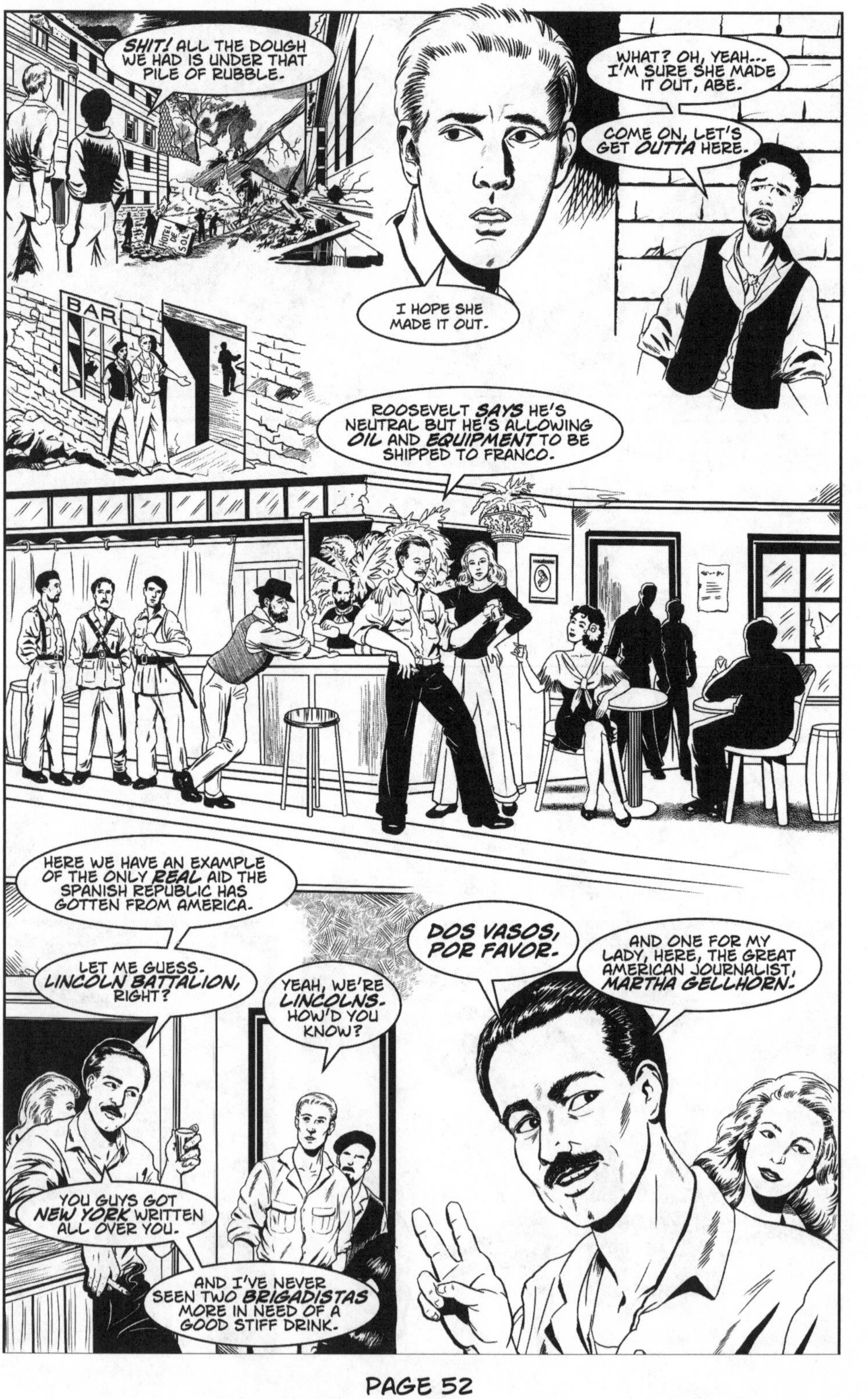

SHIT! ALL THE DOUGH WE HAD IS UNDER THAT PILE OF RUBBLE.
HOTEL DE SOL
I HOPE SHE MADE IT OUT.
WHAT? OH, YEAH... I'M SURE SHE MADE IT OUT, ABE.
COME ON, LET'S GET OUTTA HERE.
BAR
ROOSEVELT SAYS HE'S NEUTRAL BUT HE'S ALLOWING OIL AND EQUIPMENT TO BE SHIPPED TO FRANCO.
HERE WE HAVE AN EXAMPLE OF THE ONLY REAL AID THE SPANISH REPUBLIC HAS GOTTEN FROM AMERICA.
LET ME GUESS. LINCOLN BATTALION, RIGHT?
YOU GUYS GOT NEW YORK WRITTEN ALL OVER YOU.
YEAH, WE'RE LINCOLNS. HOW'D YOU KNOW?
AND I'VE NEVER SEEN TWO BRIGADISTAS MORE IN NEED OF A GOOD STIFF DRINK.
DOS VASOS, POR FAVOR.
AND ONE FOR MY LADY, HERE, THE GREAT AMERICAN JOURNALIST, MARTHA GELLHORN.

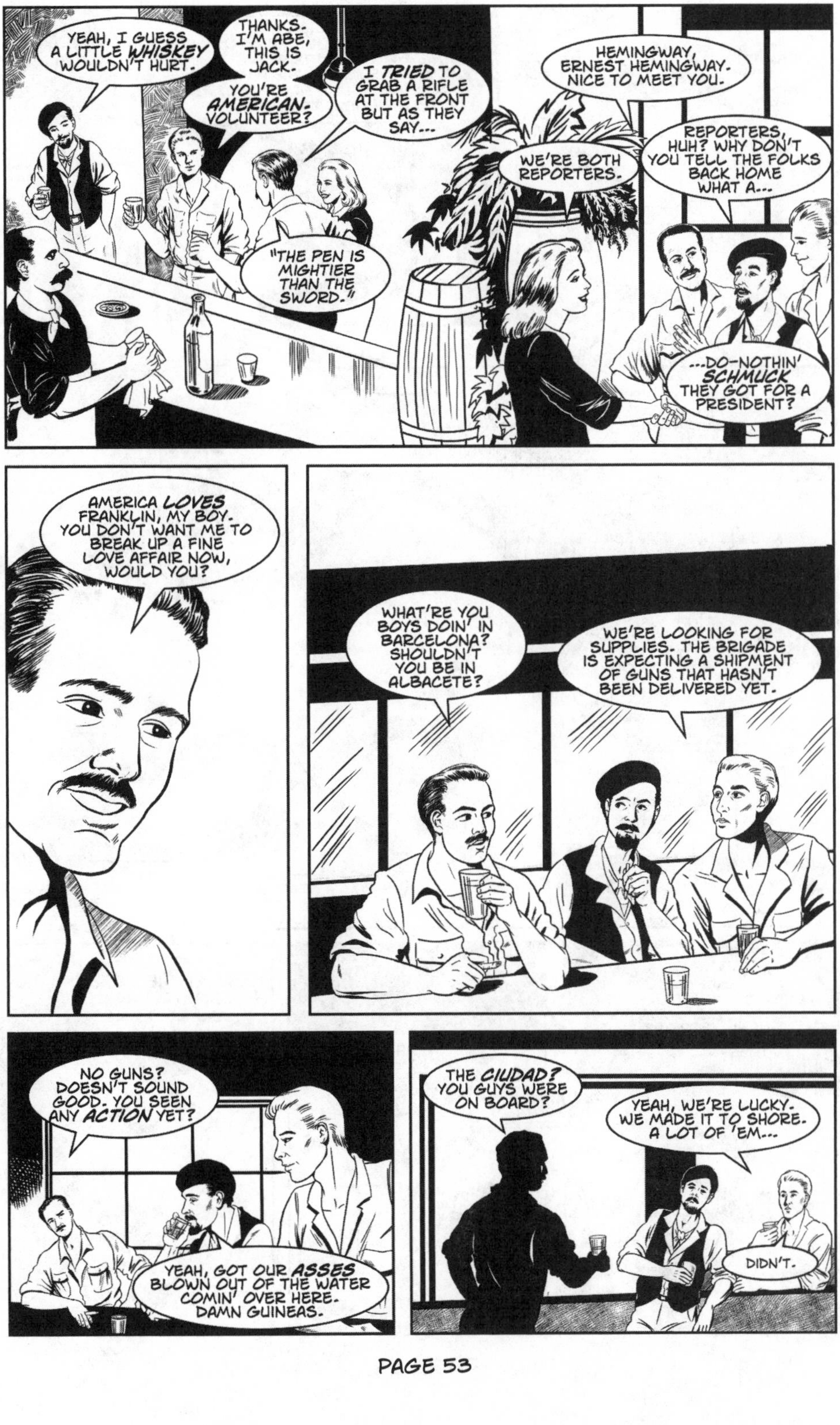
YEAH, I GUESS A LITTLE WHISKEY WOULDN'T HURT.
THANKS. I'M ABE, THIS IS JACK.
YOU'RE AMERICAN. VOLUNTEER?
I TRIED TO GRAB A RIFLE AT THE FRONT BUT AS THEY SAY...
"THE PEN IS MIGHTIER THAN THE SWORD."
HEMINGWAY, ERNEST HEMINGWAY. NICE TO MEET YOU.
WE'RE BOTH REPORTERS.
REPORTERS, HUH? WHY DON'T YOU TELL THE FOLKS BACK HOME WHAT A...
...DO-NOTHIN' SCHMUCK THEY GOT FOR A PRESIDENT?
AMERICA LOVES FRANKLIN, MY BOY. YOU DON'T WANT ME TO BREAK UP A FINE LOVE AFFAIR NOW, WOULD YOU?
WHAT'RE YOU BOYS DOIN' IN BARCELONA? SHOULDN'T YOU BE IN ALBACETE?
WE'RE LOOKING FOR SUPPLIES. THE BRIGADE IS EXPECTING A SHIPMENT OF GUNS THAT HASN'T BEEN DELIVERED YET.
NO GUNS? DOESN'T SOUND GOOD. YOU SEEN ANY ACTION YET?
YEAH, GOT OUR ASSES BLOWN OUT OF THE WATER COMIN' OVER HERE. DAMN GUINEAS.
THE CIUDAD? YOU GUYS WERE ON BOARD?
YEAH, WE'RE LUCKY. WE MADE IT TO SHORE. A LOT OF 'EM...
DIDN'T.

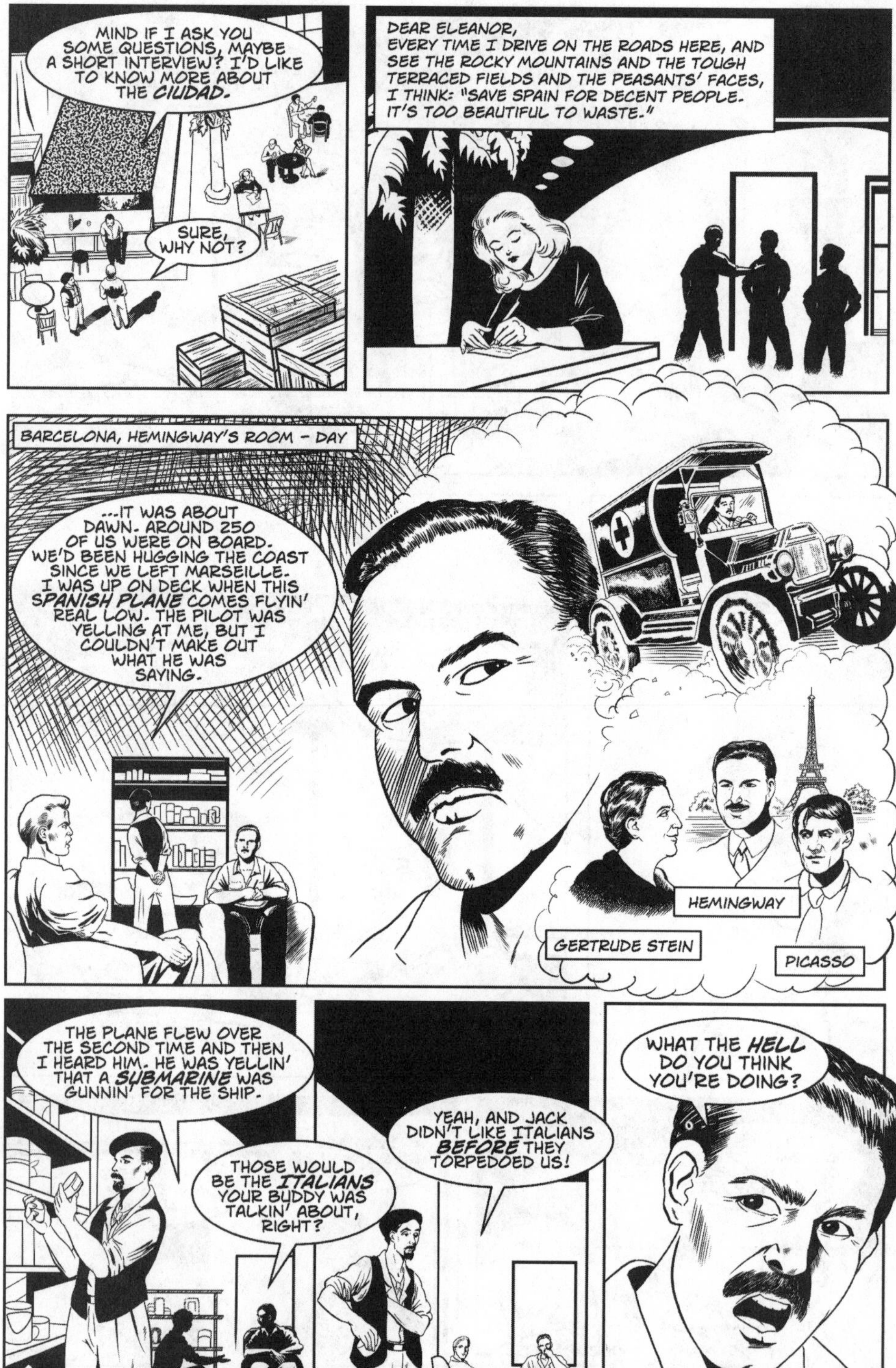
MIND IF I ASK YOU SOME QUESTIONS, MAYBE A SHORT INTERVIEW? I'D LIKE TO KNOW MORE ABOUT THE *CIUDAD*.
SURE, WHY NOT?
DEAR ELEANOR, EVERY TIME I DRIVE ON THE ROADS HERE, AND SEE THE ROCKY MOUNTAINS AND THE TOUGH TERRACED FIELDS AND THE PEASANTS' FACES, I THINK: "SAVE SPAIN FOR DECENT PEOPLE. IT'S TOO BEAUTIFUL TO WASTE."
BARCELONA, HEMINGWAY'S ROOM – DAY
...IT WAS ABOUT DAWN. AROUND 250 OF US WERE ON BOARD. WE'D BEEN HUGGING THE COAST SINCE WE LEFT MARSEILLE. I WAS UP ON DECK WHEN THIS *SPANISH PLANE* COMES FLYIN' REAL LOW. THE PILOT WAS YELLING AT ME, BUT I COULDN'T MAKE OUT WHAT HE WAS SAYING.
HEMINGWAY
GERTRUDE STEIN
PICASSO
THE PLANE FLEW OVER THE SECOND TIME AND THEN I HEARD HIM. HE WAS YELLIN' THAT A *SUBMARINE* WAS GUNNIN' FOR THE SHIP.
THOSE WOULD BE THE *ITALIANS* YOUR BUDDY WAS TALKIN' ABOUT, RIGHT?
YEAH, AND JACK DIDN'T LIKE ITALIANS *BEFORE* THEY TORPEDOED US!
WHAT THE *HELL* DO YOU THINK YOU'RE DOING?

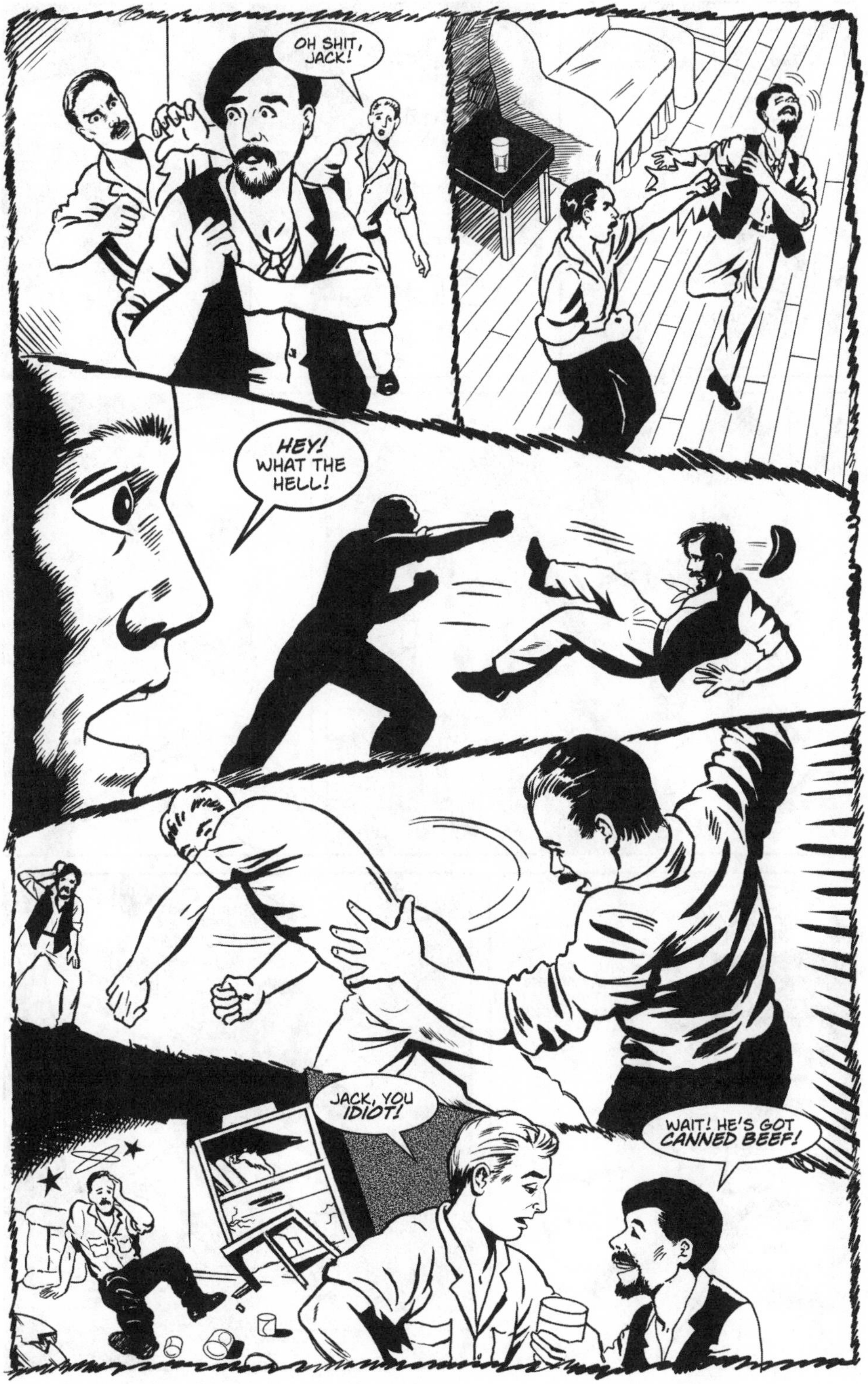
OH SHIT, JACK!
HEY! WHAT THE HELL!
JACK, YOU IDIOT!
WAIT! HE'S GOT CANNED BEEF!

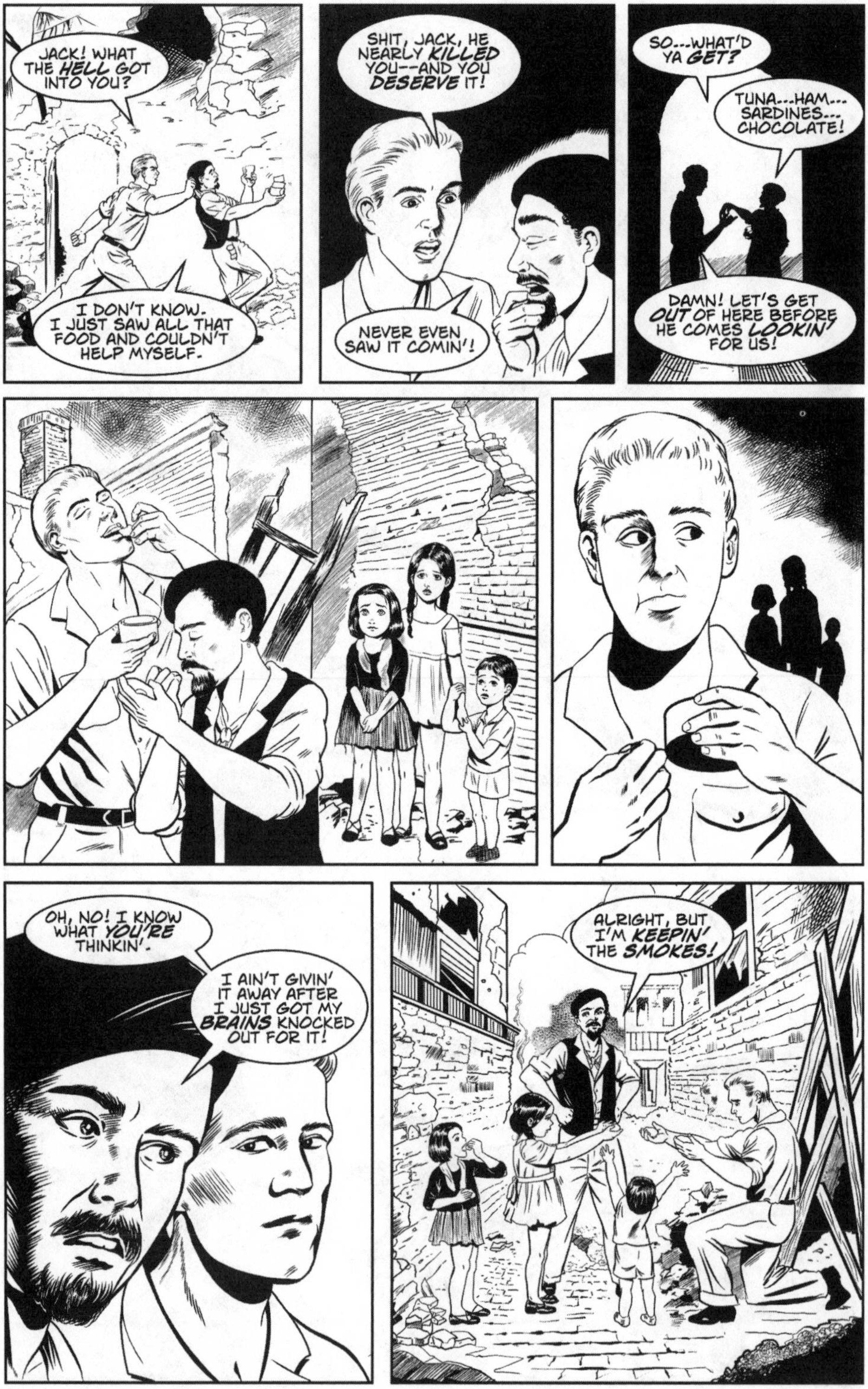
JACK! WHAT THE *HELL* GOT INTO YOU?
I DON'T KNOW. I JUST SAW ALL THAT FOOD AND COULDN'T HELP MYSELF.
SHIT, JACK, HE NEARLY *KILLED* YOU--AND YOU *DESERVE* IT!
NEVER EVEN SAW IT COMIN'!
SO...WHAT'D YA *GET?*
TUNA...HAM... SARDINES... CHOCOLATE!
DAMN! LET'S GET *OUT* OF HERE BEFORE HE COMES *LOOKIN'* FOR US!
OH, NO! I KNOW WHAT *YOU'RE* THINKIN'.
I AIN'T GIVIN' IT AWAY AFTER I JUST GOT MY *BRAINS* KNOCKED OUT FOR IT!
ALRIGHT, BUT I'M *KEEPIN'* THE *SMOKES!*

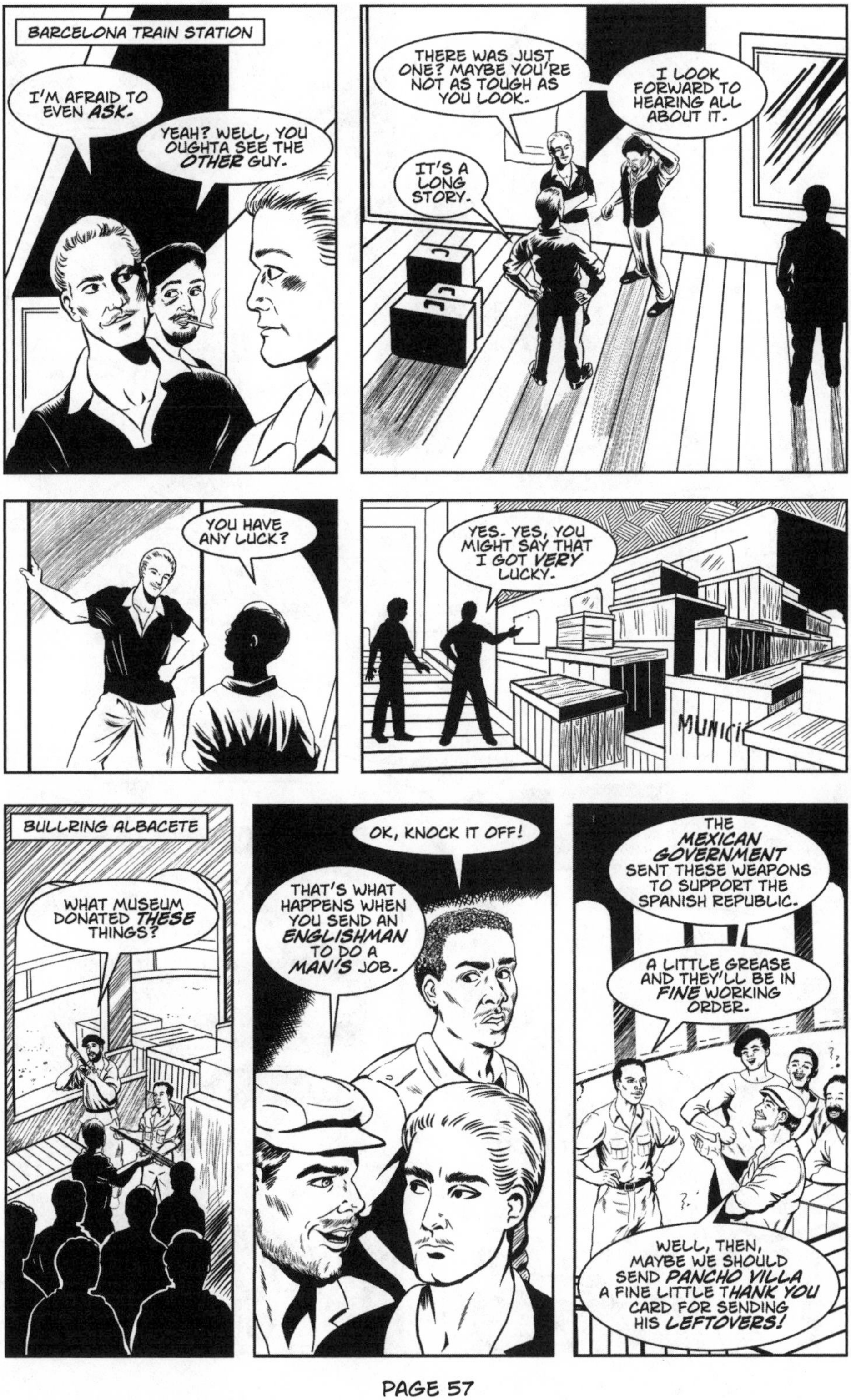
BARCELONA TRAIN STATION
I'M AFRAID TO EVEN **ASK.**
YEAH? WELL, YOU OUGHTA SEE THE **OTHER** GUY.
THERE WAS JUST ONE? MAYBE YOU'RE NOT AS TOUGH AS YOU LOOK.
I LOOK FORWARD TO HEARING ALL ABOUT IT.
IT'S A LONG STORY.
YOU HAVE ANY LUCK?
YES. YES, YOU MIGHT SAY THAT I GOT **VERY** LUCKY.
MUNICI
BULLRING ALBACETE
WHAT MUSEUM DONATED **THESE** THINGS?
OK, KNOCK IT OFF!
THAT'S WHAT HAPPENS WHEN YOU SEND AN **ENGLISHMAN** TO DO A **MAN'S** JOB.
THE **MEXICAN GOVERNMENT** SENT THESE WEAPONS TO SUPPORT THE SPANISH REPUBLIC.
A LITTLE GREASE AND THEY'LL BE IN **FINE** WORKING ORDER.
WELL, THEN, MAYBE WE SHOULD SEND **PANCHO VILLA** A FINE LITTLE T**HANK YOU** CARD FOR SENDING HIS **LEFTOVERS!**

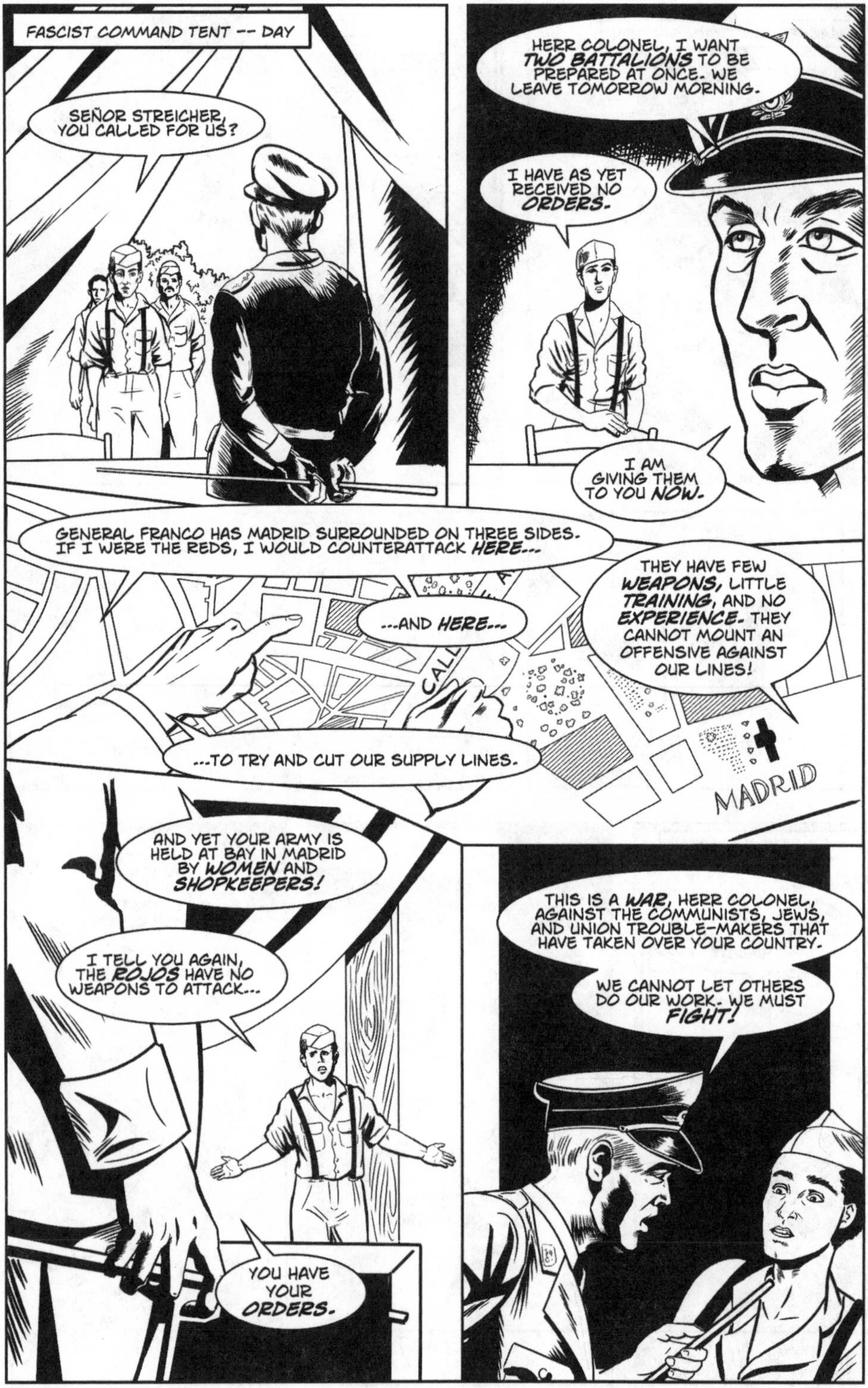
FASCIST COMMAND TENT -- DAY
SEÑOR STREICHER, YOU CALLED FOR US?
HERR COLONEL, I WANT TWO BATTALIONS TO BE PREPARED AT ONCE. WE LEAVE TOMORROW MORNING.
I HAVE AS YET RECEIVED NO ORDERS.
I AM GIVING THEM TO YOU NOW.
GENERAL FRANCO HAS MADRID SURROUNDED ON THREE SIDES. IF I WERE THE REDS, I WOULD COUNTERATTACK HERE...
...AND HERE...
...TO TRY AND CUT OUR SUPPLY LINES.
THEY HAVE FEW WEAPONS, LITTLE TRAINING, AND NO EXPERIENCE. THEY CANNOT MOUNT AN OFFENSIVE AGAINST OUR LINES!
MADRID
AND YET YOUR ARMY IS HELD AT BAY IN MADRID BY WOMEN AND SHOPKEEPERS!
I TELL YOU AGAIN, THE ROJOS HAVE NO WEAPONS TO ATTACK...
YOU HAVE YOUR ORDERS.
THIS IS A WAR, HERR COLONEL, AGAINST THE COMMUNISTS, JEWS, AND UNION TROUBLE-MAKERS THAT HAVE TAKEN OVER YOUR COUNTRY.
WE CANNOT LET OTHERS DO OUR WORK. WE MUST FIGHT!

THE RIFLES MAY BE OLD, BUT I ASSURE YOU...

THESE RUSSIAN MACHINE GUNS ARE IN *MUCH* BETTER SHAPE!

WE'VE BEEN TRAINING FOR MONTHS, GENTLEMEN, AND NOW IT'S TIME TO MOVE OUT!

WE MAY BE VOLUNTEERS, BUT THEY KNOW WE HAVE COURAGE!

THE INTERNATIONAL BRIGADES WILL BE USED TO CUT THE FASCIST SUPPLY LINES TO MADRID.

THIS IS THE REPUBLIC'S FIRST OFFENSIVE. IT'S TIME TO TAKE THE FIGHT TO THE *FASCISTS,* MEN!

PACK YOUR GEAR! WE LEAVE IN *ONE HOUR!*

WELL, ABE, IT'S *FINALLY* GOING TO HAPPEN!

IT'S ABOUT TIME!

YOU KNOW, I ALWAYS KNEW I'D FIGHT AGAINST OPPRESSION...BUT NOT AS A SOLDIER.

YOU'LL DO *FINE,* JULIUS. WE'RE JUST CONTINUING THE FIGHT WE STARTED ON THE *BREMEN.*

I GUESS SOME THINGS ARE *WORTH* DYING FOR, HUH, ABE?

PAGE 59

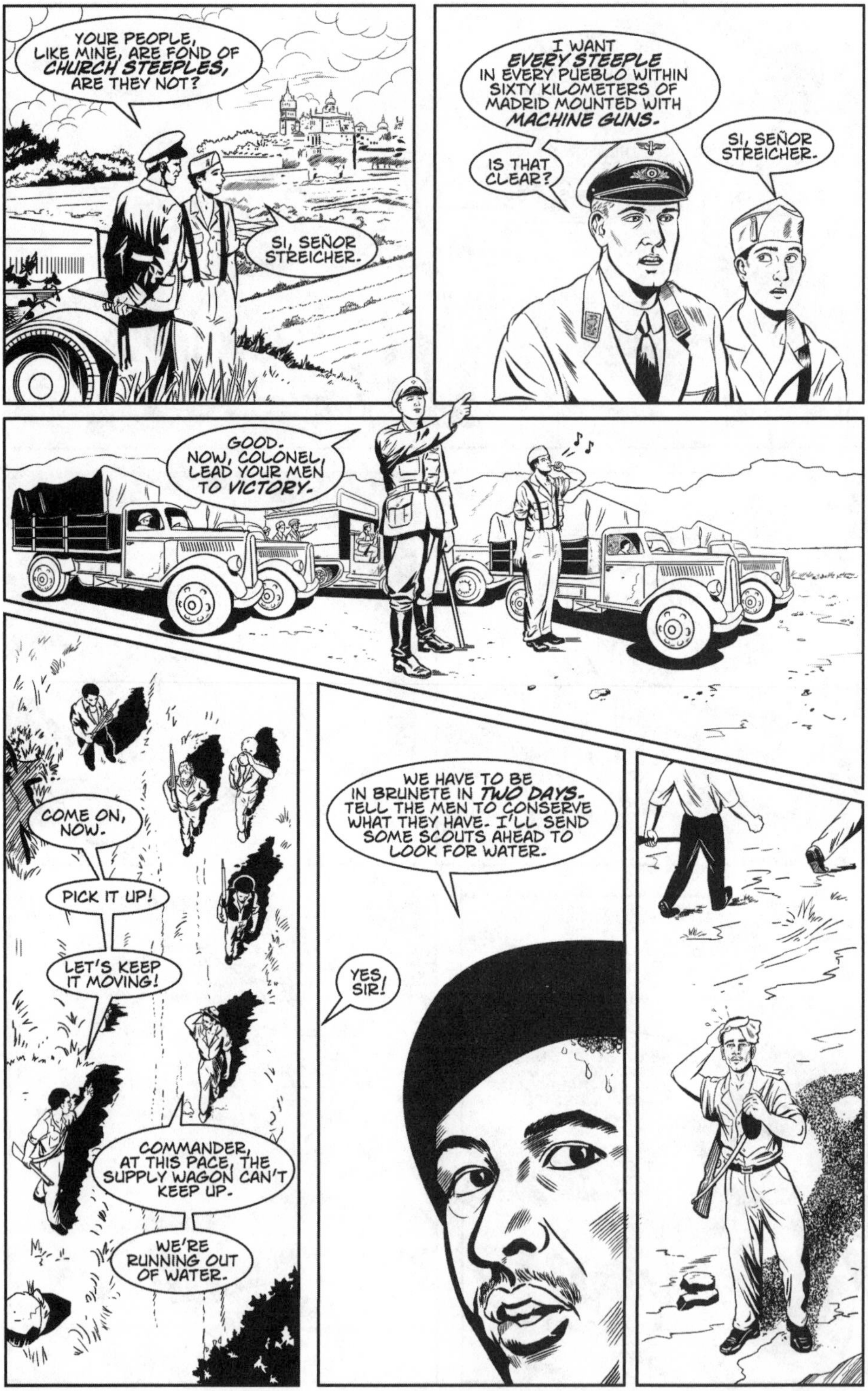
YOUR PEOPLE, LIKE MINE, ARE FOND OF CHURCH STEEPLES, ARE THEY NOT?
SI, SEÑOR STREICHER.
I WANT EVERY STEEPLE IN EVERY PUEBLO WITHIN SIXTY KILOMETERS OF MADRID MOUNTED WITH MACHINE GUNS.
IS THAT CLEAR?
SI, SEÑOR STREICHER.
GOOD. NOW, COLONEL, LEAD YOUR MEN TO VICTORY.
COME ON, NOW.
PICK IT UP!
LET'S KEEP IT MOVING!
COMMANDER, AT THIS PACE, THE SUPPLY WAGON CAN'T KEEP UP.
WE'RE RUNNING OUT OF WATER.
WE HAVE TO BE IN BRUNETE IN TWO DAYS. TELL THE MEN TO CONSERVE WHAT THEY HAVE. I'LL SEND SOME SCOUTS AHEAD TO LOOK FOR WATER.
YES SIR!

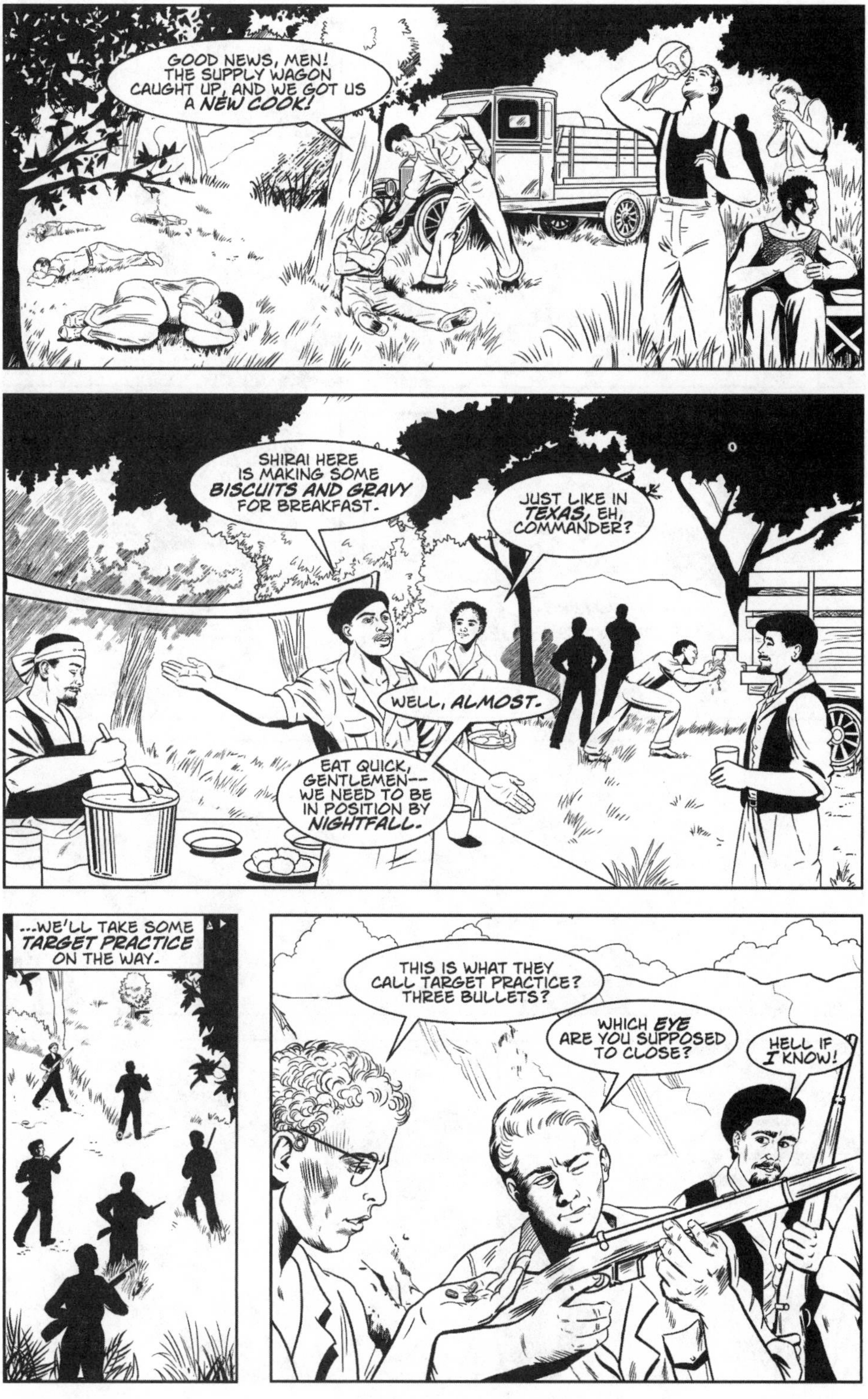
GOOD NEWS, MEN! THE SUPPLY WAGON CAUGHT UP, AND WE GOT US A *NEW COOK!*
SHIRAI HERE IS MAKING SOME *BISCUITS AND GRAVY* FOR BREAKFAST.
JUST LIKE IN *TEXAS,* EH, COMMANDER?
WELL, *ALMOST.*
EAT QUICK, GENTLEMEN-- WE NEED TO BE IN POSITION BY *NIGHTFALL.*
...WE'LL TAKE SOME *TARGET PRACTICE* ON THE WAY.
THIS IS WHAT THEY CALL TARGET PRACTICE? THREE BULLETS?
WHICH *EYE* ARE YOU SUPPOSED TO CLOSE?
HELL IF *I* KNOW!

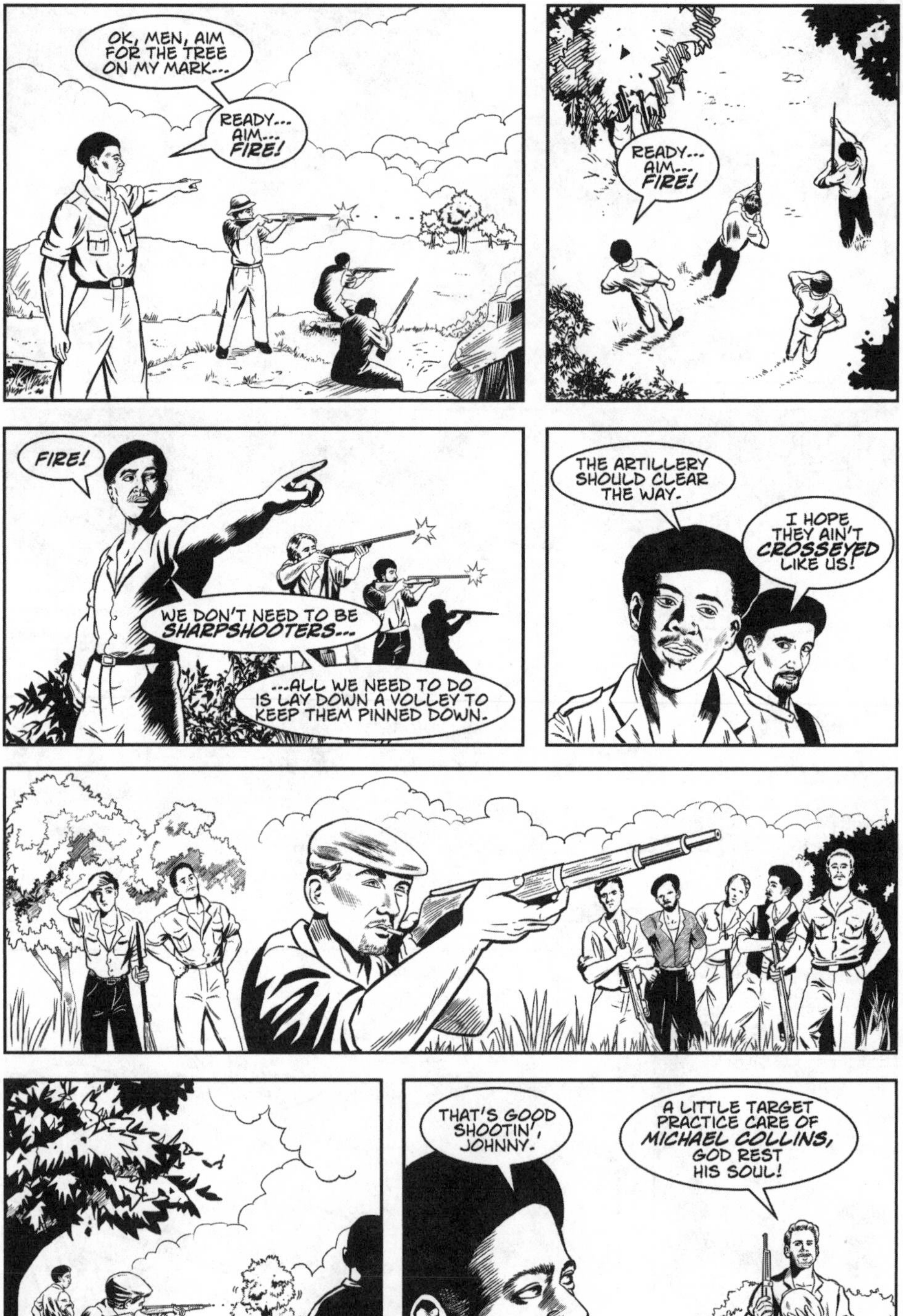
OK, MEN, AIM FOR THE TREE ON MY MARK...
READY... AIM... FIRE!
READY... AIM... FIRE!
FIRE!
WE DON'T NEED TO BE SHARPSHOOTERS...
...ALL WE NEED TO DO IS LAY DOWN A VOLLEY TO KEEP THEM PINNED DOWN.
THE ARTILLERY SHOULD CLEAR THE WAY.
I HOPE THEY AIN'T CROSSEYED LIKE US!
THAT'S GOOD SHOOTIN', JOHNNY.
A LITTLE TARGET PRACTICE CARE OF MICHAEL COLLINS, GOD REST HIS SOUL!

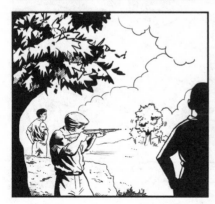

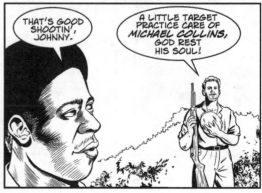

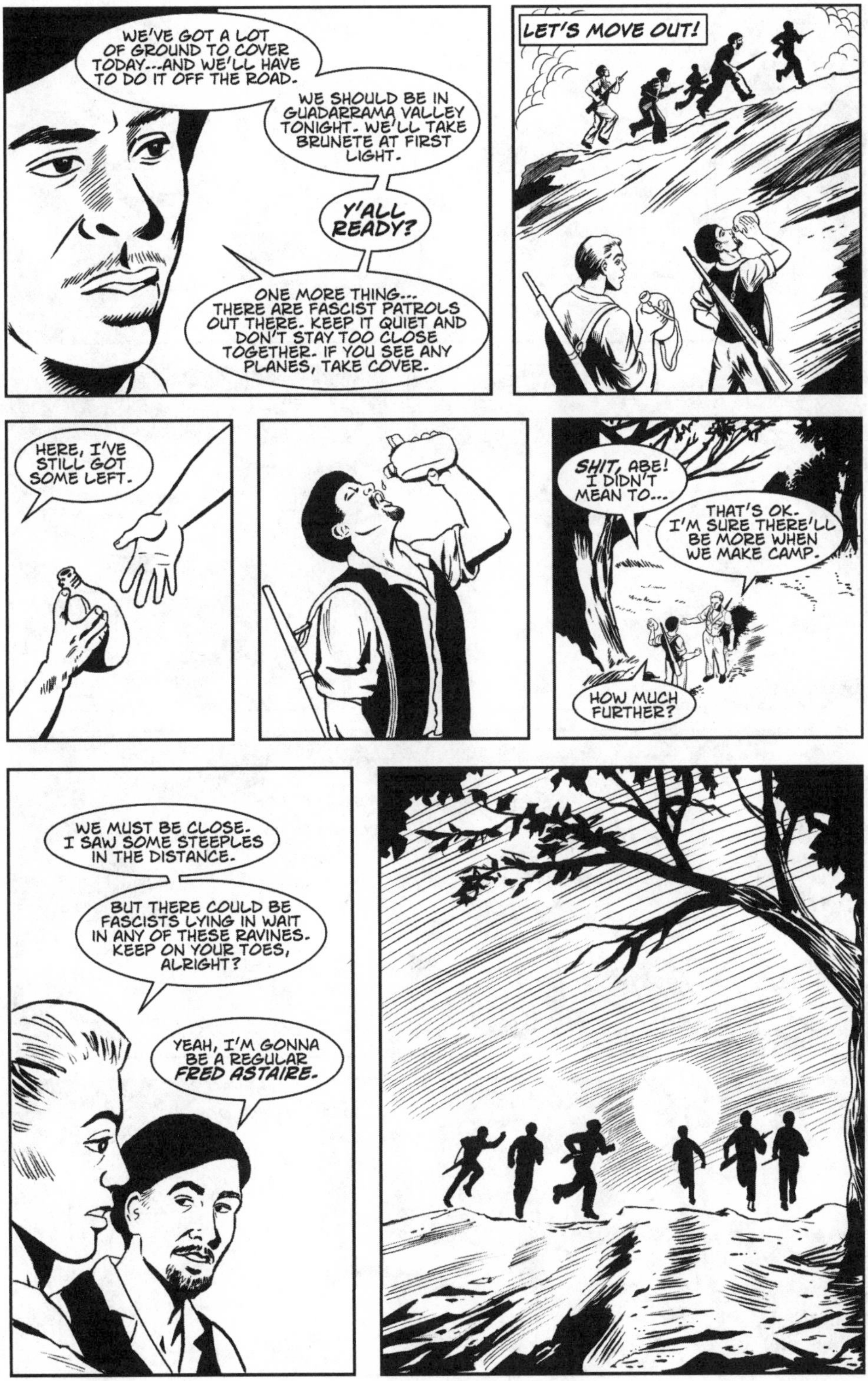
WE'VE GOT A LOT OF GROUND TO COVER TODAY---AND WE'LL HAVE TO DO IT OFF THE ROAD.
WE SHOULD BE IN GUADARRAMA VALLEY TONIGHT. WE'LL TAKE BRUNETE AT FIRST LIGHT.
Y'ALL READY?
ONE MORE THING... THERE ARE FASCIST PATROLS OUT THERE. KEEP IT QUIET AND DON'T STAY TOO CLOSE TOGETHER. IF YOU SEE ANY PLANES, TAKE COVER.
LET'S MOVE OUT!
HERE, I'VE STILL GOT SOME LEFT.
SHIT, ABE! I DIDN'T MEAN TO...
THAT'S OK. I'M SURE THERE'LL BE MORE WHEN WE MAKE CAMP.
HOW MUCH FURTHER?
WE MUST BE CLOSE. I SAW SOME STEEPLES IN THE DISTANCE.
BUT THERE COULD BE FASCISTS LYING IN WAIT IN ANY OF THESE RAVINES. KEEP ON YOUR TOES, ALRIGHT?
YEAH, I'M GONNA BE A REGULAR FRED ASTAIRE.

WE'RE GONNA TAKE COVER HERE FOR THE NIGHT.
IN THE MORNING, WE SHOULD HAVE SOME AIR COVER AND ARTILLERY SUPPORT.
WHEN THAT HAPPENS, WE GO OVER THE TOP.
WHAT ABOUT WATER? WE'RE DYIN' OF THIRST HERE.
I KNOW. I KNOW. WE'RE WORKIN' ON IT.
YOU GUYS HANG IN THERE.
JACK, YOU OKAY, BUDDY?
WHEN WE WAS ON THAT BOAT, I COMPLAINED ABOUT BEIN' SURROUNDED BY WATER.
NOW LOOK AT US.
NOT A DROP IN SIGHT.

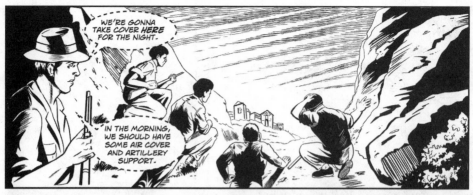

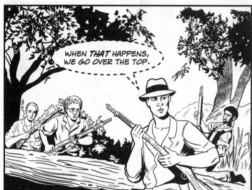

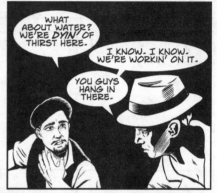

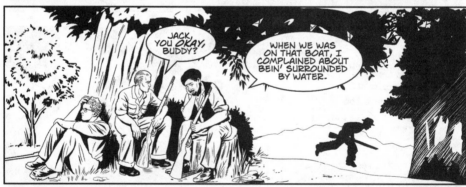

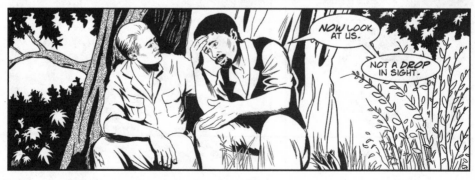

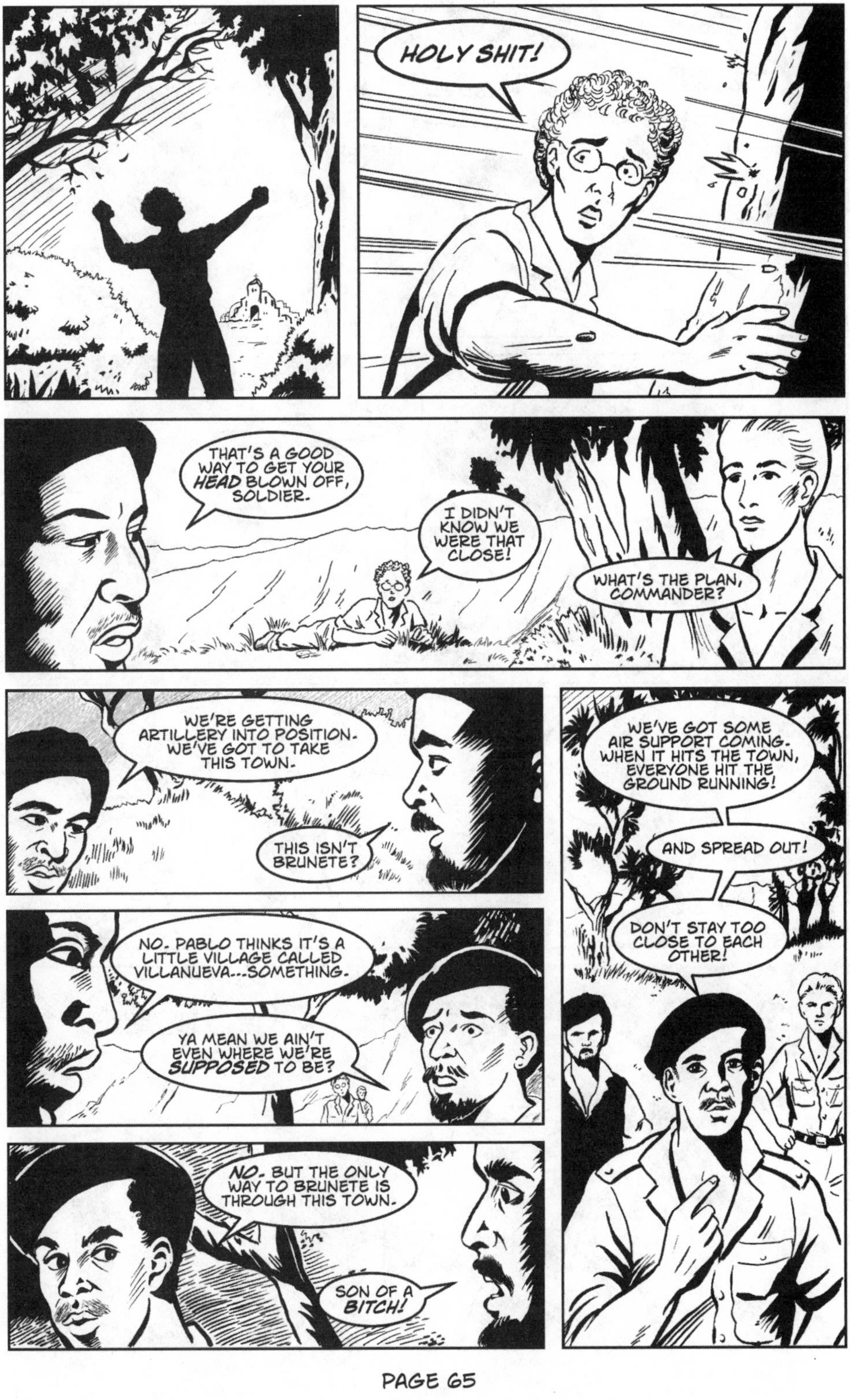
HOLY SHIT!
THAT'S A GOOD WAY TO GET YOUR HEAD BLOWN OFF, SOLDIER.
I DIDN'T KNOW WE WERE THAT CLOSE!
WHAT'S THE PLAN, COMMANDER?
WE'RE GETTING ARTILLERY INTO POSITION. WE'VE GOT TO TAKE THIS TOWN.
THIS ISN'T BRUNETE?
NO. PABLO THINKS IT'S A LITTLE VILLAGE CALLED VILLANUEVA...SOMETHING.
YA MEAN WE AIN'T EVEN WHERE WE'RE SUPPOSED TO BE?
NO. BUT THE ONLY WAY TO BRUNETE IS THROUGH THIS TOWN.
SON OF A BITCH!
WE'VE GOT SOME AIR SUPPORT COMING. WHEN IT HITS THE TOWN, EVERYONE HIT THE GROUND RUNNING!
AND SPREAD OUT!
DON'T STAY TOO CLOSE TO EACH OTHER!

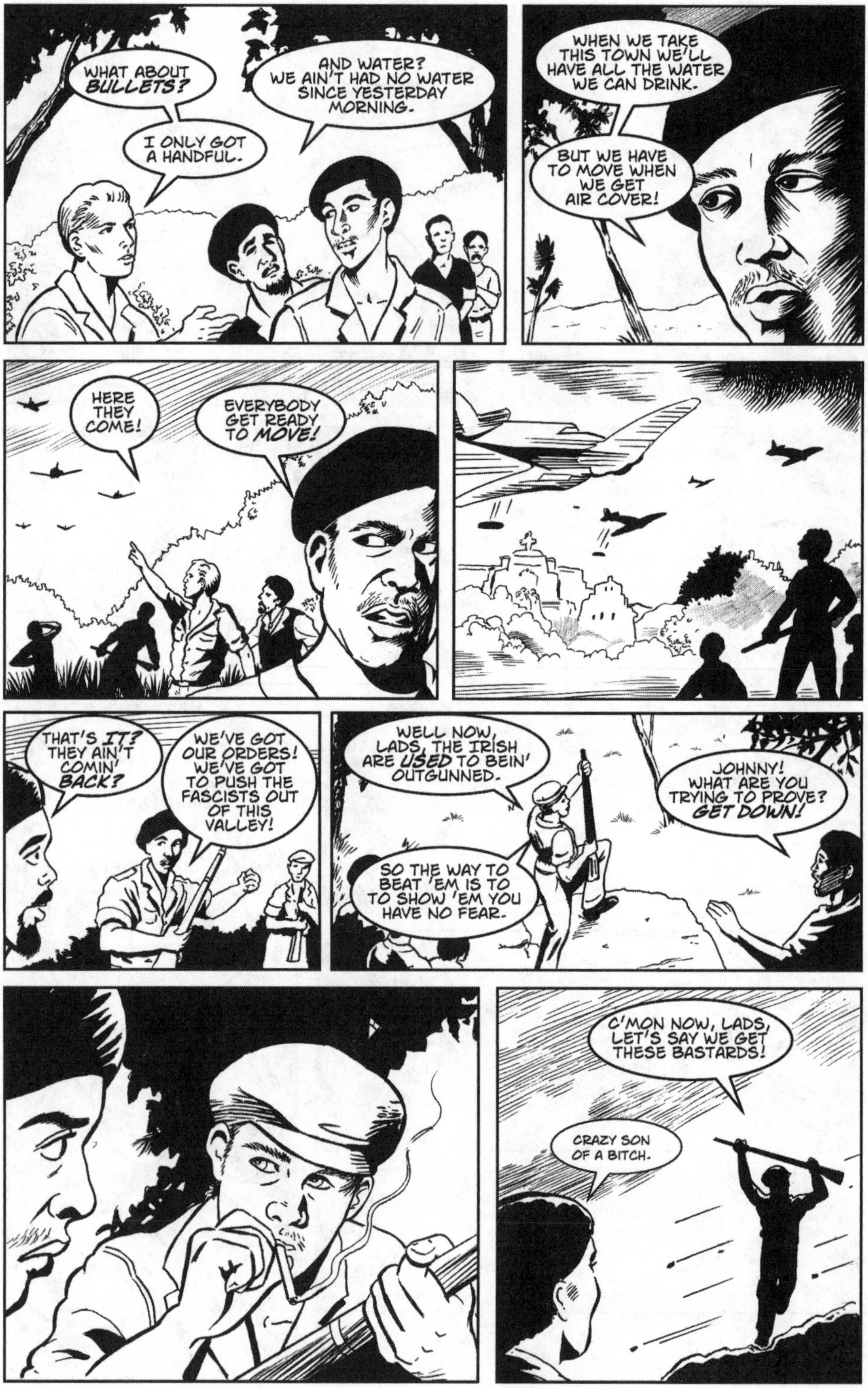
WHAT ABOUT BULLETS?
I ONLY GOT A HANDFUL.
AND WATER? WE AIN'T HAD NO WATER SINCE YESTERDAY MORNING.
WHEN WE TAKE THIS TOWN WE'LL HAVE ALL THE WATER WE CAN DRINK.
BUT WE HAVE TO MOVE WHEN WE GET AIR COVER!
HERE THEY COME!
EVERYBODY GET READY TO MOVE!
THAT'S IT? THEY AIN'T COMIN' BACK?
WE'VE GOT OUR ORDERS! WE'VE GOT TO PUSH THE FASCISTS OUT OF THIS VALLEY!
WELL NOW, LADS, THE IRISH ARE USED TO BEIN' OUTGUNNED.
SO THE WAY TO BEAT 'EM IS TO TO SHOW 'EM YOU HAVE NO FEAR.
JOHNNY! WHAT ARE YOU TRYING TO PROVE? GET DOWN!
C'MON NOW, LADS, LET'S SAY WE GET THESE BASTARDS!
CRAZY SON OF A BITCH.

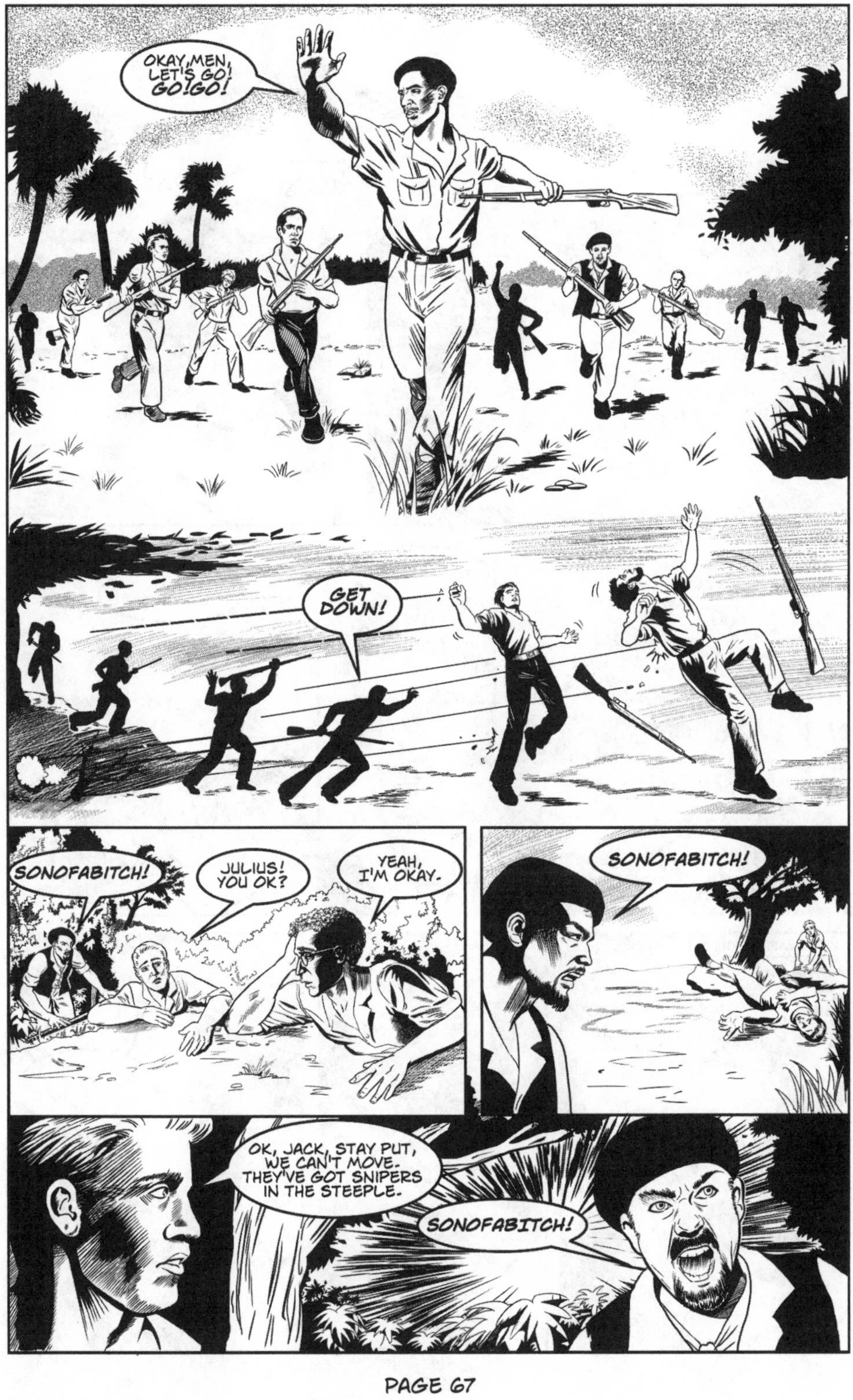
OKAY, MEN, LET'S GO! GO!GO!
GET DOWN!
SONOFABITCH!
JULIUS! YOU OK?
YEAH, I'M OKAY.
SONOFABITCH!
OK, JACK, STAY PUT, WE CAN'T MOVE. THEY'VE GOT SNIPERS IN THE STEEPLE.
SONOFABITCH!

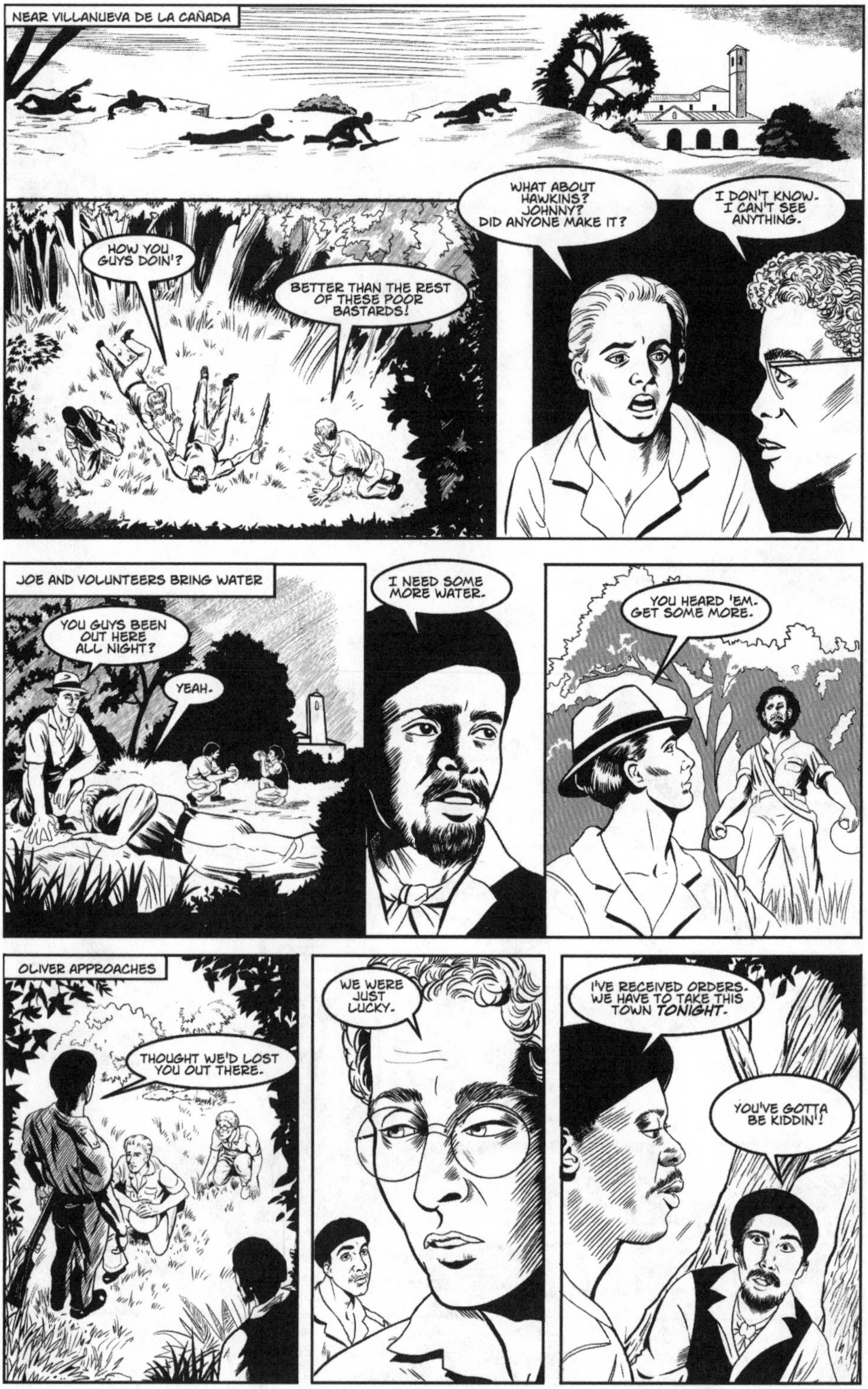
NEAR VILLANUEVA DE LA CAÑADA
HOW YOU GUYS DOIN'?
BETTER THAN THE REST OF THESE POOR BASTARDS!
WHAT ABOUT HAWKINS? JOHNNY? DID ANYONE MAKE IT?
I DON'T KNOW. I CAN'T SEE ANYTHING.
JOE AND VOLUNTEERS BRING WATER
YOU GUYS BEEN OUT HERE ALL NIGHT?
YEAH.
I NEED SOME MORE WATER.
YOU HEARD 'EM. GET SOME MORE.
OLIVER APPROACHES
THOUGHT WE'D LOST YOU OUT THERE.
WE WERE JUST LUCKY.
I'VE RECEIVED ORDERS. WE HAVE TO TAKE THIS TOWN *TONIGHT*.
YOU'VE GOTTA BE KIDDIN'!

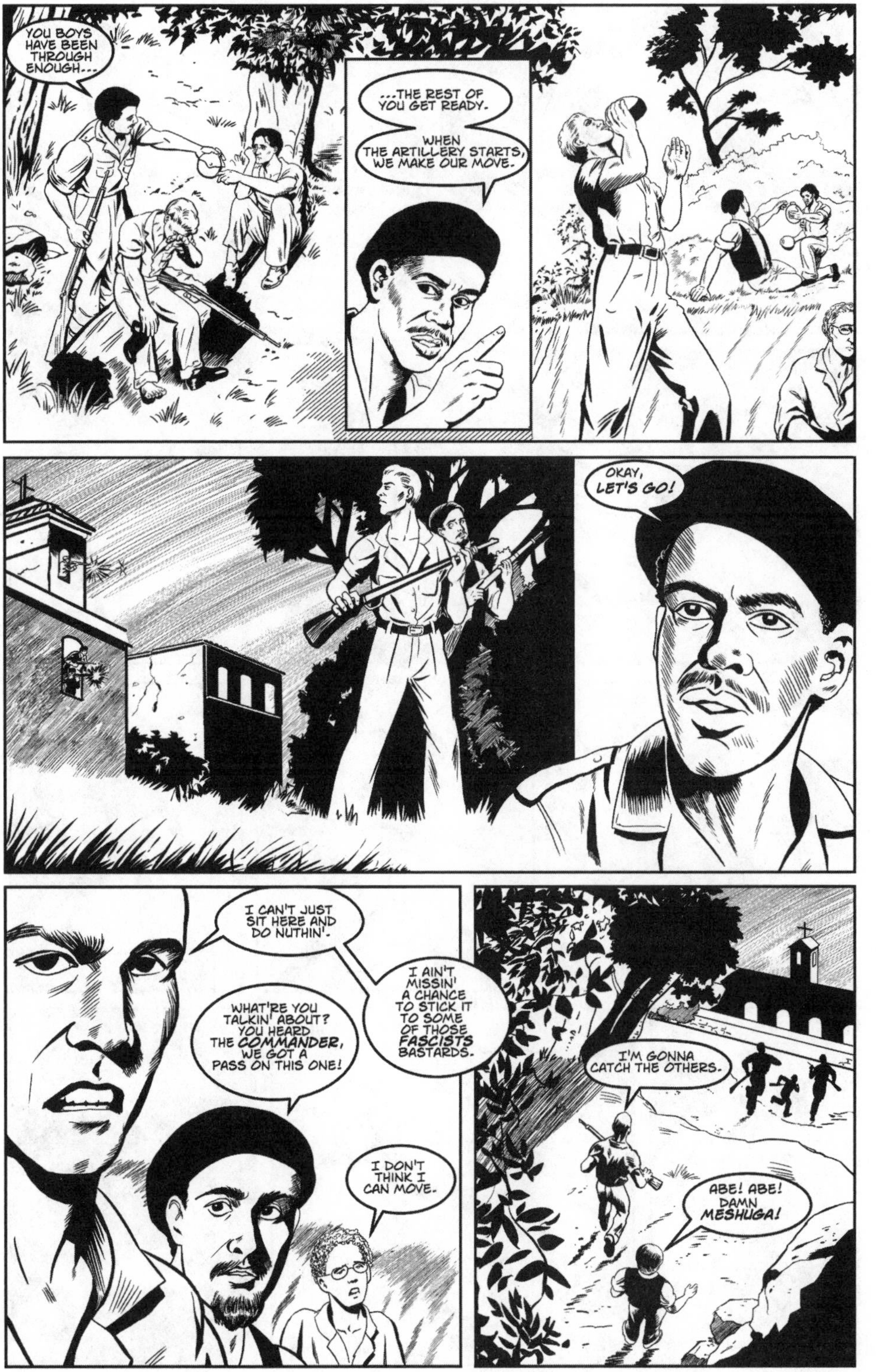
YOU BOYS HAVE BEEN THROUGH ENOUGH...
...THE REST OF YOU GET READY.
WHEN THE ARTILLERY STARTS, WE MAKE OUR MOVE.
OKAY, LET'S GO!
I CAN'T JUST SIT HERE AND DO NUTHIN'.
WHAT'RE YOU TALKIN' ABOUT? YOU HEARD THE COMMANDER, WE GOT A PASS ON THIS ONE!
I AIN'T MISSIN' A CHANCE TO STICK IT TO SOME OF THOSE FASCISTS BASTARDS.
I DON'T THINK I CAN MOVE.
I'M GONNA CATCH THE OTHERS.
ABE! ABE! DAMN MESHUGA!

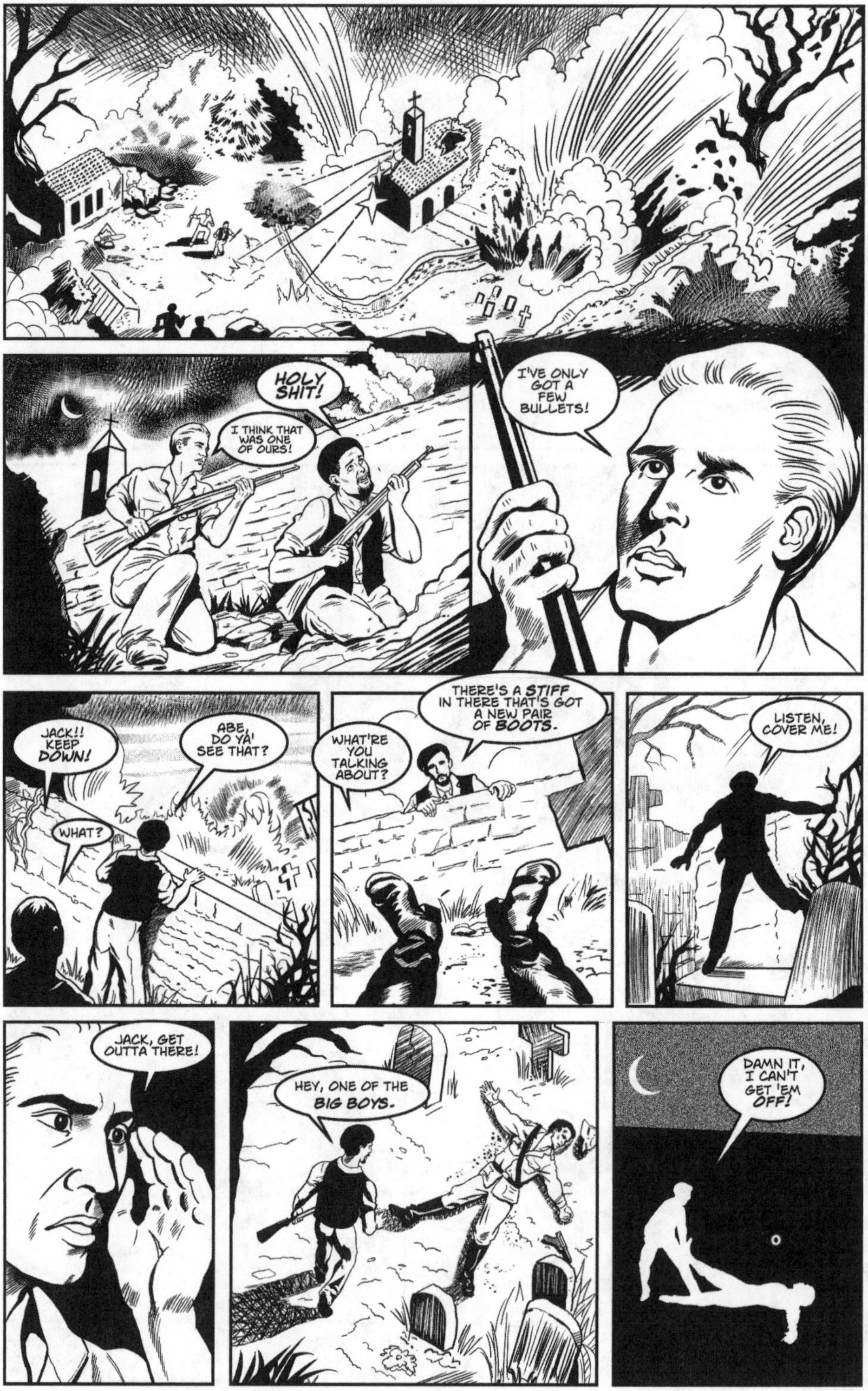
HOLY SHIT!
I THINK THAT WAS ONE OF OURS!
I'VE ONLY GOT A FEW BULLETS!
JACK!! KEEP DOWN!
ABE, DO YA' SEE THAT?
WHAT?
WHAT'RE YOU TALKING ABOUT?
THERE'S A STIFF IN THERE THAT'S GOT A NEW PAIR OF BOOTS.
LISTEN, COVER ME!
JACK, GET OUTTA THERE!
HEY, ONE OF THE BIG BOYS.
DAMN IT, I CAN'T GET 'EM OFF!

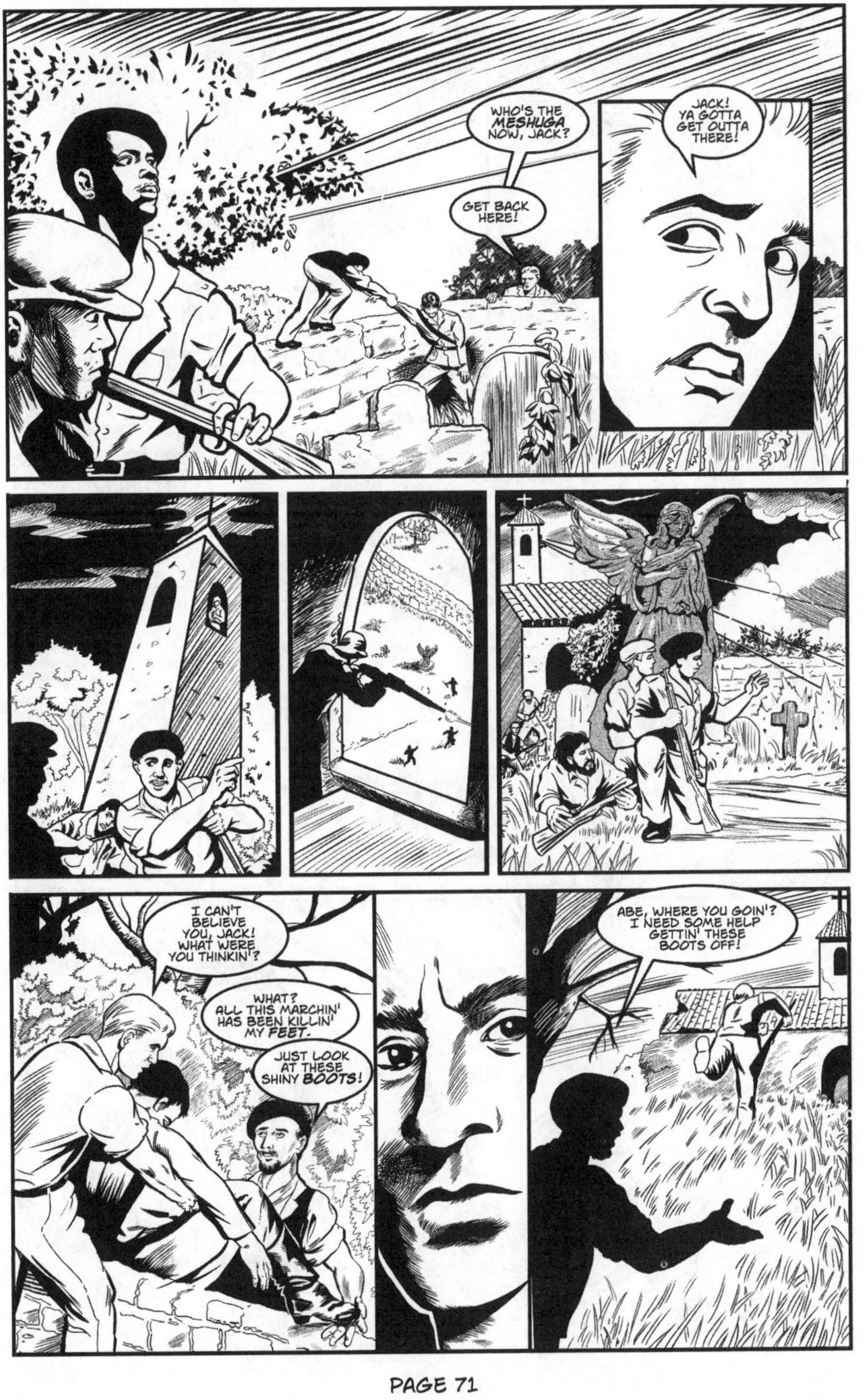
WHO'S THE MESHUGA NOW, JACK?
GET BACK HERE!
JACK! YA GOTTA GET OUTTA THERE!
I CAN'T BELIEVE YOU, JACK! WHAT WERE YOU THINKIN'?
WHAT? ALL THIS MARCHIN' HAS BEEN KILLIN' MY FEET.
JUST LOOK AT THESE SHINY BOOTS!
ABE, WHERE YOU GOIN'? I NEED SOME HELP GETTIN' THESE BOOTS OFF!

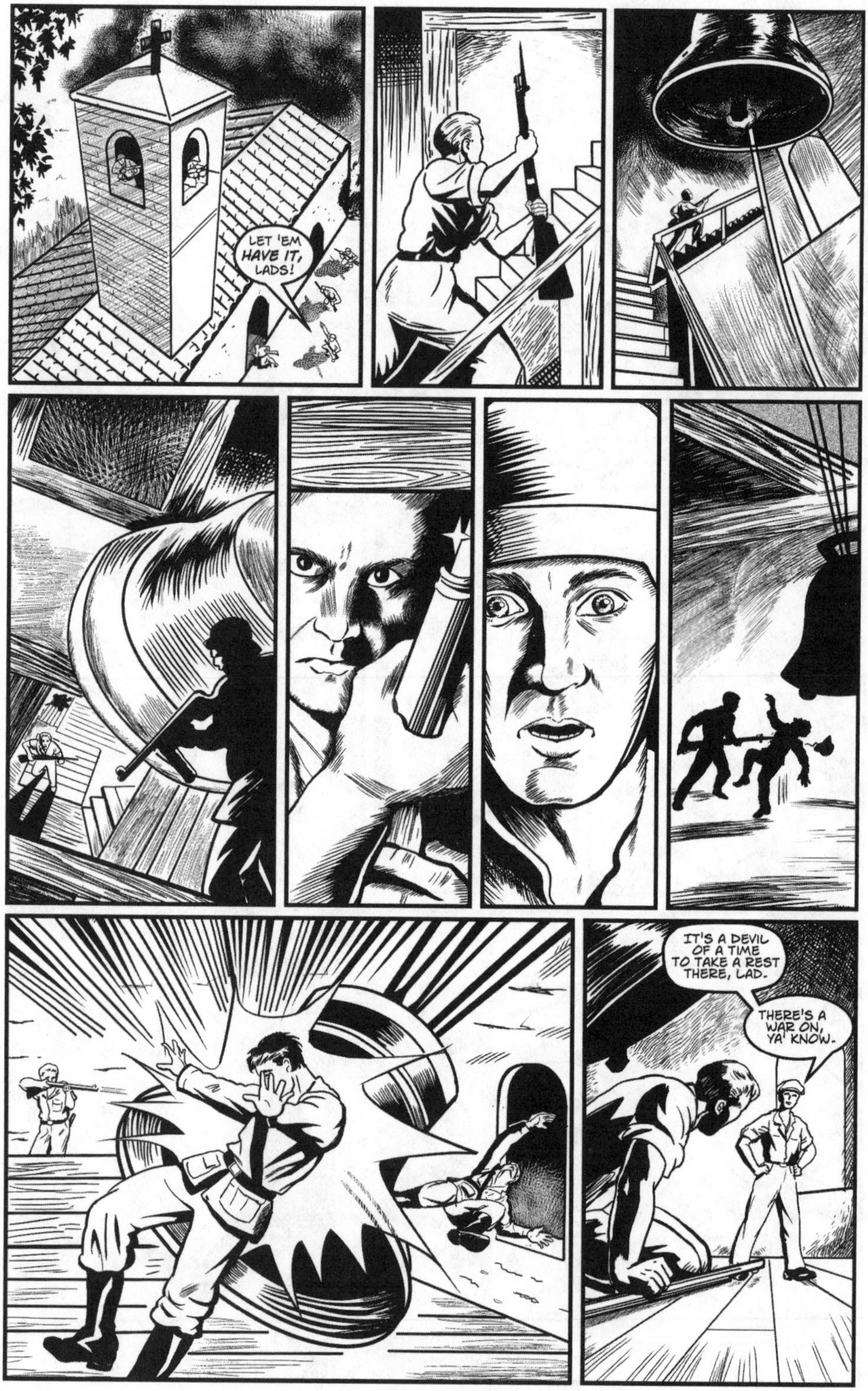
LET 'EM HAVE IT, LADS!
IT'S A DEVIL OF A TIME TO TAKE A REST THERE, LAD.
THERE'S A WAR ON, YA' KNOW.

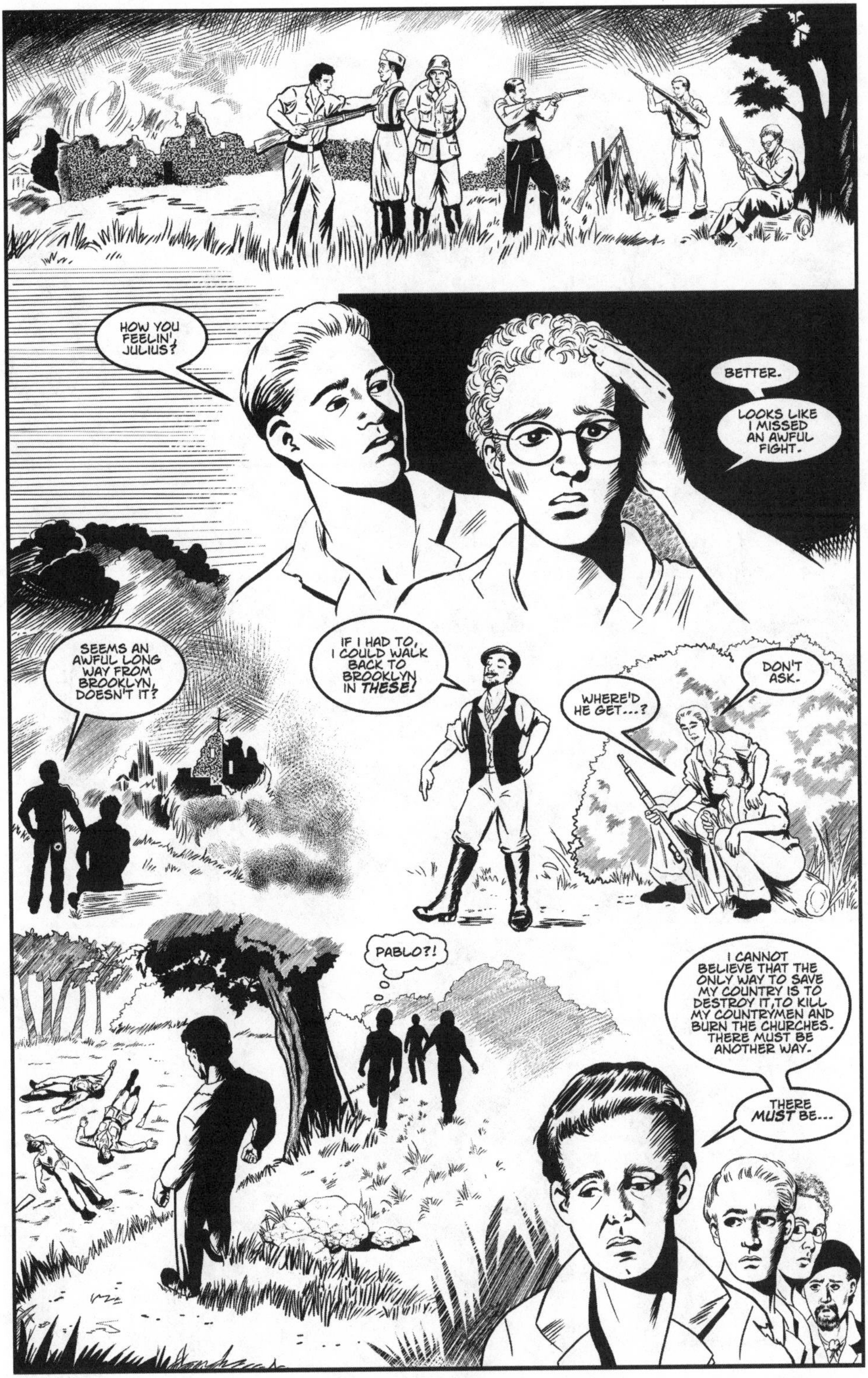
HOW YOU FEELIN', JULIUS?
BETTER.
LOOKS LIKE I MISSED AN AWFUL FIGHT.
SEEMS AN AWFUL LONG WAY FROM BROOKLYN, DOESN'T IT?
IF I HAD TO, I COULD WALK BACK TO BROOKLYN IN *THESE!*
WHERE'D HE GET...?
DON'T ASK.
PABLO?!
I CANNOT BELIEVE THAT THE ONLY WAY TO SAVE MY COUNTRY IS TO DESTROY IT, TO KILL MY COUNTRYMEN AND BURN THE CHURCHES. THERE MUST BE ANOTHER WAY.
THERE *MUST* BE...

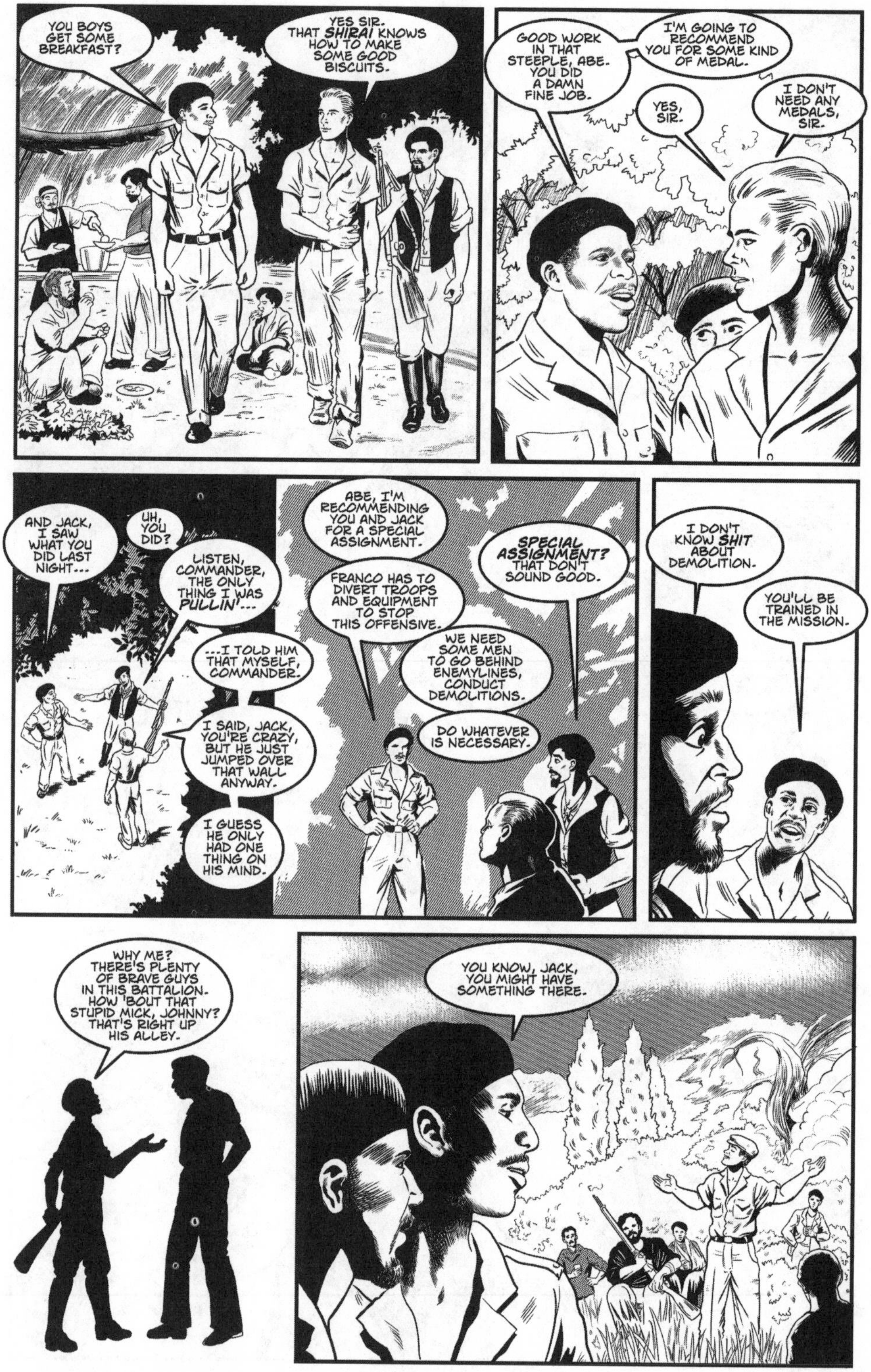
YOU BOYS GET SOME BREAKFAST?
YES SIR. THAT SHIRAI KNOWS HOW TO MAKE SOME GOOD BISCUITS.
GOOD WORK IN THAT STEEPLE, ABE. YOU DID A DAMN FINE JOB.
I'M GOING TO RECOMMEND YOU FOR SOME KIND OF MEDAL.
YES, SIR.
I DON'T NEED ANY MEDALS, SIR.
AND JACK, I SAW WHAT YOU DID LAST NIGHT...
UH, YOU DID?
LISTEN, COMMANDER, THE ONLY THING I WAS PULLIN'...
...I TOLD HIM THAT MYSELF, COMMANDER.
I SAID, JACK, YOU'RE CRAZY, BUT HE JUST JUMPED OVER THAT WALL ANYWAY.
I GUESS HE ONLY HAD ONE THING ON HIS MIND.
ABE, I'M RECOMMENDING YOU AND JACK FOR A SPECIAL ASSIGNMENT.
FRANCO HAS TO DIVERT TROOPS AND EQUIPMENT TO STOP THIS OFFENSIVE.
WE NEED SOME MEN TO GO BEHIND ENEMYLINES, CONDUCT DEMOLITIONS.
DO WHATEVER IS NECESSARY.
SPECIAL ASSIGNMENT? THAT DON'T SOUND GOOD.
I DON'T KNOW SHIT ABOUT DEMOLITION.
YOU'LL BE TRAINED IN THE MISSION.
WHY ME? THERE'S PLENTY OF BRAVE GUYS IN THIS BATTALION. HOW 'BOUT THAT STUPID MICK, JOHNNY? THAT'S RIGHT UP HIS ALLEY.
YOU KNOW, JACK, YOU MIGHT HAVE SOMETHING THERE.

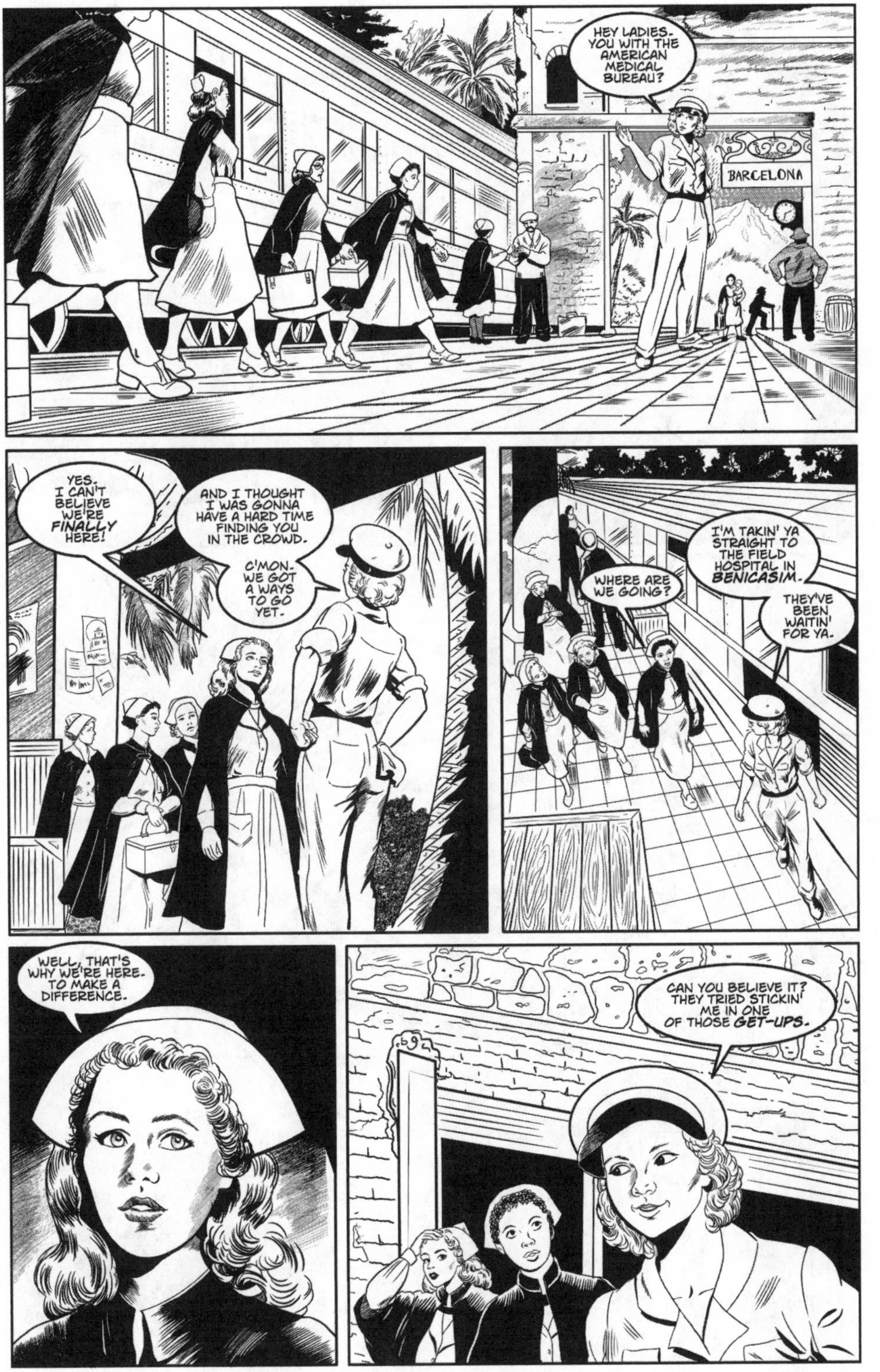
HEY LADIES. YOU WITH THE AMERICAN MEDICAL BUREAU?
BARCELONA
YES. I CAN'T BELIEVE WE'RE **FINALLY** HERE!
AND I THOUGHT I WAS GONNA HAVE A HARD TIME FINDING YOU IN THE CROWD.
C'MON. WE GOT A WAYS TO GO YET.
WHERE ARE WE GOING?
I'M TAKIN' YA STRAIGHT TO THE FIELD HOSPITAL IN **BENICASIM**.
THEY'VE BEEN WAITIN' FOR YA.
WELL, THAT'S WHY WE'RE HERE. TO MAKE A DIFFERENCE.
CAN YOU BELIEVE IT? THEY TRIED STICKIN' ME IN ONE OF THOSE **GET-UPS**.

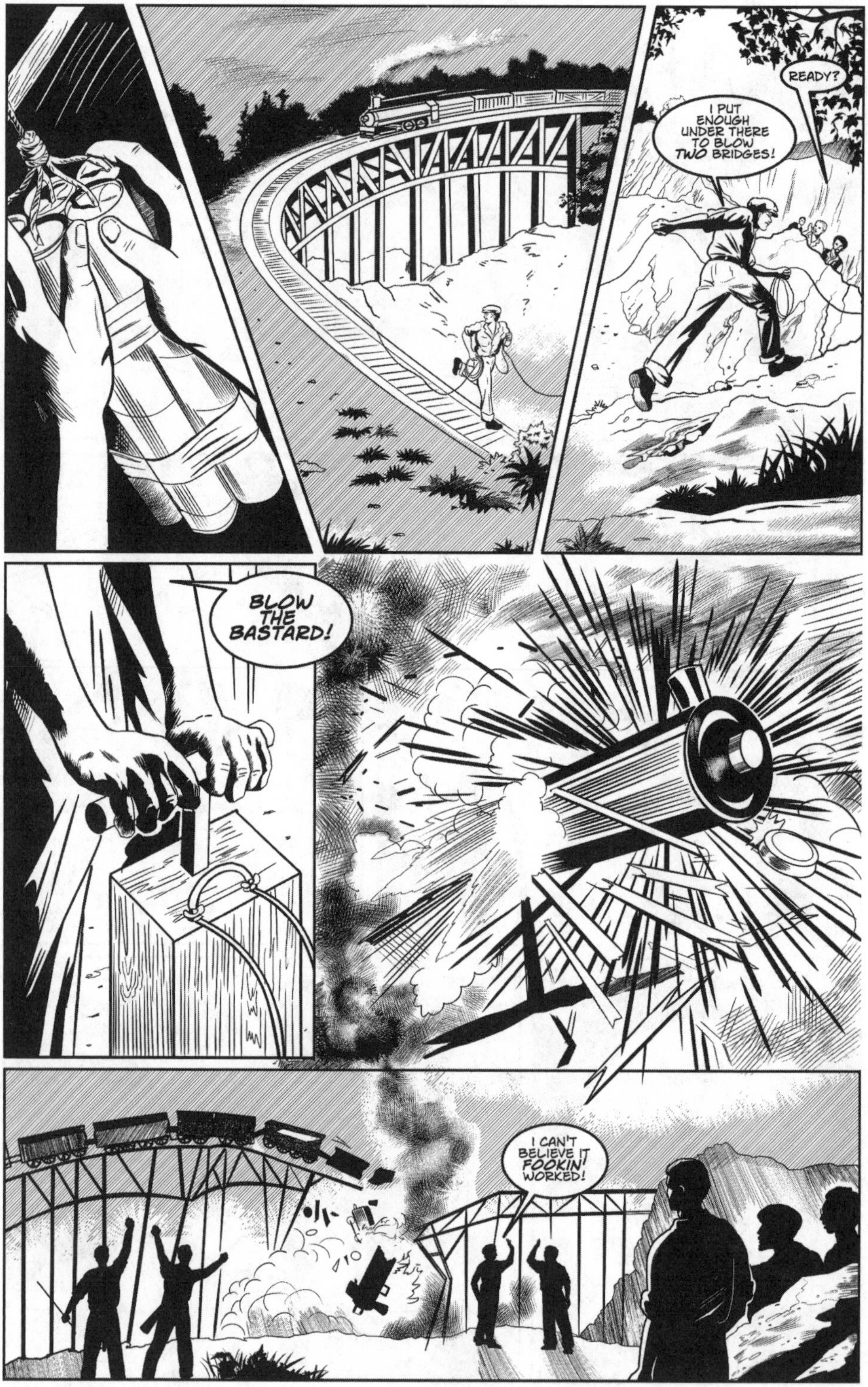
I PUT ENOUGH UNDER THERE TO BLOW TWO BRIDGES!
READY?
BLOW THE BASTARD!
I CAN'T BELIEVE IT FOOKIN' WORKED!

FASCIST HEADQUARTERS, NORTH OF MADRID.

TWO BRIDGES *AND* A SUPPLY TRAIN?

IT MUST BE A SMALL BAND OF *SABOTEURS.* MY MEN HAVE BEEN PATROLLING THE ROADS AND HAVE SEEN NOTHING.

THE REDS ARE DOING EXACTLY WHAT I PREDICTED, AND YET YOU *CANNOT* STOP THEM!

OF THAT I'M SURE.

DOUBLE THE GUARDS AT EVERY BRIDGE.

I'LL TAKE SOME MEN ON HORSEBACK AND FIND THESE SABOTEURS.

AND WHEN I FIND THEM...

CLICK

THE LINCOLN BRIGADE IS ON THE MARCH.

DAMN, THIS HAS TO BE THE *HOTTEST* PLACE ON THE PLANET!

YOU'VE NEVER BEEN TO *TEXAS* THEN, HAVE YOU SON?

NO, SIR. I'VE NEVER BEEN OUT OF NEW YORK CITY.

PAGE 77

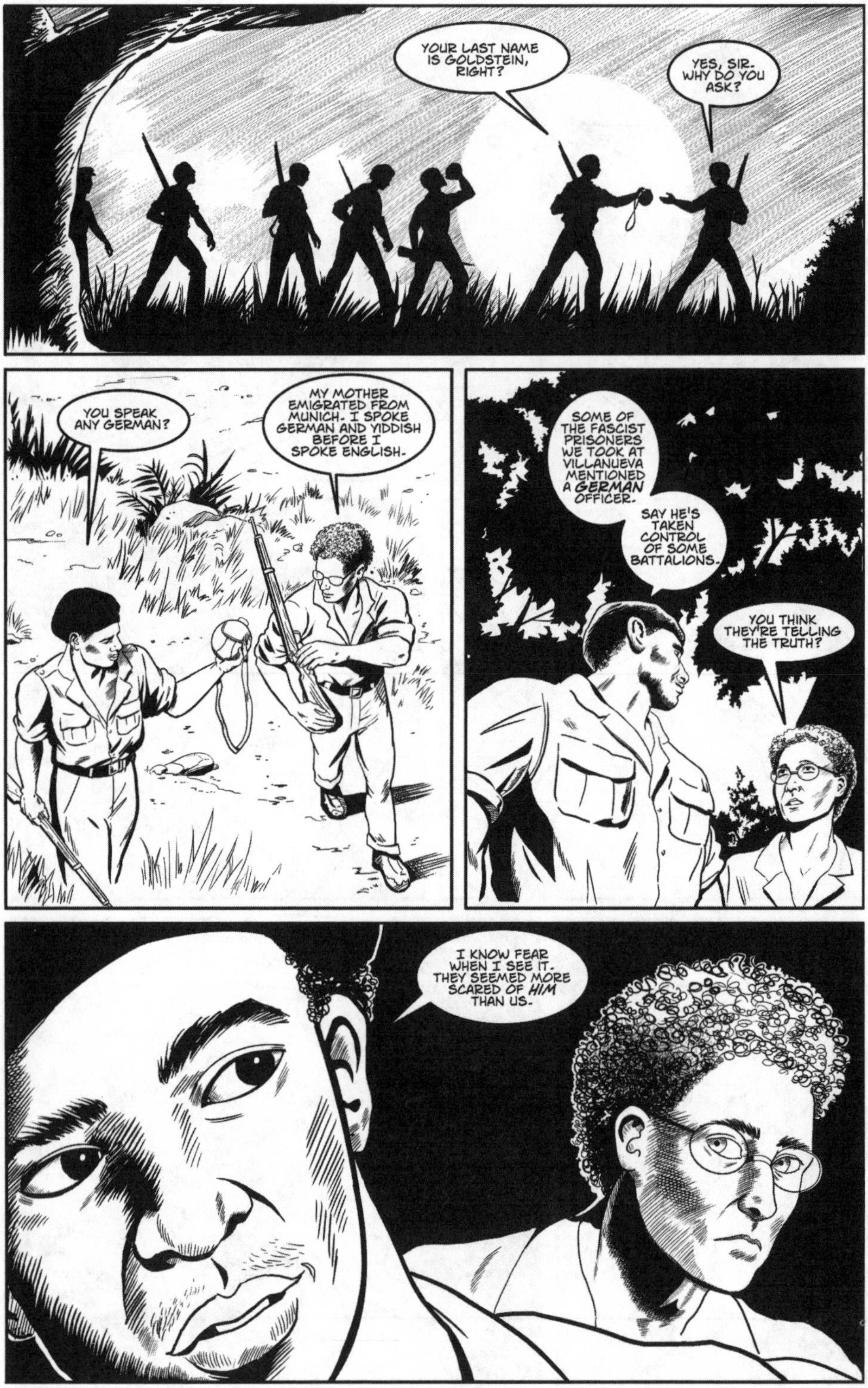
YOUR LAST NAME IS GOLDSTEIN, RIGHT?
YES, SIR. WHY DO YOU ASK?
YOU SPEAK ANY GERMAN?
MY MOTHER EMIGRATED FROM MUNICH. I SPOKE GERMAN AND YIDDISH BEFORE I SPOKE ENGLISH.
SOME OF THE FASCIST PRISONERS WE TOOK AT VILLANUEVA MENTIONED A GERMAN OFFICER.
SAY HE'S TAKEN CONTROL OF SOME BATTALIONS.
YOU THINK THEY'RE TELLING THE TRUTH?
I KNOW FEAR WHEN I SEE IT. THEY SEEMED MORE SCARED OF HIM THAN US.

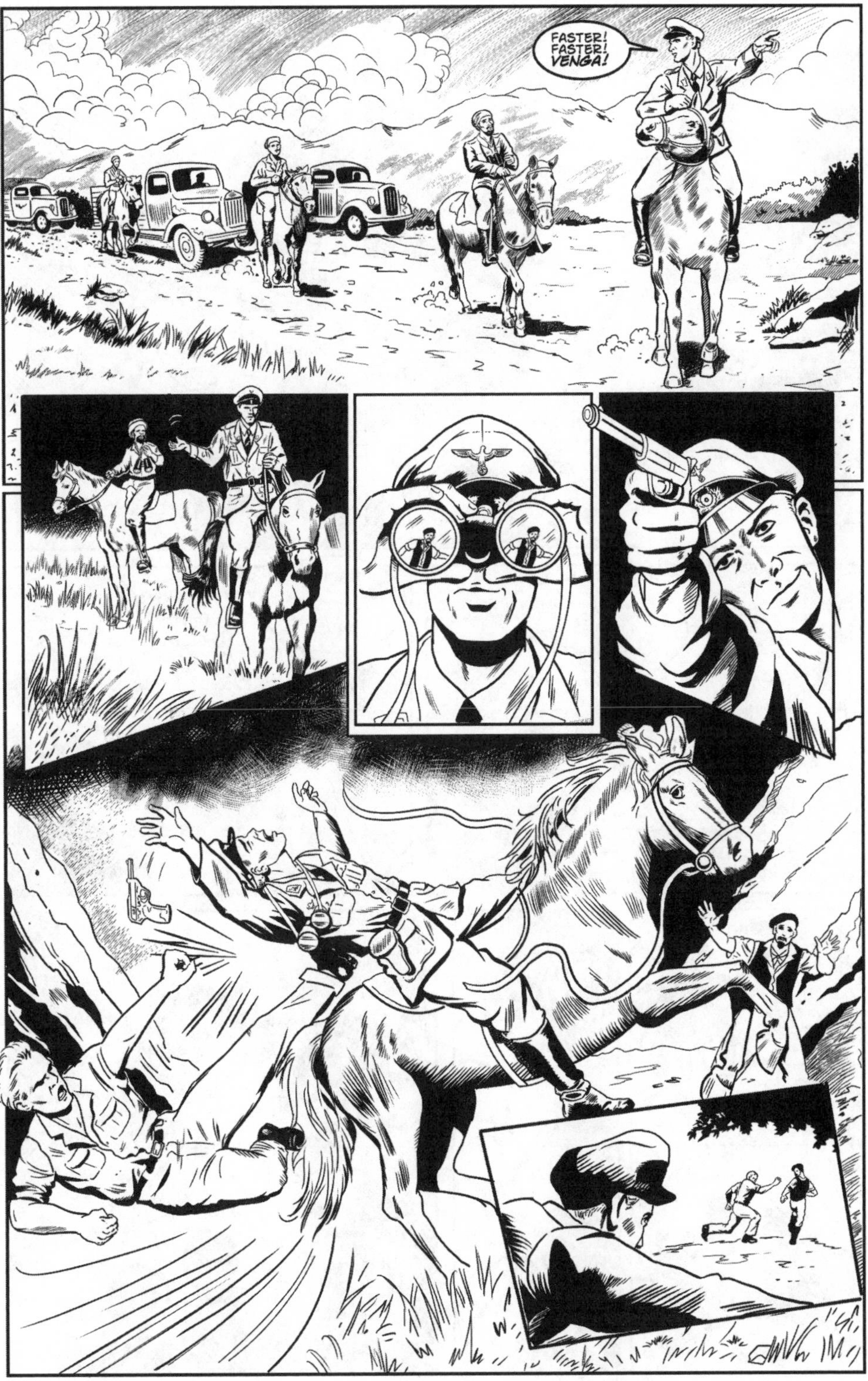
FASTER! FASTER! VENGA!

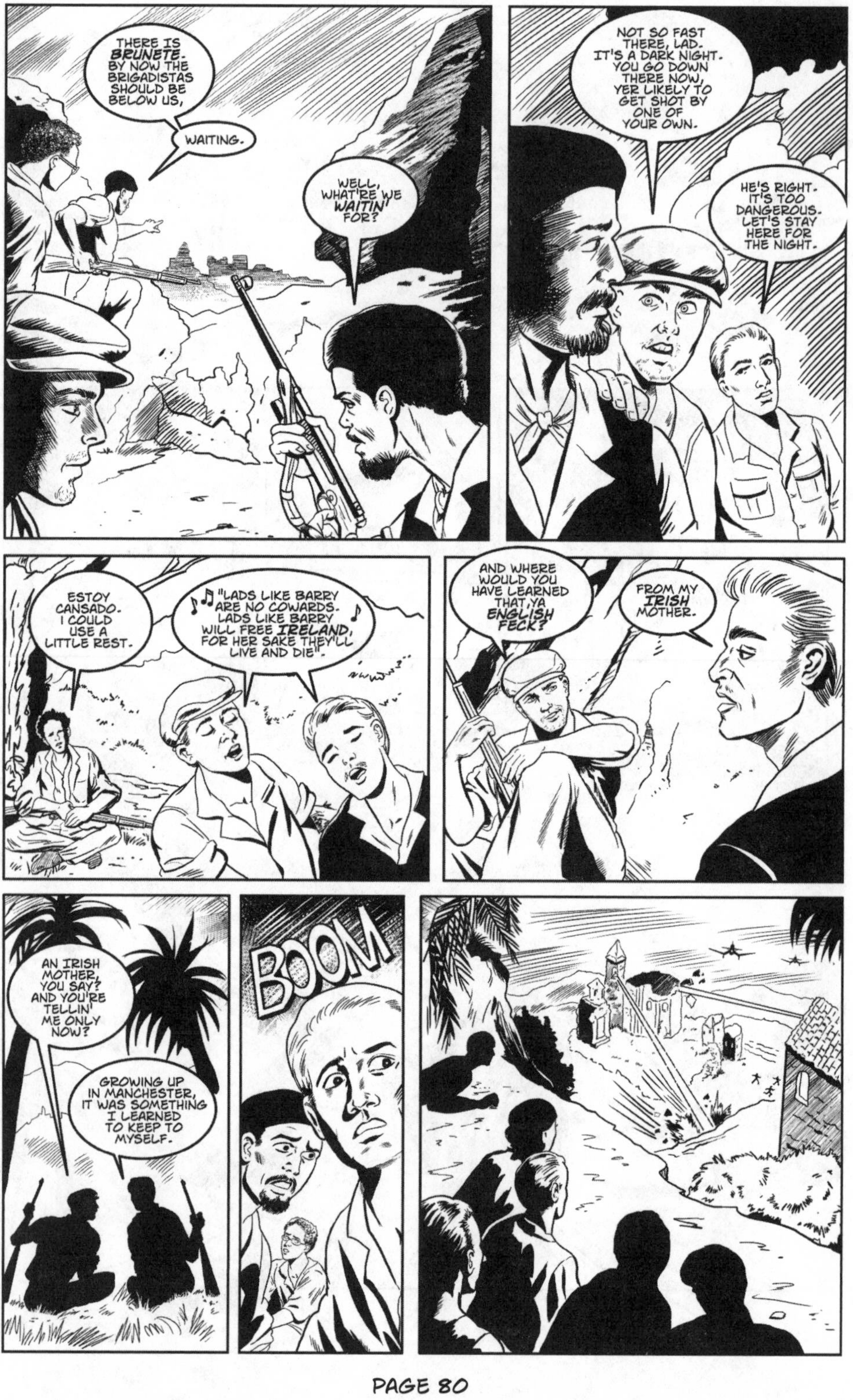
THERE IS BRUNETE. BY NOW THE BRIGADISTAS SHOULD BE BELOW US,
WAITING.
WELL, WHAT'RE WE WAITIN' FOR?
NOT SO FAST THERE, LAD. IT'S A DARK NIGHT. YOU GO DOWN THERE NOW, YER LIKELY TO GET SHOT BY ONE OF YOUR OWN.
HE'S RIGHT. IT'S TOO DANGEROUS. LET'S STAY HERE FOR THE NIGHT.
ESTOY CANSADO. I COULD USE A LITTLE REST.
♪♫ "LADS LIKE BARRY ARE NO COWARDS. LADS LIKE BARRY WILL FREE IRELAND, FOR HER SAKE THEY'LL LIVE AND DIE". ♪
AND WHERE WOULD YOU HAVE LEARNED THAT, YA ENGLISH FECK?
FROM MY IRISH MOTHER.
AN IRISH MOTHER, YOU SAY? AND YOU'RE TELLIN' ME ONLY NOW?
GROWING UP IN MANCHESTER, IT WAS SOMETHING I LEARNED TO KEEP TO MYSELF.
BOOM

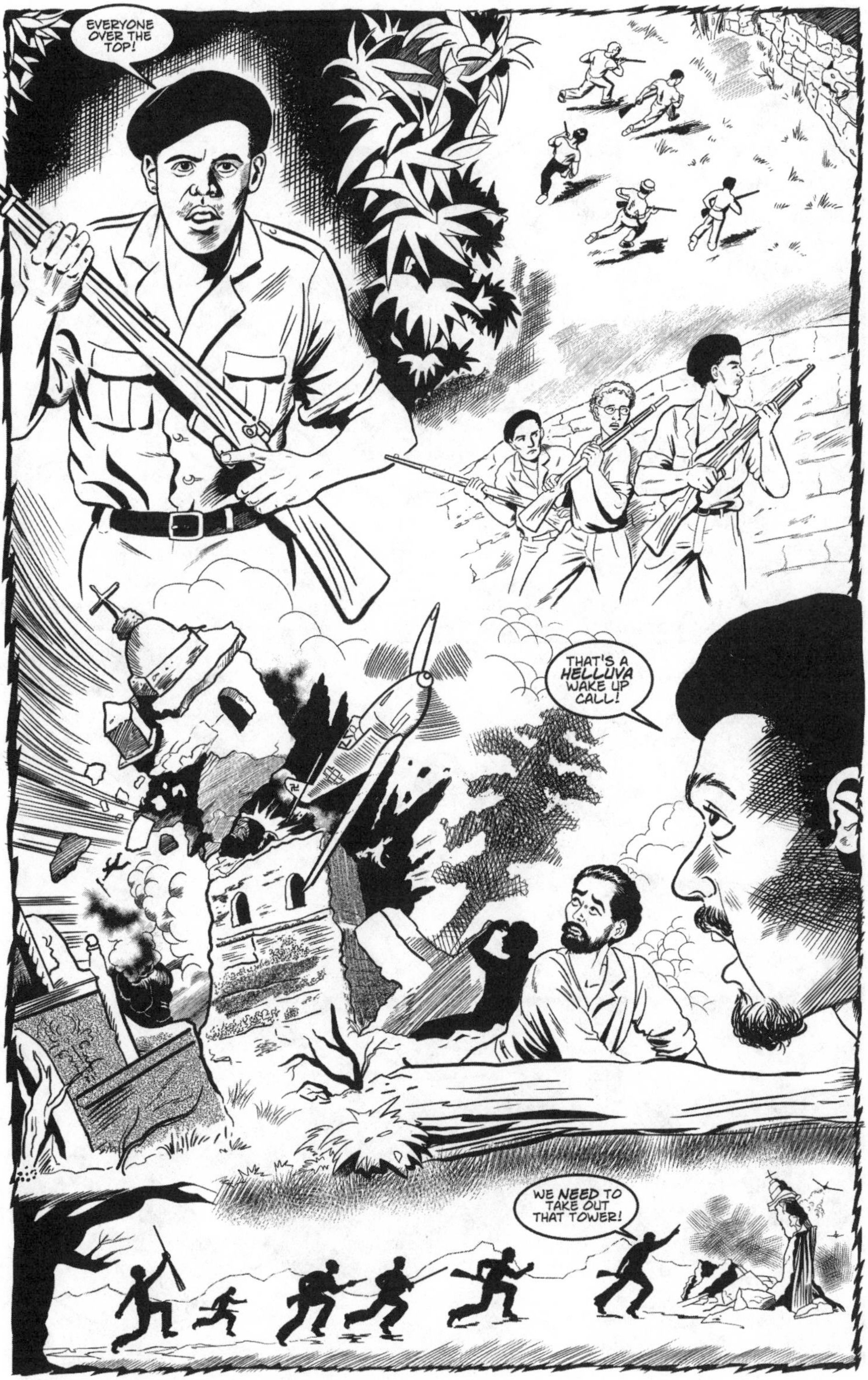
EVERYONE OVER THE TOP!
THAT'S A HELLUVA WAKE UP CALL!
WE NEED TO TAKE OUT THAT TOWER!

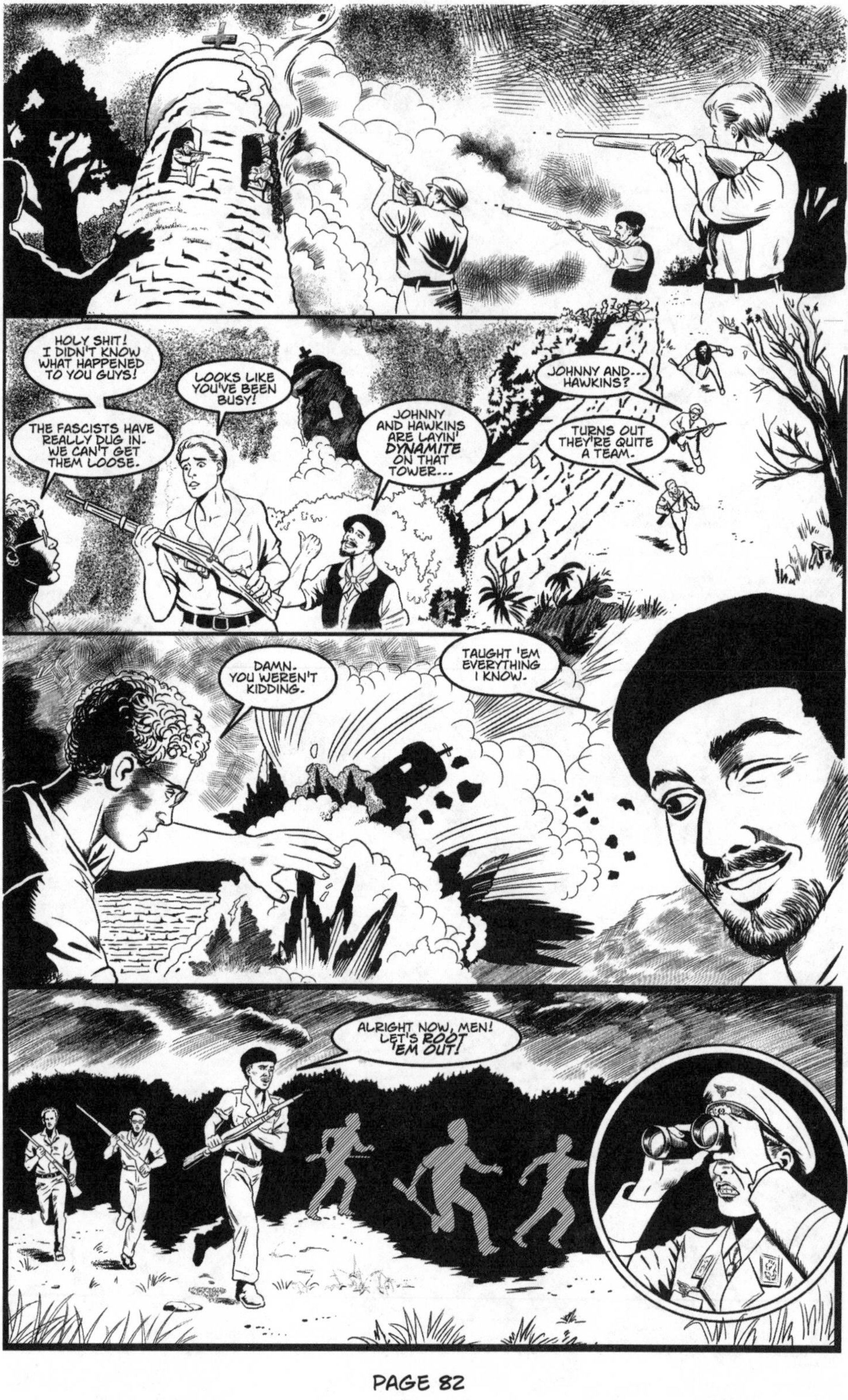
HOLY SHIT! I DIDN'T KNOW WHAT HAPPENED TO YOU GUYS!
THE FASCISTS HAVE REALLY DUG IN. WE CAN'T GET THEM LOOSE.
LOOKS LIKE YOU'VE BEEN BUSY!
JOHNNY AND HAWKINS ARE LAYIN' DYNAMITE ON THAT TOWER...
JOHNNY AND... HAWKINS?
TURNS OUT THEY'RE QUITE A TEAM.
DAMN. YOU WEREN'T KIDDING.
TAUGHT 'EM EVERYTHING I KNOW.
ALRIGHT NOW, MEN! LET'S ROOT 'EM OUT!

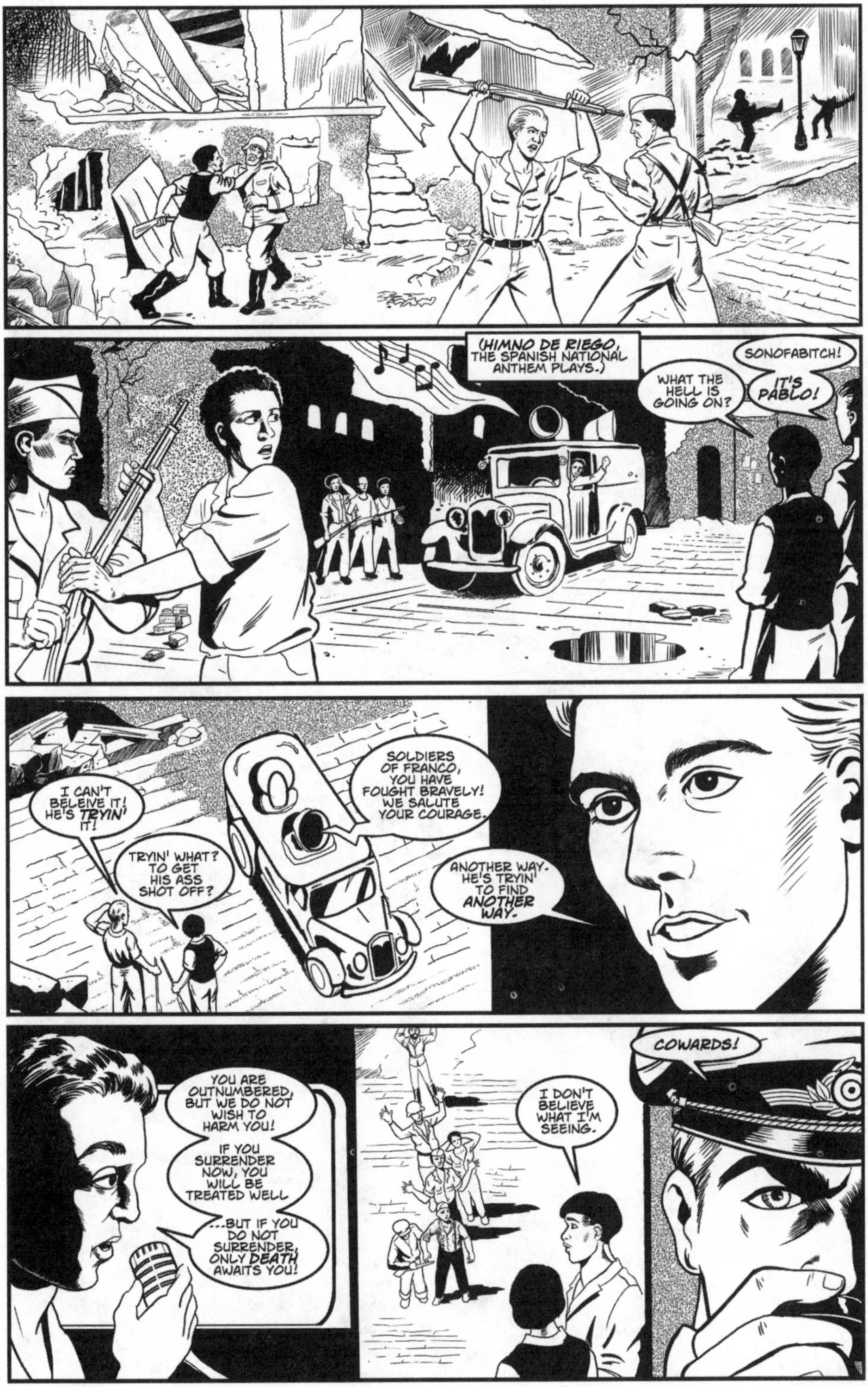
(HIMNO DE RIEGO, THE SPANISH NATIONAL ANTHEM PLAYS.)
WHAT THE HELL IS GOING ON?
SONOFABITCH!
IT'S PABLO!
I CAN'T BELEIVE IT! HE'S TRYIN' IT!
TRYIN' WHAT? TO GET HIS ASS SHOT OFF?
SOLDIERS OF FRANCO, YOU HAVE FOUGHT BRAVELY! WE SALUTE YOUR COURAGE.
ANOTHER WAY. HE'S TRYIN' TO FIND ANOTHER WAY.
YOU ARE OUTNUMBERED, BUT WE DO NOT WISH TO HARM YOU!
IF YOU SURRENDER NOW, YOU WILL BE TREATED WELL
...BUT IF YOU DO NOT SURRENDER, ONLY DEATH AWAITS YOU!
I DON'T BELIEVE WHAT I'M SEEING.
COWARDS!

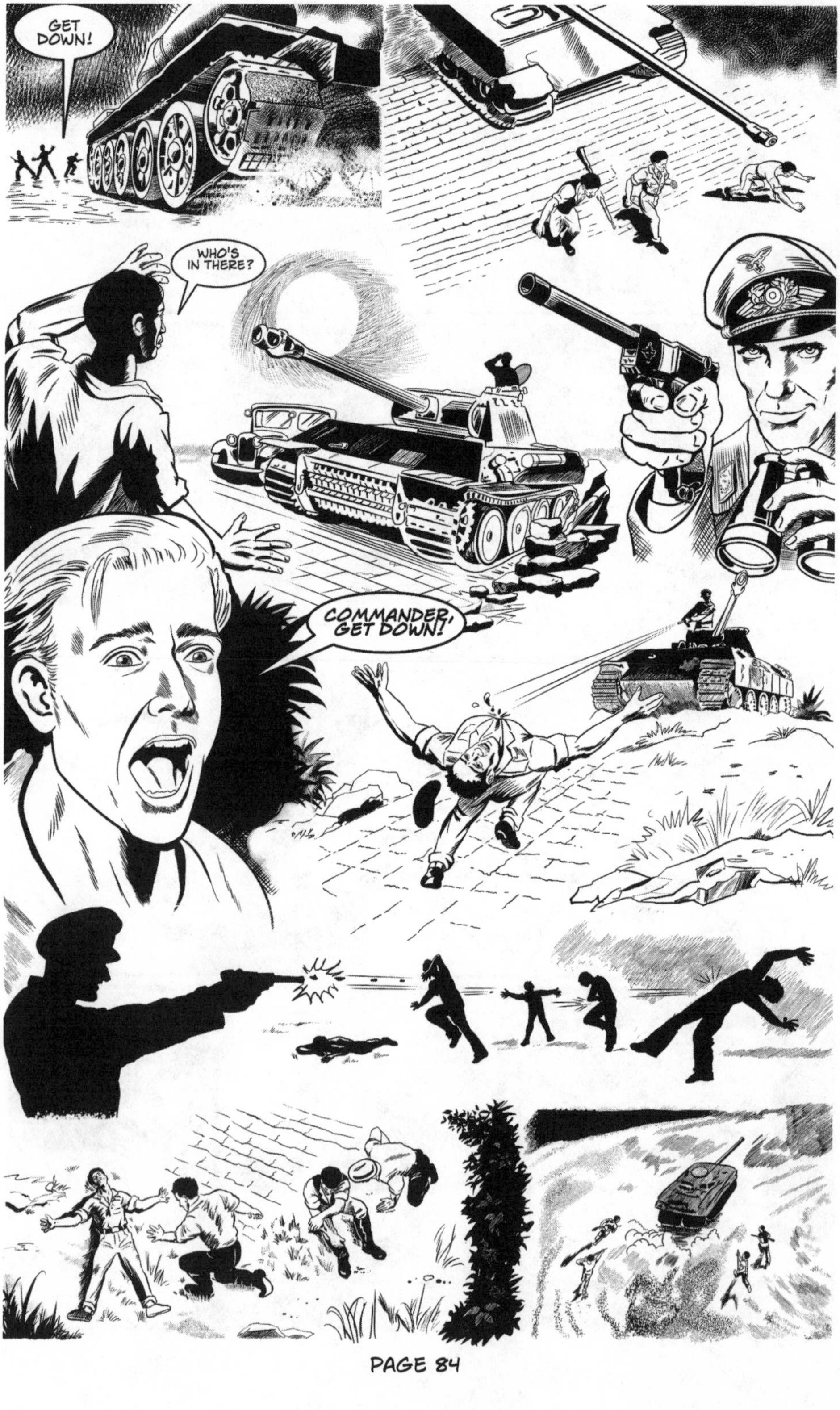
GET DOWN!
WHO'S IN THERE?
COMMANDER, GET DOWN!

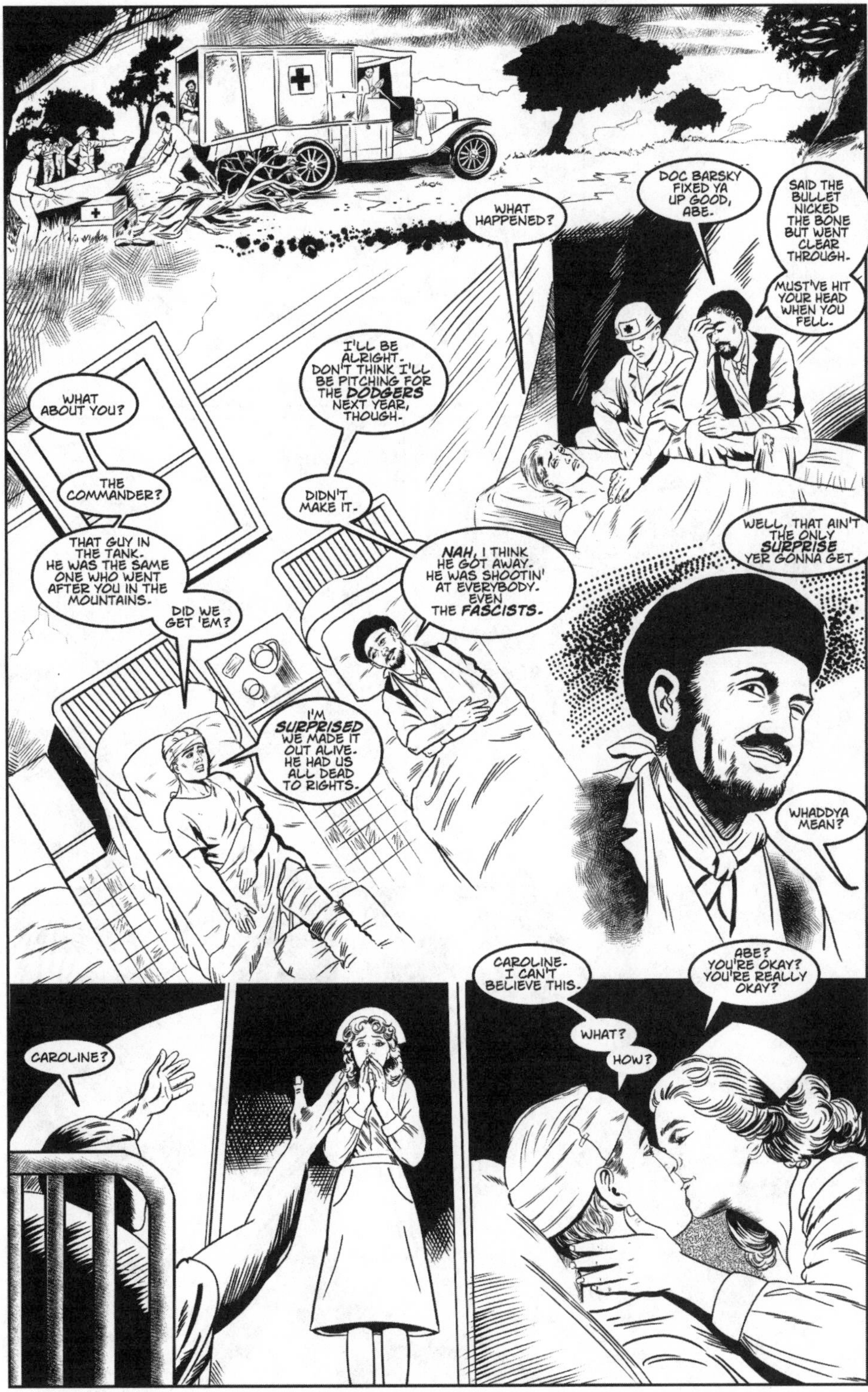

WHAT HAPPENED?
DOC BARSKY FIXED YA UP GOOD, ABE.
SAID THE BULLET NICKED THE BONE BUT WENT CLEAR THROUGH.
MUST'VE HIT YOUR HEAD WHEN YOU FELL.
WHAT ABOUT YOU?
I'LL BE ALRIGHT. DON'T THINK I'LL BE PITCHING FOR THE DODGERS NEXT YEAR, THOUGH.
THE COMMANDER?
DIDN'T MAKE IT.
THAT GUY IN THE TANK. HE WAS THE SAME ONE WHO WENT AFTER YOU IN THE MOUNTAINS.
DID WE GET 'EM?
NAH, I THINK HE GOT AWAY. HE WAS SHOOTIN' AT EVERYBODY. EVEN THE FASCISTS.
I'M SURPRISED WE MADE IT OUT ALIVE. HE HAD US ALL DEAD TO RIGHTS.
WELL, THAT AIN'T THE ONLY SURPRISE YER GONNA GET.
WHADDYA MEAN?
CAROLINE?
CAROLINE. I CAN'T BELIEVE THIS.
ABE? YOU'RE OKAY? YOU'RE REALLY OKAY?
WHAT?
HOW?

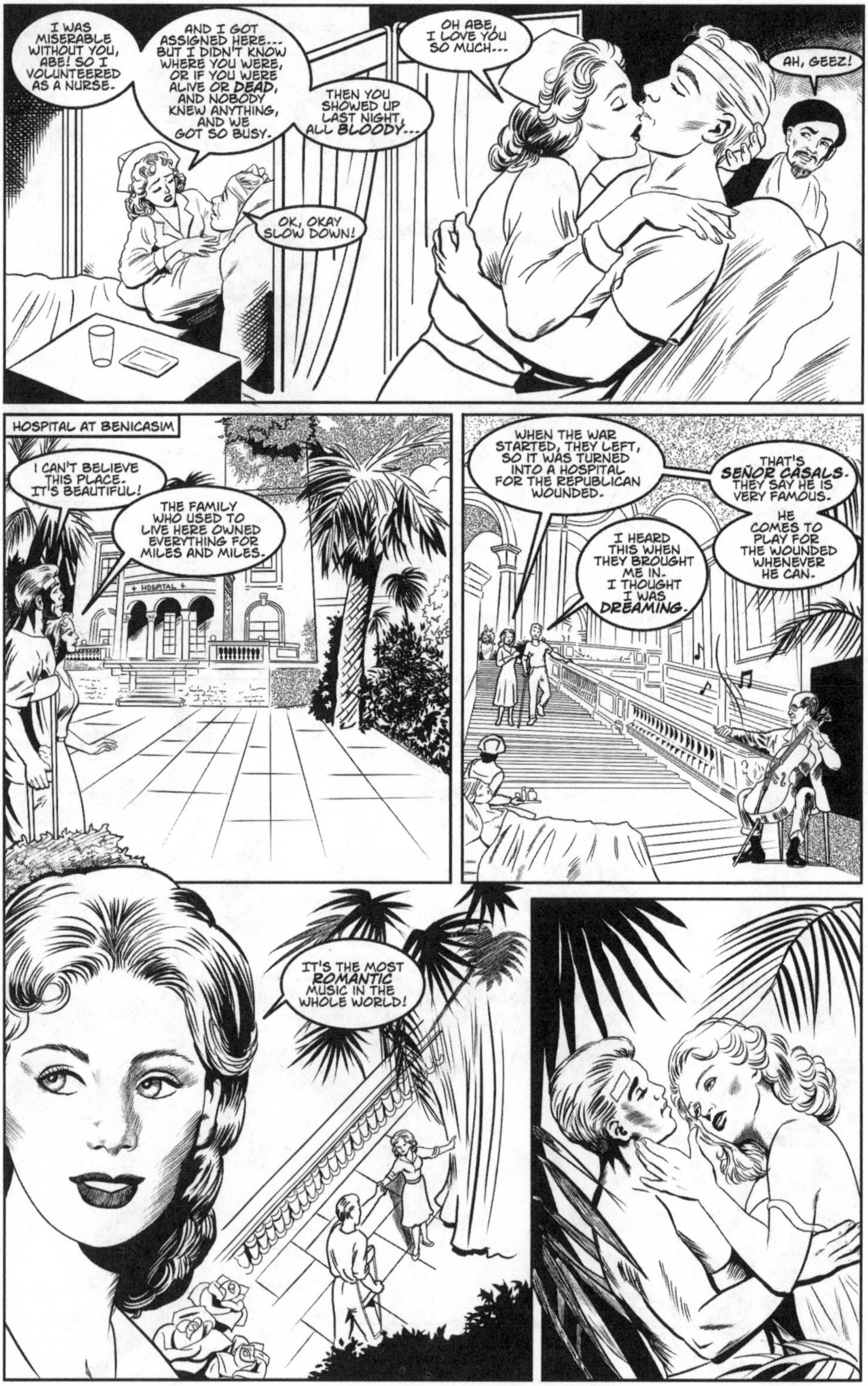
I WAS MISERABLE WITHOUT YOU, ABE! SO I VOLUNTEERED AS A NURSE.
AND I GOT ASSIGNED HERE... BUT I DIDN'T KNOW WHERE YOU WERE, OR IF YOU WERE ALIVE OR DEAD, AND NOBODY KNEW ANYTHING, AND WE GOT SO BUSY.
THEN YOU SHOWED UP LAST NIGHT, ALL BLOODY...
OK, OKAY SLOW DOWN!
OH ABE, I LOVE YOU SO MUCH...
AH, GEEZ!
HOSPITAL AT BENICASIM
I CAN'T BELIEVE THIS PLACE. IT'S BEAUTIFUL!
THE FAMILY WHO USED TO LIVE HERE OWNED EVERYTHING FOR MILES AND MILES.
+ HOSPITAL +
WHEN THE WAR STARTED, THEY LEFT, SO IT WAS TURNED INTO A HOSPITAL FOR THE REPUBLICAN WOUNDED.
I HEARD THIS WHEN THEY BROUGHT ME IN. I THOUGHT I WAS DREAMING.
THAT'S SEÑOR CASALS. THEY SAY HE IS VERY FAMOUS.
HE COMES TO PLAY FOR THE WOUNDED WHENEVER HE CAN.
IT'S THE MOST ROMANTIC MUSIC IN THE WHOLE WORLD!

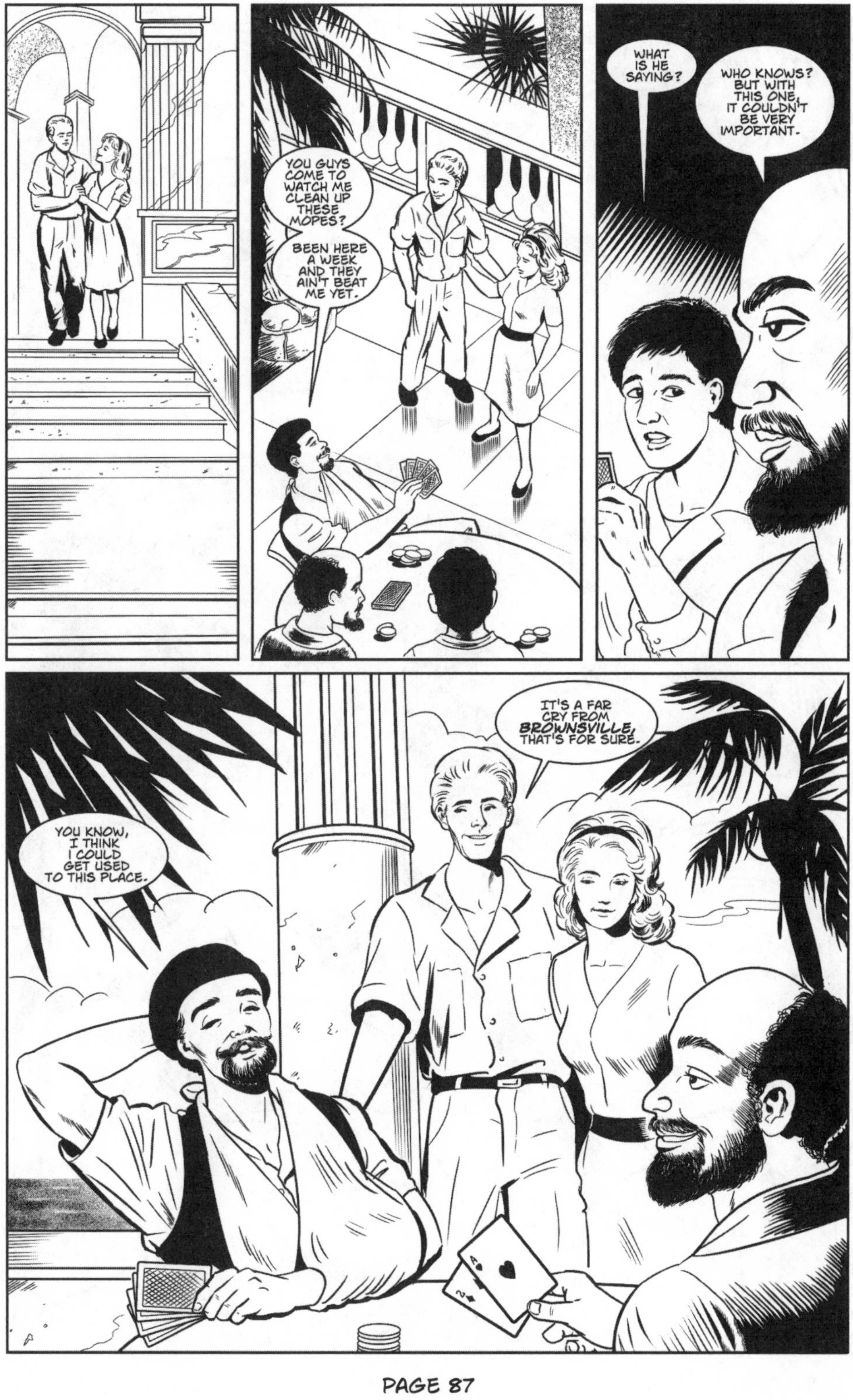
YOU GUYS COME TO WATCH ME CLEAN UP THESE MOPES?
BEEN HERE A WEEK AND THEY AIN'T BEAT ME YET.
WHAT IS HE SAYING?
WHO KNOWS? BUT WITH THIS ONE, IT COULDN'T BE VERY IMPORTANT.
YOU KNOW, I THINK I COULD GET USED TO THIS PLACE.
IT'S A FAR CRY FROM BROWNSVILLE, THAT'S FOR SURE.

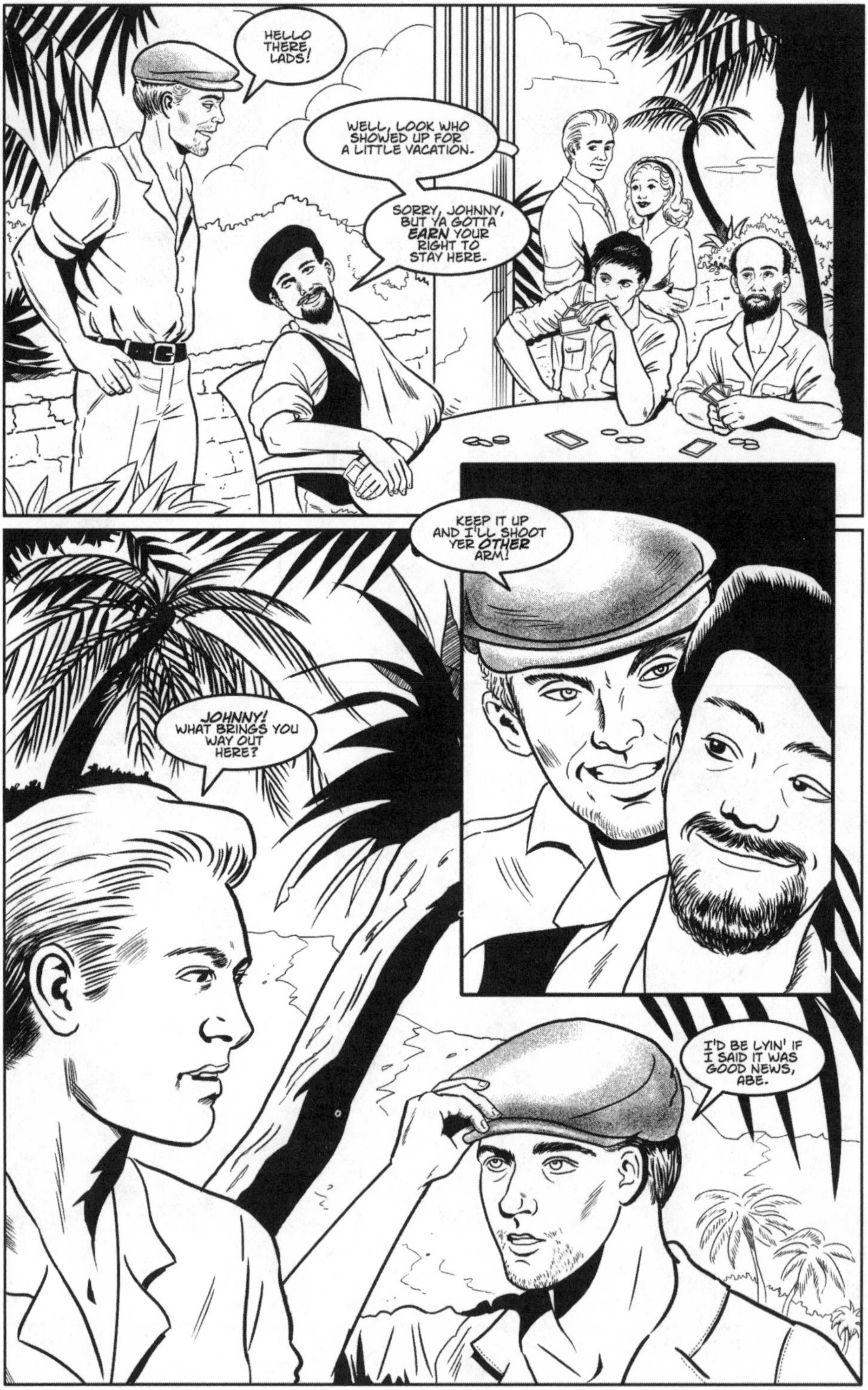
HELLO THERE, LADS!
WELL, LOOK WHO SHOWED UP FOR A LITTLE VACATION.
SORRY, JOHNNY, BUT YA GOTTA EARN YOUR RIGHT TO STAY HERE.
JOHNNY! WHAT BRINGS YOU WAY OUT HERE?
KEEP IT UP AND I'LL SHOOT YER OTHER ARM!
I'D BE LYIN' IF I SAID IT WAS GOOD NEWS, ABE.

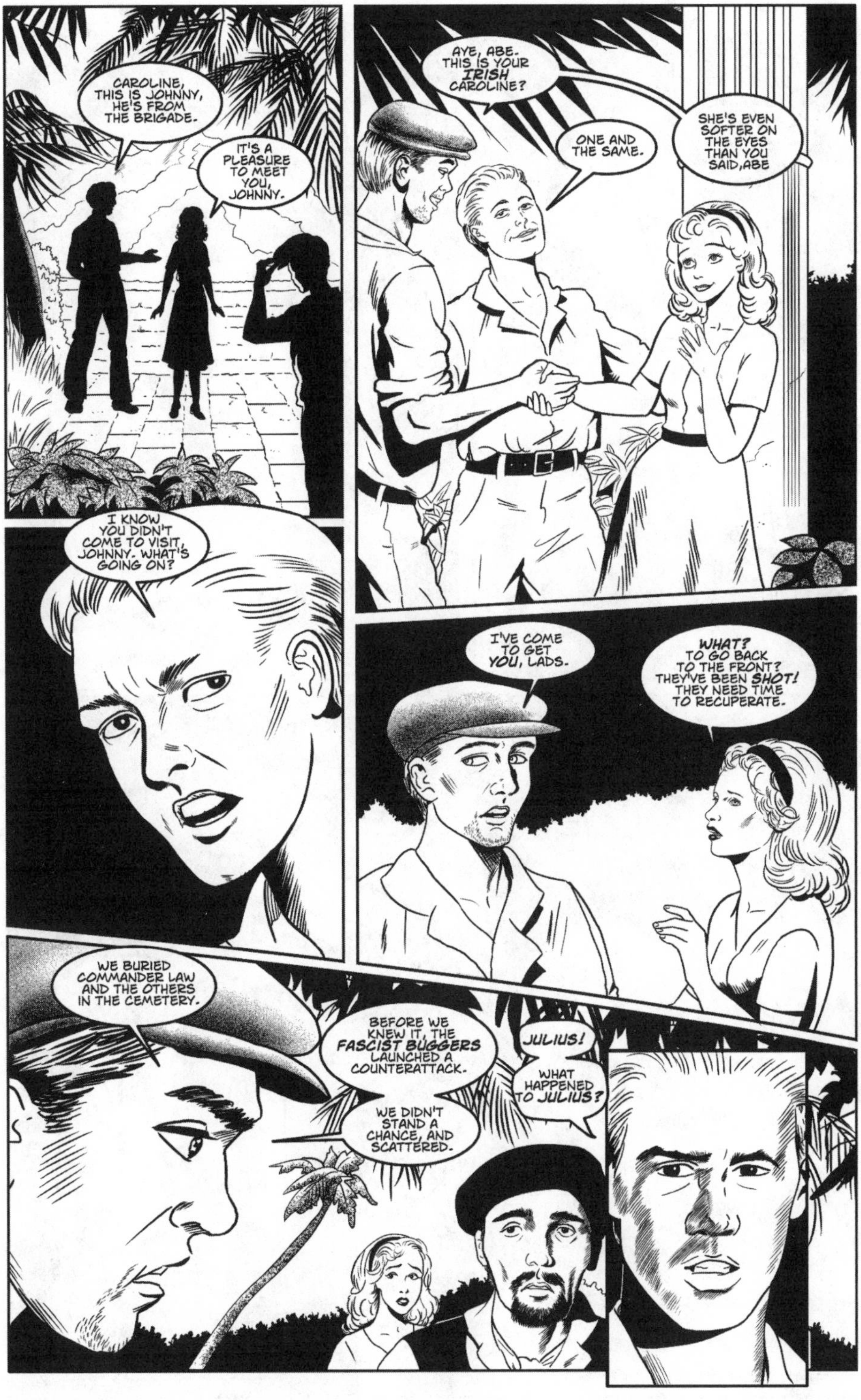
CAROLINE, THIS IS JOHNNY, HE'S FROM THE BRIGADE.
IT'S A PLEASURE TO MEET YOU, JOHNNY.
AYE, ABE. THIS IS YOUR IRISH CAROLINE?
ONE AND THE SAME.
SHE'S EVEN SOFTER ON THE EYES THAN YOU SAID, ABE
I KNOW YOU DIDN'T COME TO VISIT, JOHNNY. WHAT'S GOING ON?
I'VE COME TO GET YOU, LADS.
WHAT? TO GO BACK TO THE FRONT? THEY'VE BEEN SHOT! THEY NEED TIME TO RECUPERATE.
WE BURIED COMMANDER LAW AND THE OTHERS IN THE CEMETERY.
BEFORE WE KNEW IT, THE FASCIST BUGGERS LAUNCHED A COUNTERATTACK.
WE DIDN'T STAND A CHANCE, AND SCATTERED.
JULIUS!
WHAT HAPPENED TO JULIUS?

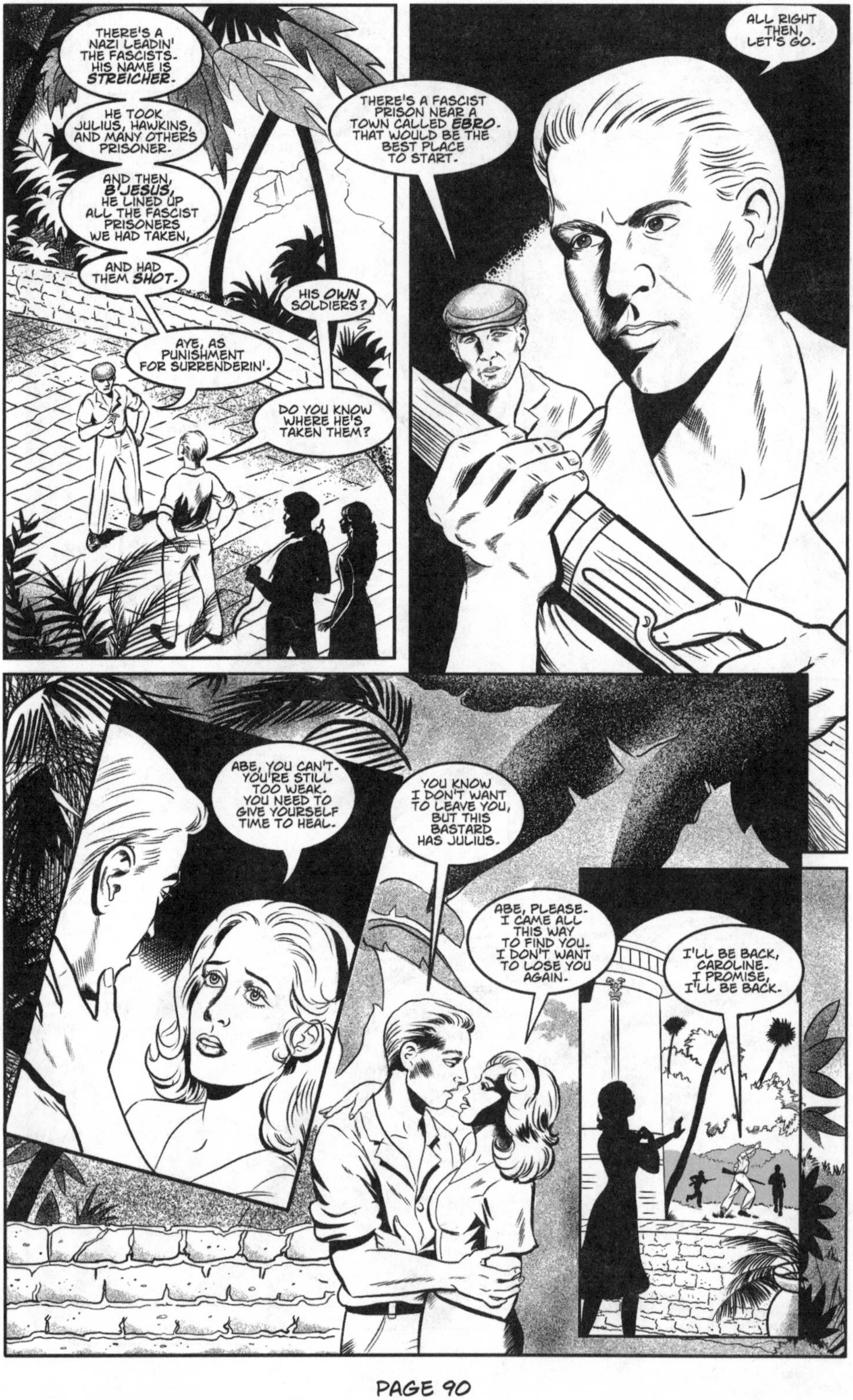
THERE'S A NAZI LEADIN' THE FASCISTS- HIS NAME IS STREICHER.
HE TOOK JULIUS, HAWKINS, AND MANY OTHERS PRISONER.
AND THEN, B'JESUS, HE LINED UP ALL THE FASCIST PRISONERS WE HAD TAKEN,
AND HAD THEM SHOT.
HIS OWN SOLDIERS?
AYE, AS PUNISHMENT FOR SURRENDERIN'.
DO YOU KNOW WHERE HE'S TAKEN THEM?
ALL RIGHT THEN, LET'S GO.
THERE'S A FASCIST PRISON NEAR A TOWN CALLED EBRO. THAT WOULD BE THE BEST PLACE TO START.
ABE, YOU CAN'T. YOU'RE STILL TOO WEAK. YOU NEED TO GIVE YOURSELF TIME TO HEAL.
YOU KNOW I DON'T WANT TO LEAVE YOU, BUT THIS BASTARD HAS JULIUS.
ABE, PLEASE. I CAME ALL THIS WAY TO FIND YOU. I DON'T WANT TO LOSE YOU AGAIN.
I'LL BE BACK, CAROLINE. I PROMISE, I'LL BE BACK.

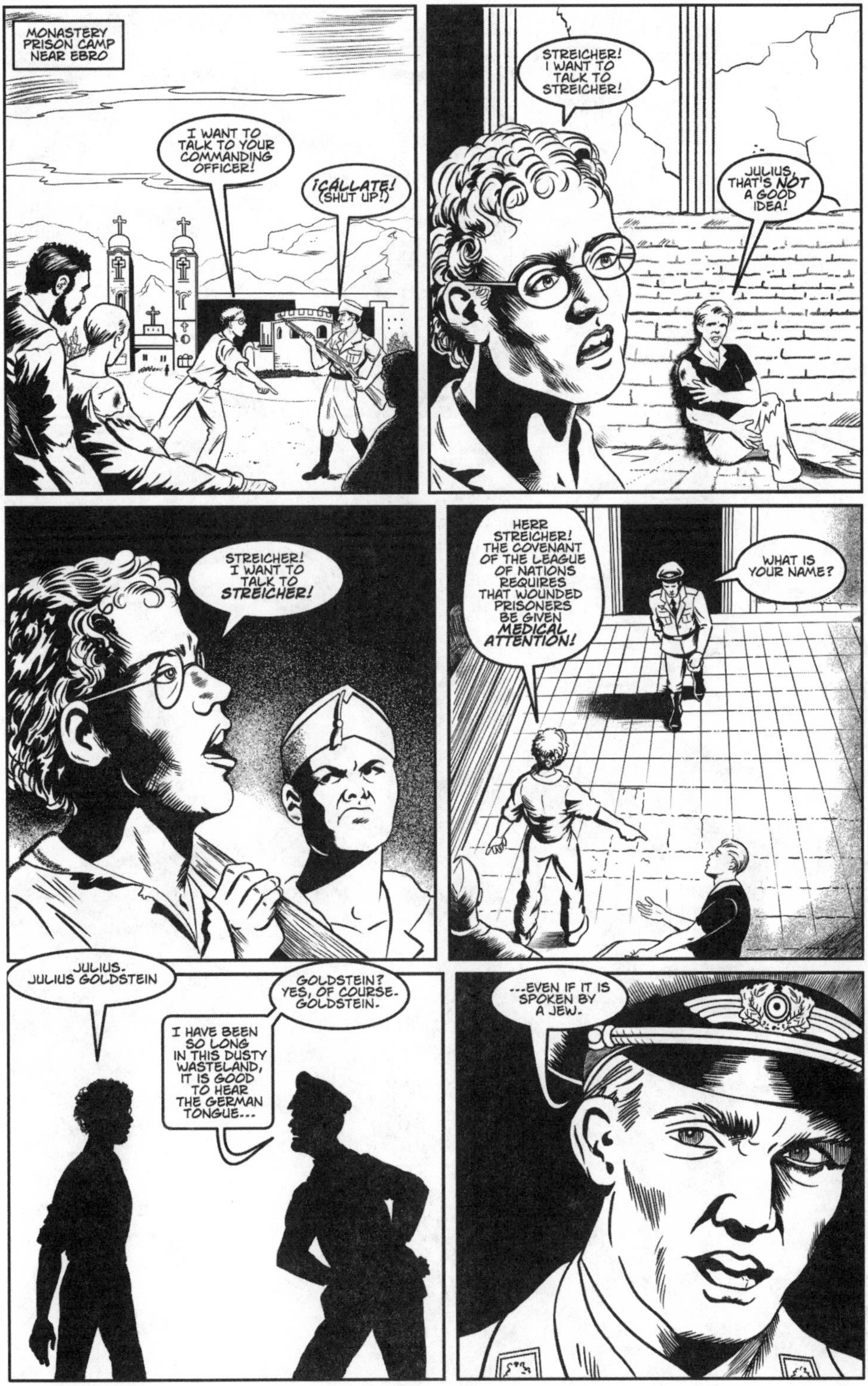
MONASTERY PRISON CAMP NEAR EBRO
I WANT TO TALK TO YOUR COMMANDING OFFICER!
¡CÁLLATE! (SHUT UP!)
STREICHER! I WANT TO TALK TO STREICHER!
JULIUS, THAT'S NOT A GOOD IDEA!
STREICHER! I WANT TO TALK TO STREICHER!
HERR STREICHER! THE COVENANT OF THE LEAGUE OF NATIONS REQUIRES THAT WOUNDED PRISONERS BE GIVEN MEDICAL ATTENTION!
WHAT IS YOUR NAME?
JULIUS. JULIUS GOLDSTEIN
GOLDSTEIN? YES, OF COURSE. GOLDSTEIN.
I HAVE BEEN SO LONG IN THIS DUSTY WASTELAND, IT IS GOOD TO HEAR THE GERMAN TONGUE...
...EVEN IF IT IS SPOKEN BY A JEW.

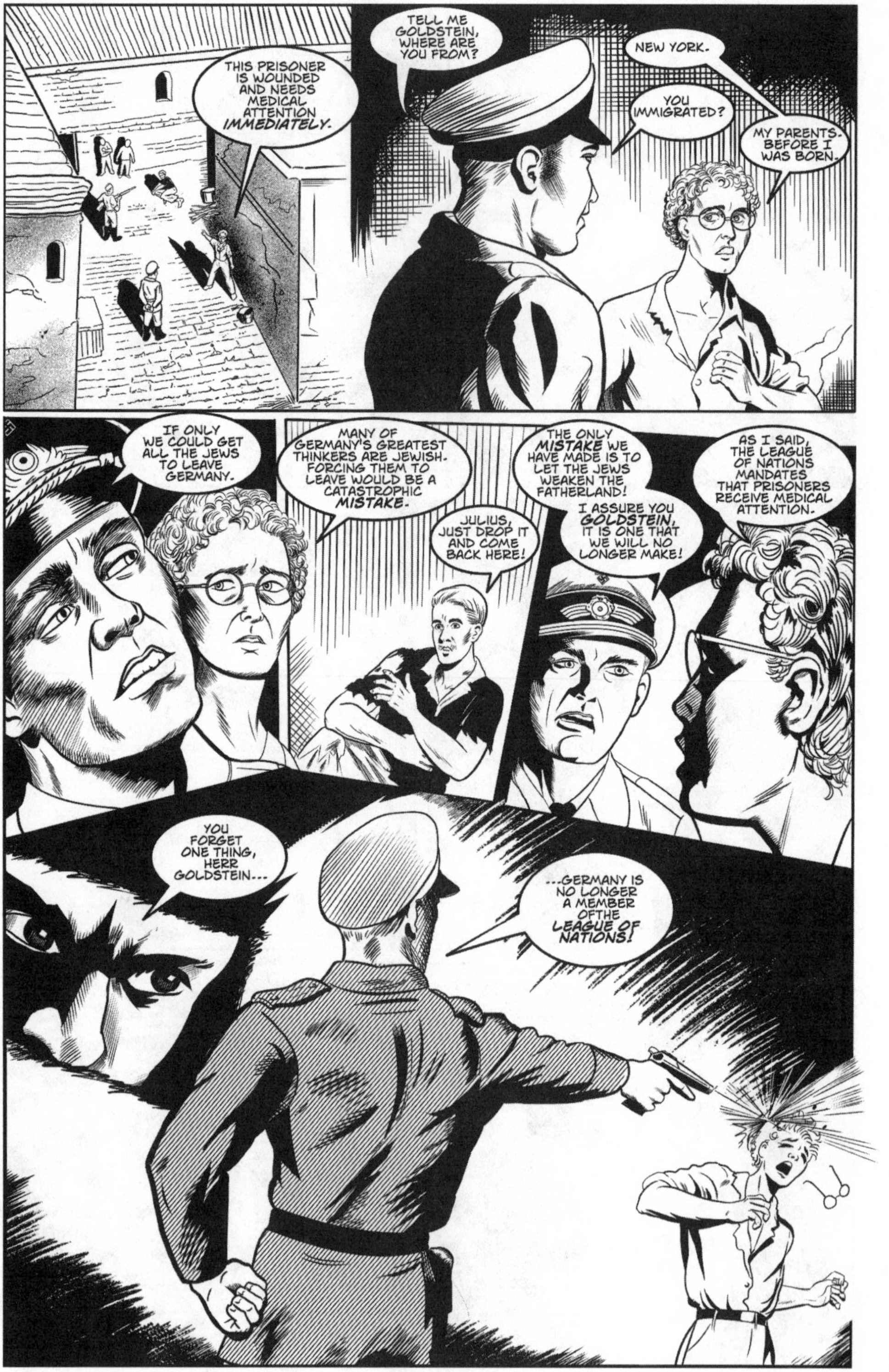
THIS PRISONER IS WOUNDED AND NEEDS MEDICAL ATTENTION IMMEDIATELY.
TELL ME GOLDSTEIN, WHERE ARE YOU FROM?
NEW YORK.
YOU IMMIGRATED?
MY PARENTS. BEFORE I WAS BORN.
IF ONLY WE COULD GET ALL THE JEWS TO LEAVE GERMANY.
MANY OF GERMANY'S GREATEST THINKERS ARE JEWISH. FORCING THEM TO LEAVE WOULD BE A CATASTROPHIC MISTAKE.
JULIUS, JUST DROP IT AND COME BACK HERE!
THE ONLY MISTAKE WE HAVE MADE IS TO LET THE JEWS WEAKEN THE FATHERLAND!
I ASSURE YOU GOLDSTEIN, IT IS ONE THAT WE WILL NO LONGER MAKE!
AS I SAID, THE LEAGUE OF NATIONS MANDATES THAT PRISONERS RECEIVE MEDICAL ATTENTION.
YOU FORGET ONE THING, HERR GOLDSTEIN...
...GERMANY IS NO LONGER A MEMBER OF THE LEAGUE OF NATIONS!

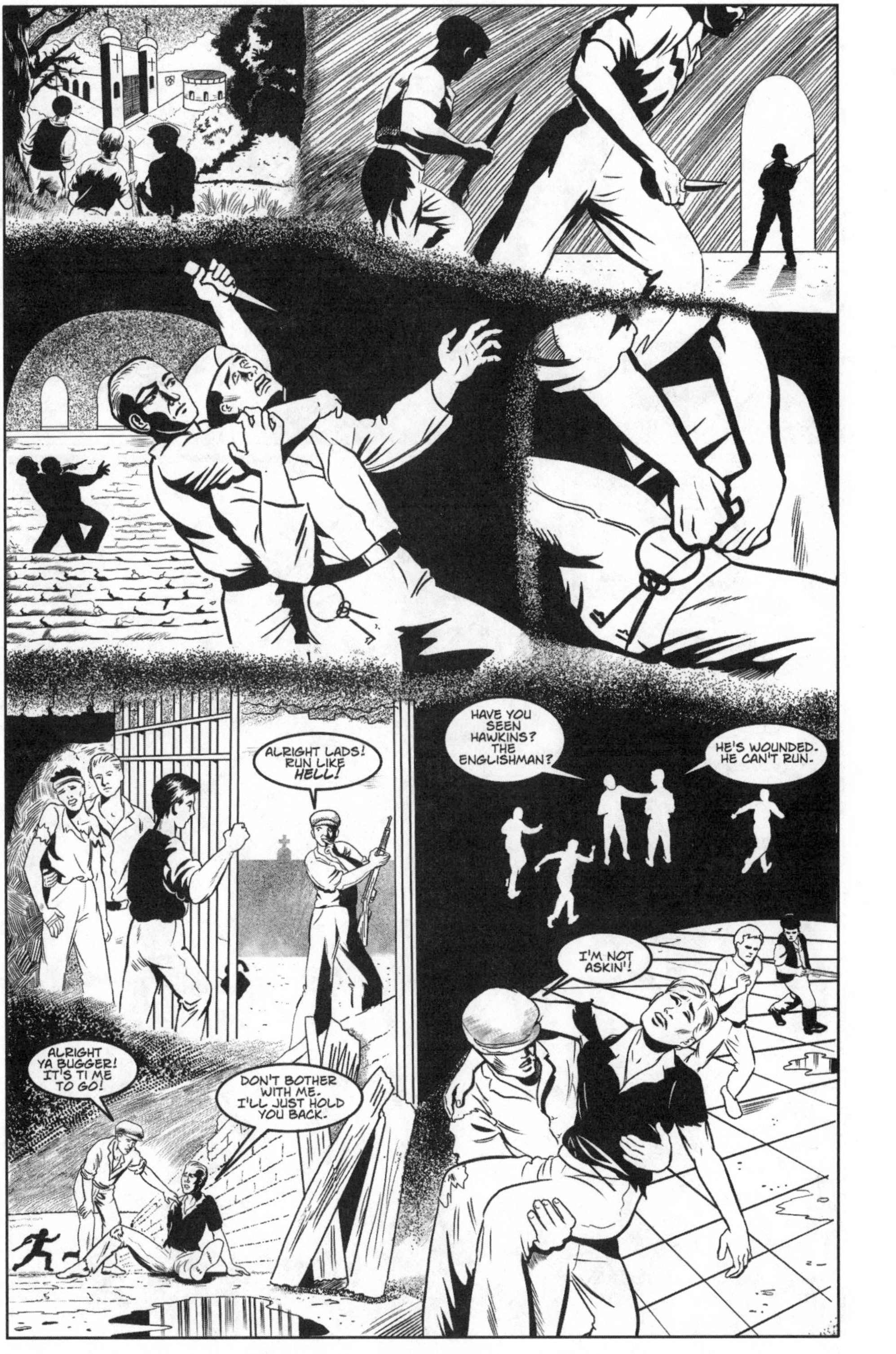

ALRIGHT LADS! RUN LIKE *HELL!*
ALRIGHT YA BUGGER! IT'S TI ME TO GO!
DON'T BOTHER WITH ME. I'LL JUST HOLD YOU BACK.
HAVE YOU SEEN HAWKINS? THE ENGLISHMAN?
HE'S WOUNDED. HE CAN'T RUN.
I'M NOT ASKIN'!

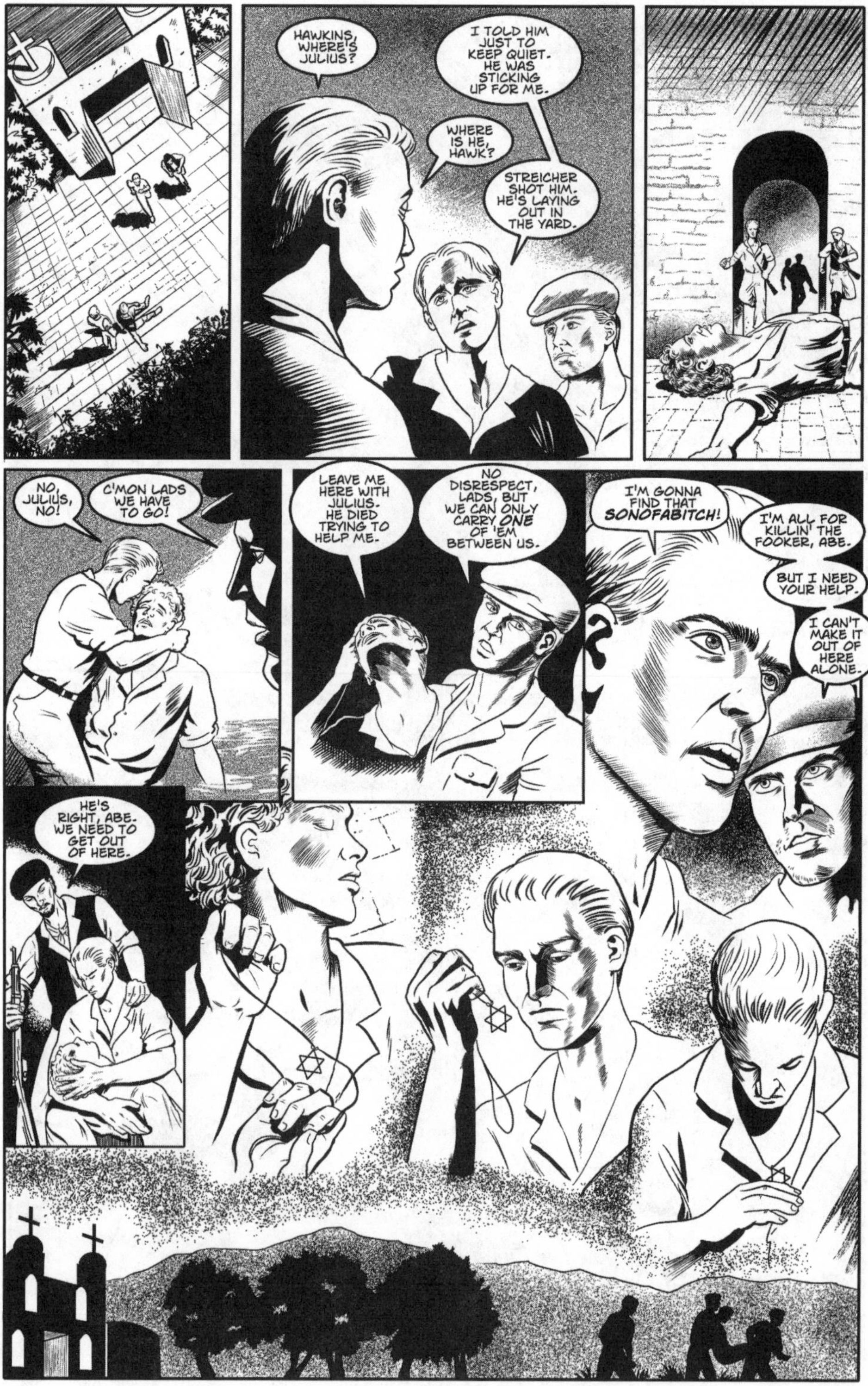
HAWKINS, WHERE'S JULIUS?
I TOLD HIM JUST TO KEEP QUIET. HE WAS STICKING UP FOR ME.
WHERE IS HE, HAWK?
STREICHER SHOT HIM. HE'S LAYING OUT IN THE YARD.
NO, JULIUS, NO!
C'MON LADS WE HAVE TO GO!
LEAVE ME HERE WITH JULIUS. HE DIED TRYING TO HELP ME.
NO DISRESPECT, LADS, BUT WE CAN ONLY CARRY ONE OF 'EM BETWEEN US.
I'M GONNA FIND THAT SONOFABITCH!
I'M ALL FOR KILLIN' THE FOOKER, ABE.
BUT I NEED YOUR HELP.
I CAN'T MAKE IT OUT OF HERE ALONE.
HE'S RIGHT, ABE. WE NEED TO GET OUT OF HERE.

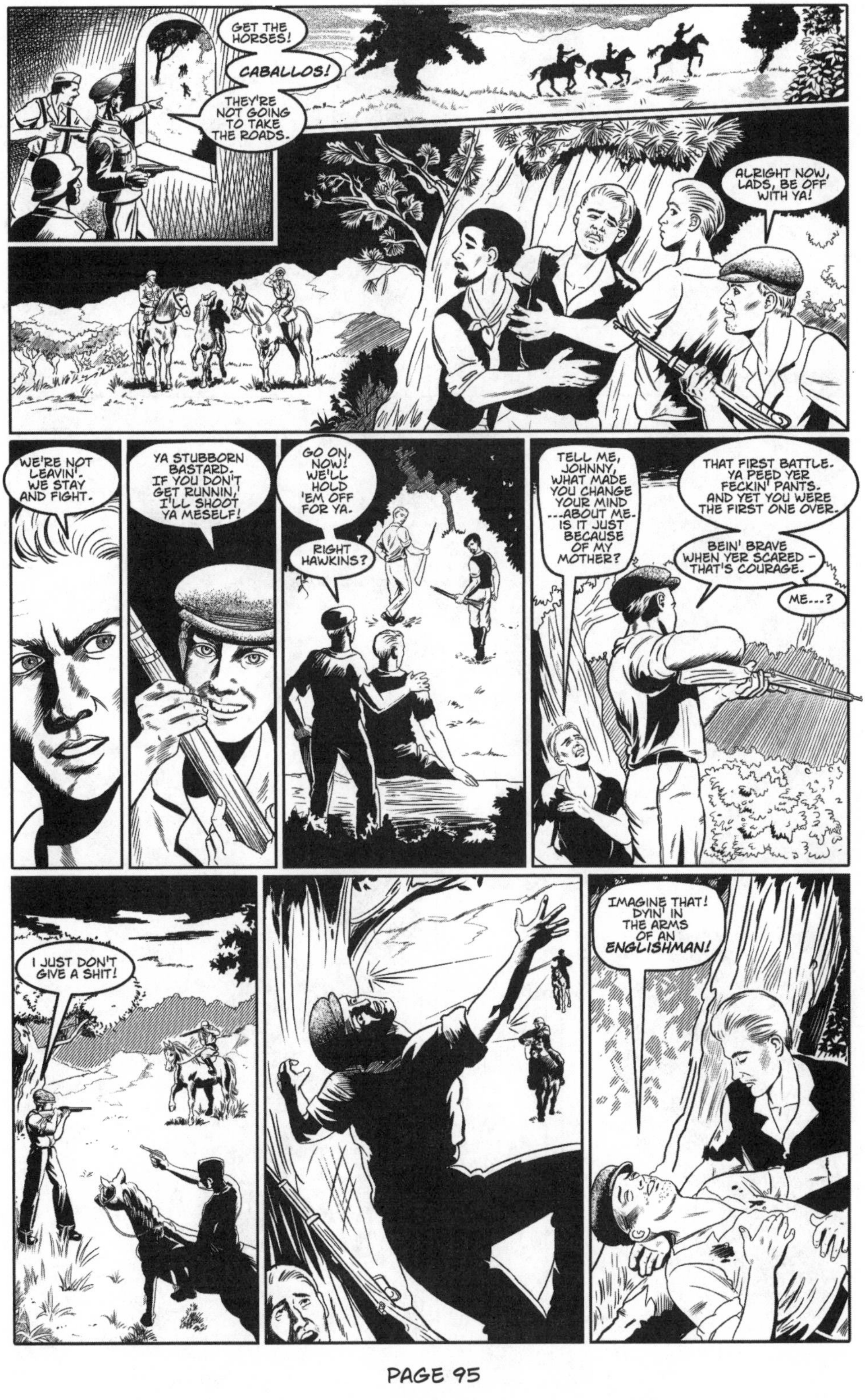
GET THE HORSES!
CABALLOS!
THEY'RE NOT GOING TO TAKE THE ROADS.
ALRIGHT NOW, LADS, BE OFF WITH YA!
WE'RE NOT LEAVIN'. WE STAY AND FIGHT.
YA STUBBORN BASTARD. IF YOU DON'T GET RUNNIN', I'LL SHOOT YA MESELF!
GO ON, NOW! WE'LL HOLD 'EM OFF FOR YA.
RIGHT HAWKINS?
TELL ME, JOHNNY, WHAT MADE YOU CHANGE YOUR MIND ---ABOUT ME. IS IT JUST BECAUSE OF MY MOTHER?
THAT FIRST BATTLE. YA PEED YER FECKIN' PANTS. AND YET YOU WERE THE FIRST ONE OVER.
BEIN' BRAVE WHEN YER SCARED - THAT'S COURAGE.
ME...?
I JUST DON'T GIVE A SHIT!
IMAGINE THAT! DYIN' IN THE ARMS OF AN ENGLISHMAN!

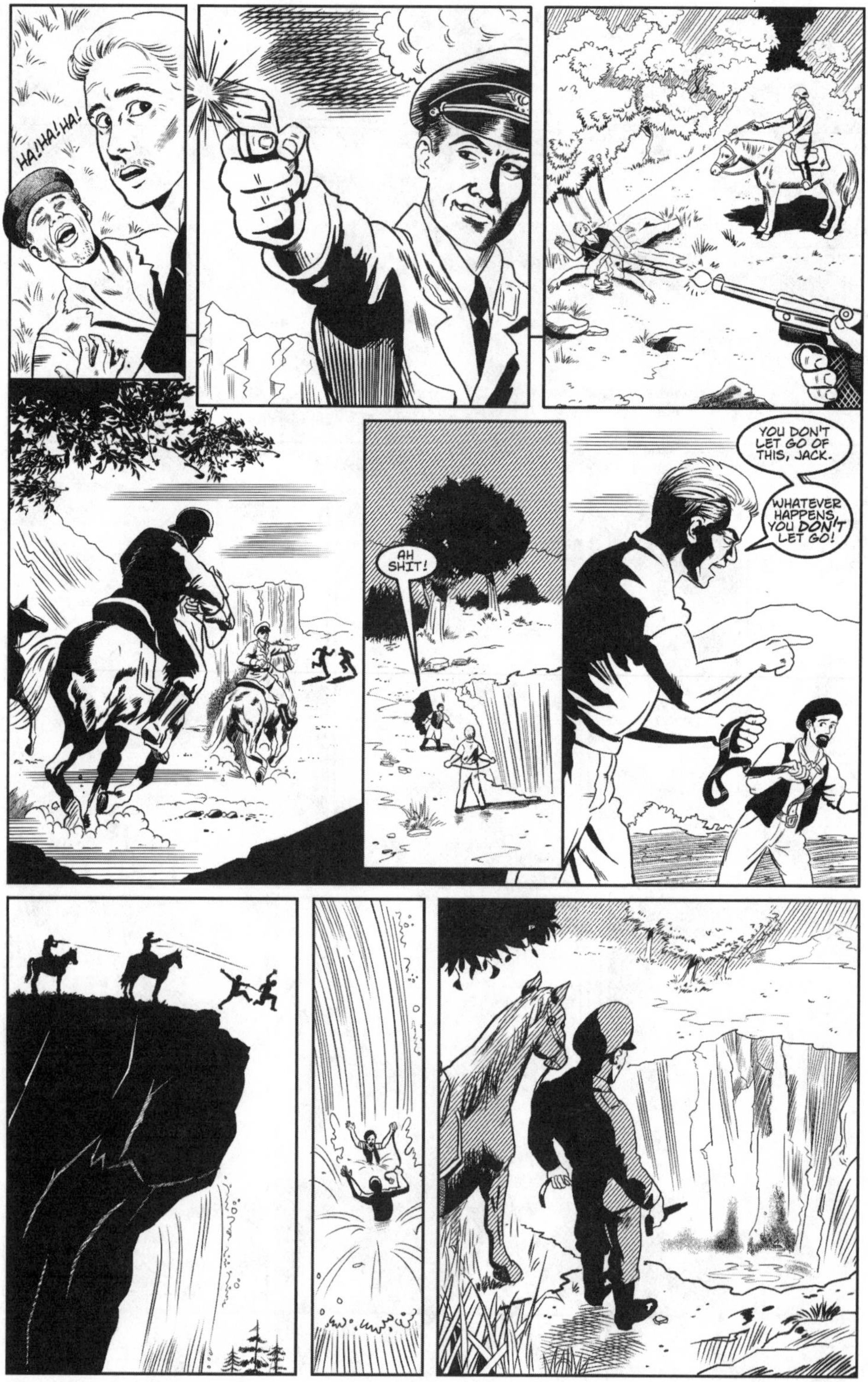
HA! HA! HA!
AH SHIT!
YOU DON'T LET GO OF THIS, JACK.
WHATEVER HAPPENS, YOU DON'T LET GO!

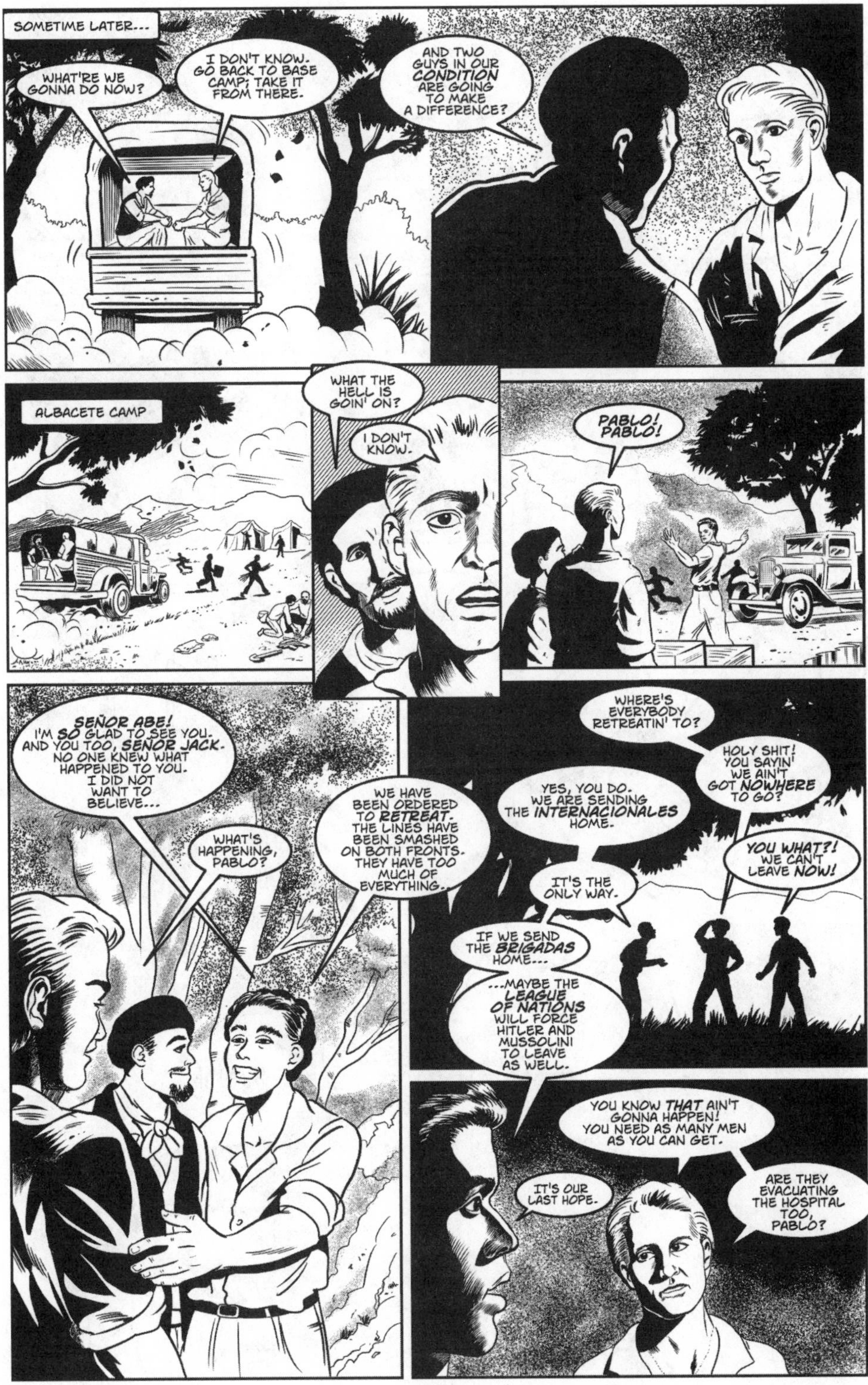
SOMETIME LATER...
WHAT'RE WE GONNA DO NOW?
I DON'T KNOW. GO BACK TO BASE CAMP; TAKE IT FROM THERE.
AND TWO GUYS IN OUR CONDITION ARE GOING TO MAKE A DIFFERENCE?
ALBACETE CAMP
WHAT THE HELL IS GOIN' ON?
I DON'T KNOW.
PABLO! PABLO!
SEÑOR ABE! I'M SO GLAD TO SEE YOU. AND YOU TOO, SEÑOR JACK. NO ONE KNEW WHAT HAPPENED TO YOU. I DID NOT WANT TO BELIEVE...
WHAT'S HAPPENING, PABLO?
WE HAVE BEEN ORDERED TO RETREAT. THE LINES HAVE BEEN SMASHED ON BOTH FRONTS. THEY HAVE TOO MUCH OF EVERYTHING.
WHERE'S EVERYBODY RETREATIN' TO?
HOLY SHIT! YOU SAYIN' WE AIN'T GOT NOWHERE TO GO?
YES, YOU DO. WE ARE SENDING THE INTERNACIONALES HOME.
YOU WHAT?! WE CAN'T LEAVE NOW!
IT'S THE ONLY WAY.
IF WE SEND THE BRIGADAS HOME...
...MAYBE THE LEAGUE OF NATIONS WILL FORCE HITLER AND MUSSOLINI TO LEAVE AS WELL.
YOU KNOW THAT AIN'T GONNA HAPPEN! YOU NEED AS MANY MEN AS YOU CAN GET.
IT'S OUR LAST HOPE.
ARE THEY EVACUATING THE HOSPITAL TOO, PABLO?

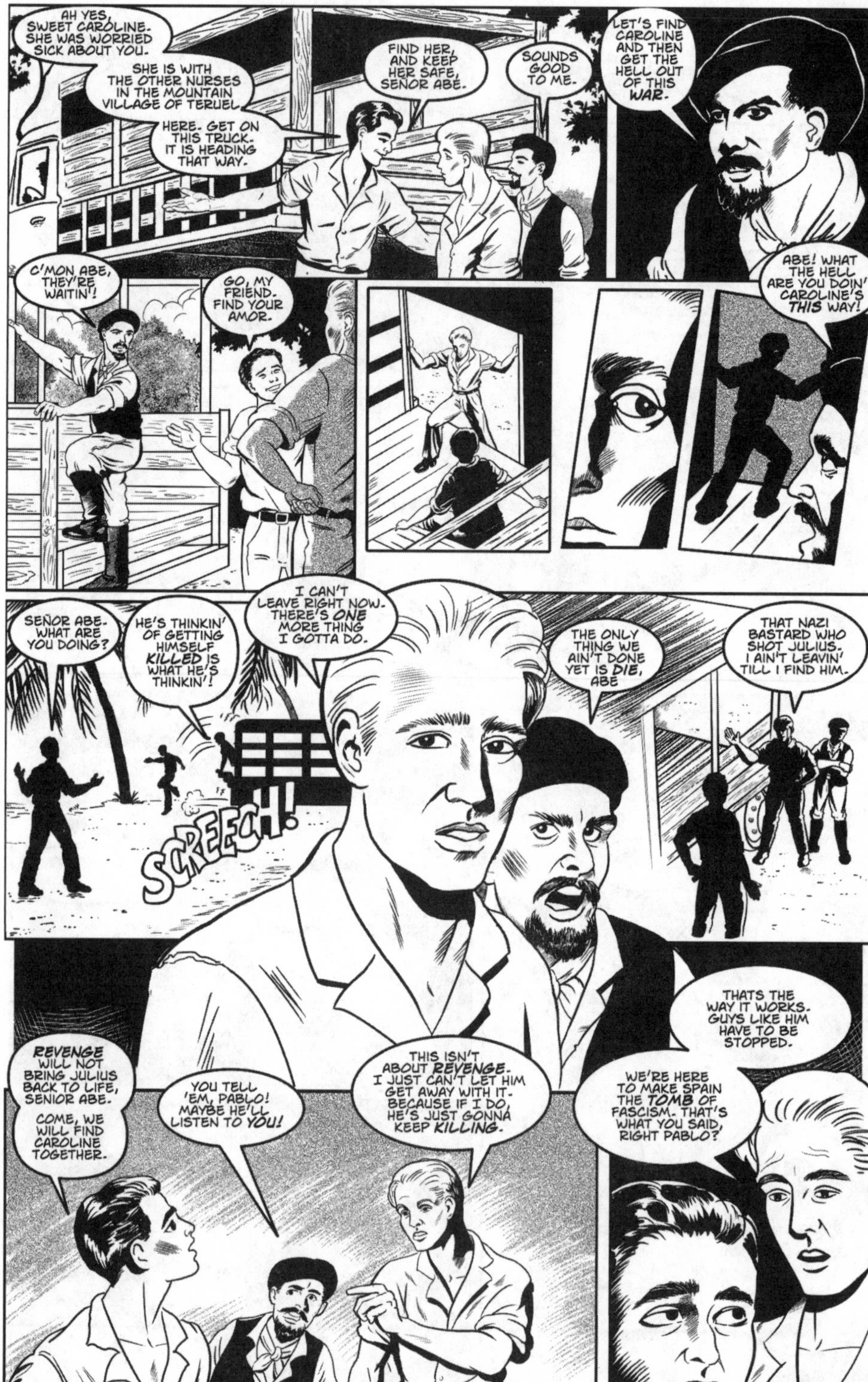
AH YES, SWEET CAROLINE. SHE WAS WORRIED SICK ABOUT YOU.
SHE IS WITH THE OTHER NURSES IN THE MOUNTAIN VILLAGE OF TERUEL.
HERE. GET ON THIS TRUCK. IT IS HEADING THAT WAY.
FIND HER, AND KEEP HER SAFE, SENOR ABE.
SOUNDS GOOD TO ME.
LET'S FIND CAROLINE AND THEN GET THE HELL OUT OF THIS WAR.
C'MON ABE, THEY'RE WAITIN'!
GO, MY FRIEND. FIND YOUR AMOR.
ABE! WHAT THE HELL ARE YOU DOIN'? CAROLINE'S THIS WAY!
SEÑOR ABE. WHAT ARE YOU DOING?
HE'S THINKIN' OF GETTING HIMSELF KILLED IS WHAT HE'S THINKIN'!
I CAN'T LEAVE RIGHT NOW. THERE'S ONE MORE THING I GOTTA DO.
SCREECH!
THE ONLY THING WE AIN'T DONE YET IS DIE, ABE
THAT NAZI BASTARD WHO SHOT JULIUS. I AIN'T LEAVIN' TILL I FIND HIM.
REVENGE WILL NOT BRING JULIUS BACK TO LIFE, SENIOR ABE.
COME, WE WILL FIND CAROLINE TOGETHER.
YOU TELL 'EM, PABLO! MAYBE HE'LL LISTEN TO YOU!
THIS ISN'T ABOUT REVENGE. I JUST CAN'T LET HIM GET AWAY WITH IT. BECAUSE IF I DO, HE'S JUST GONNA KEEP KILLING.
THATS THE WAY IT WORKS. GUYS LIKE HIM HAVE TO BE STOPPED.
WE'RE HERE TO MAKE SPAIN THE TOMB OF FASCISM. THAT'S WHAT YOU SAID, RIGHT PABLO?

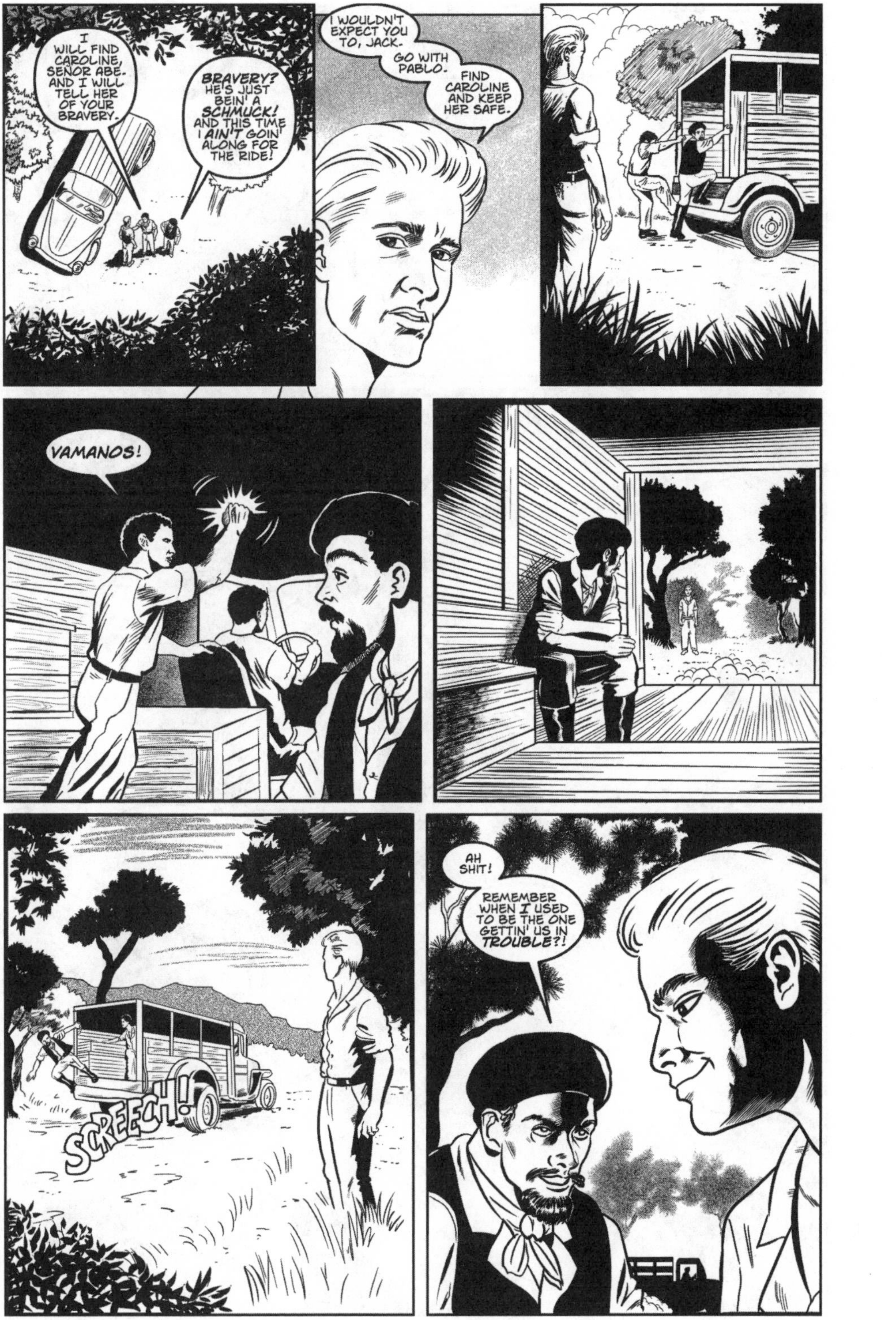
I WILL FIND CAROLINE, SEÑOR ABE. AND I WILL TELL HER OF YOUR BRAVERY.
BRAVERY? HE'S JUST BEIN' A SCHMUCK! AND THIS TIME I AIN'T GOIN' ALONG FOR THE RIDE!
I WOULDN'T EXPECT YOU TO, JACK.
GO WITH PABLO.
FIND CAROLINE AND KEEP HER SAFE.
VAMANOS!
SCREECH!!
AH SHIT!
REMEMBER WHEN I USED TO BE THE ONE GETTIN' US IN TROUBLE?!

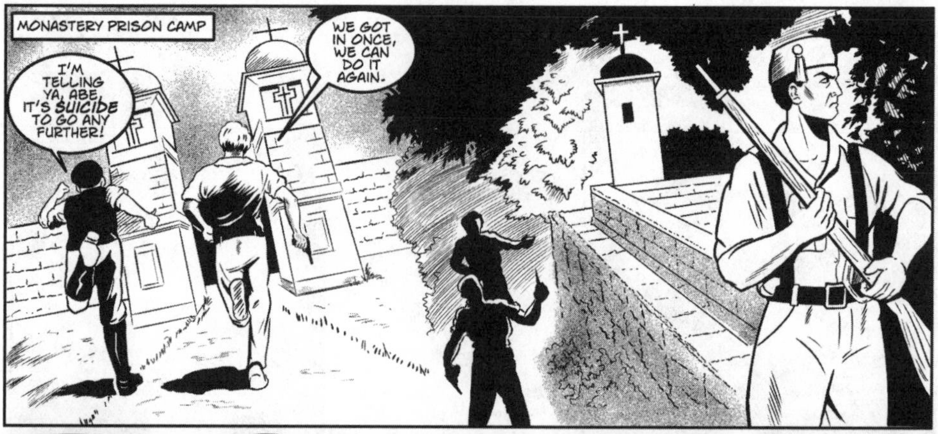
MONASTERY PRISON CAMP
I'M TELLING YA, ABE IT'S SUICIDE TO GO ANY FURTHER!
WE GOT IN ONCE, WE CAN DO IT AGAIN.

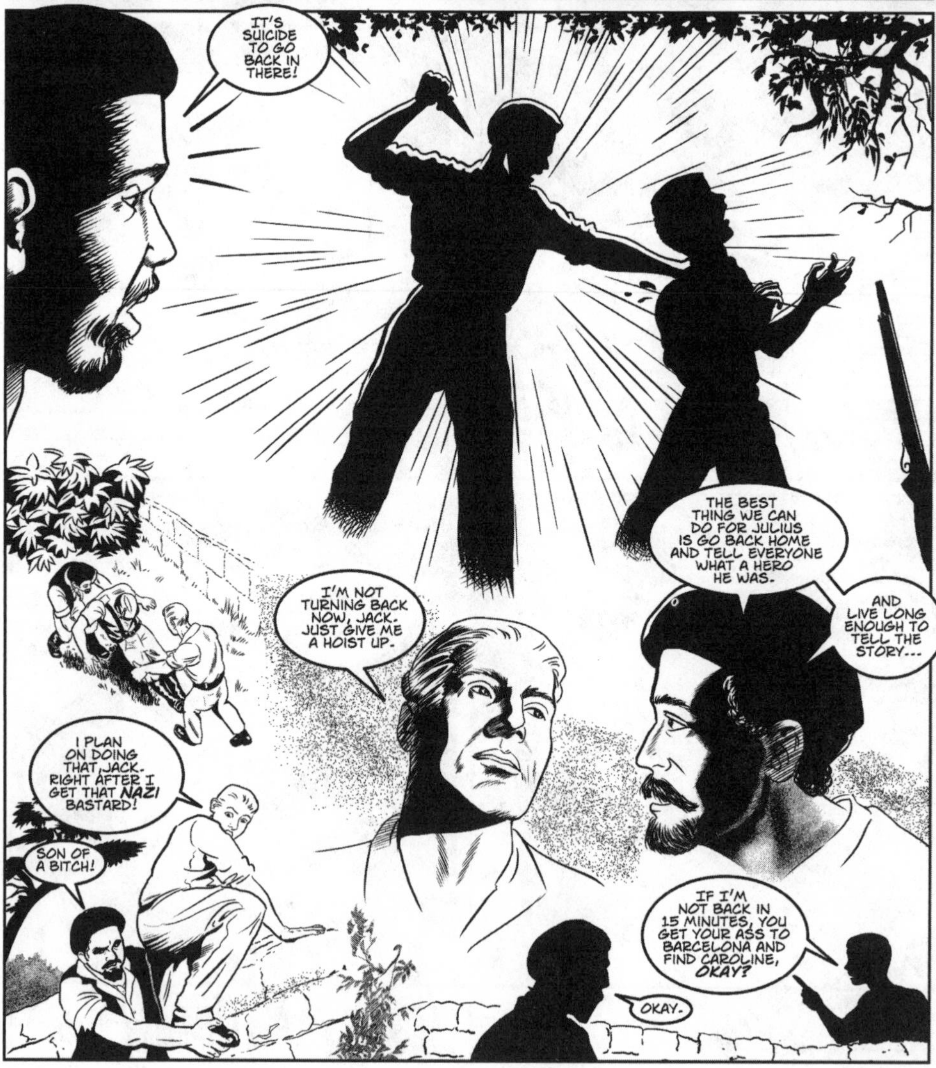
IT'S SUICIDE TO GO BACK IN THERE!
THE BEST THING WE CAN DO FOR JULIUS IS GO BACK HOME AND TELL EVERYONE WHAT A HERO HE WAS.
I'M NOT TURNING BACK NOW, JACK. JUST GIVE ME A HOIST UP.
AND LIVE LONG ENOUGH TO TELL THE STORY...
I PLAN ON DOING THAT, JACK. RIGHT AFTER I GET THAT NAZI BASTARD!
SON OF A BITCH!
IF I'M NOT BACK IN 15 MINUTES, YOU GET YOUR ASS TO BARCELONA AND FIND CAROLINE, OKAY?
OKAY.

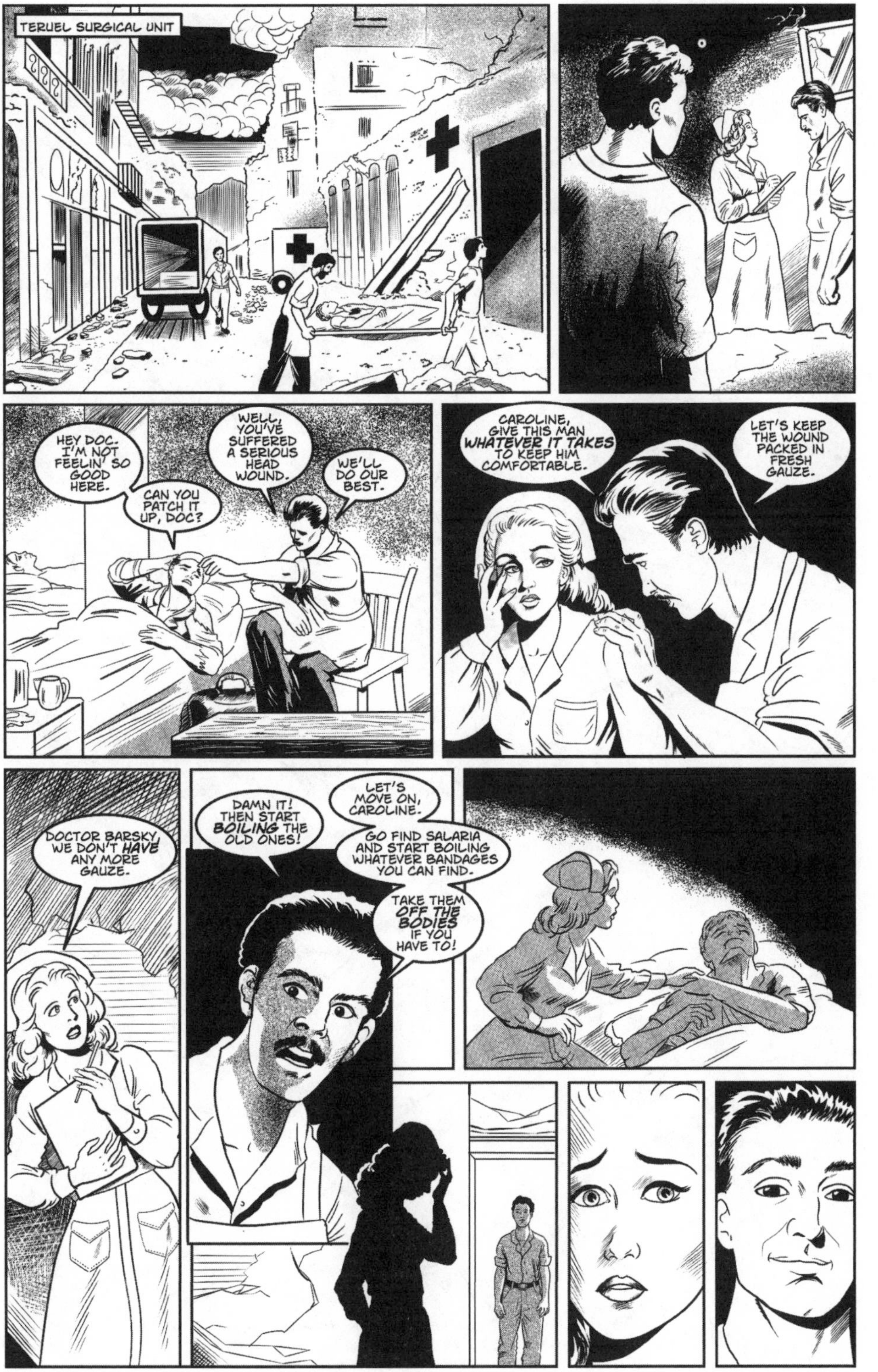
TERUEL SURGICAL UNIT
HEY DOC. I'M NOT FEELIN' SO GOOD HERE.
CAN YOU PATCH IT UP, DOC?
WELL, YOU'VE SUFFERED A SERIOUS HEAD WOUND.
WE'LL DO OUR BEST.
CAROLINE, GIVE THIS MAN **WHATEVER IT TAKES** TO KEEP HIM COMFORTABLE.
LET'S KEEP THE WOUND PACKED IN FRESH GAUZE.
DOCTOR BARSKY, WE DON'T **HAVE** ANY MORE GAUZE.
DAMN IT! THEN START **BOILING** THE OLD ONES!
LET'S MOVE ON, CAROLINE.
GO FIND SALARIA AND START BOILING WHATEVER BANDAGES YOU CAN FIND.
TAKE THEM **OFF THE BODIES** IF YOU HAVE TO!

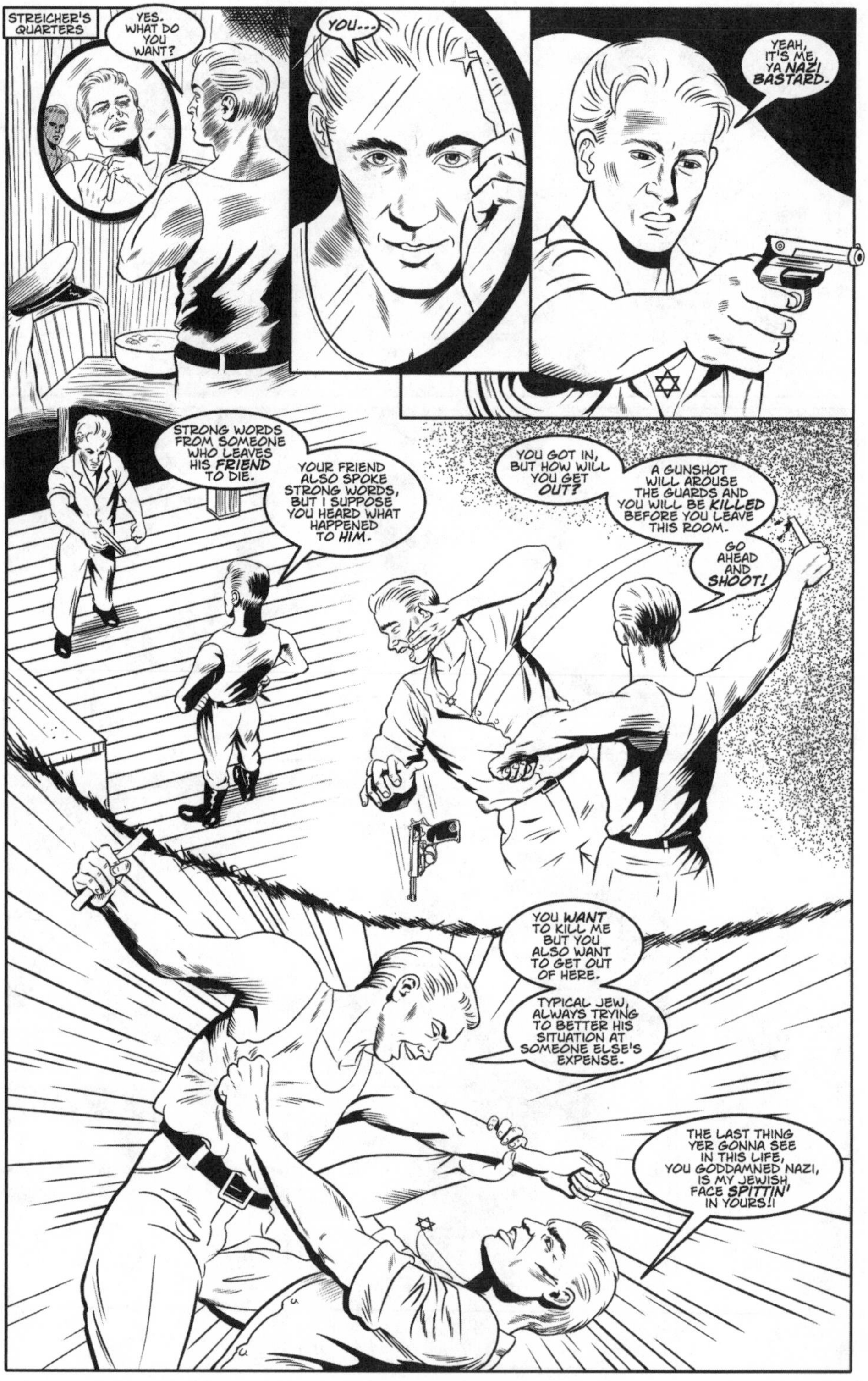
STREICHER'S QUARTERS
YES. WHAT DO YOU WANT?
YOU...
YEAH, IT'S ME, YA NAZI BASTARD.
STRONG WORDS FROM SOMEONE WHO LEAVES HIS FRIEND TO DIE.
YOUR FRIEND ALSO SPOKE STRONG WORDS, BUT I SUPPOSE YOU HEARD WHAT HAPPENED TO HIM.
YOU GOT IN, BUT HOW WILL YOU GET OUT?
A GUNSHOT WILL AROUSE THE GUARDS AND YOU WILL BE KILLED BEFORE YOU LEAVE THIS ROOM.
GO AHEAD AND SHOOT!
YOU WANT TO KILL ME BUT YOU ALSO WANT TO GET OUT OF HERE.
TYPICAL JEW, ALWAYS TRYING TO BETTER HIS SITUATION AT SOMEONE ELSE'S EXPENSE.
THE LAST THING YER GONNA SEE IN THIS LIFE, YOU GODDAMNED NAZI, IS MY JEWISH FACE SPITTIN' IN YOURS!!

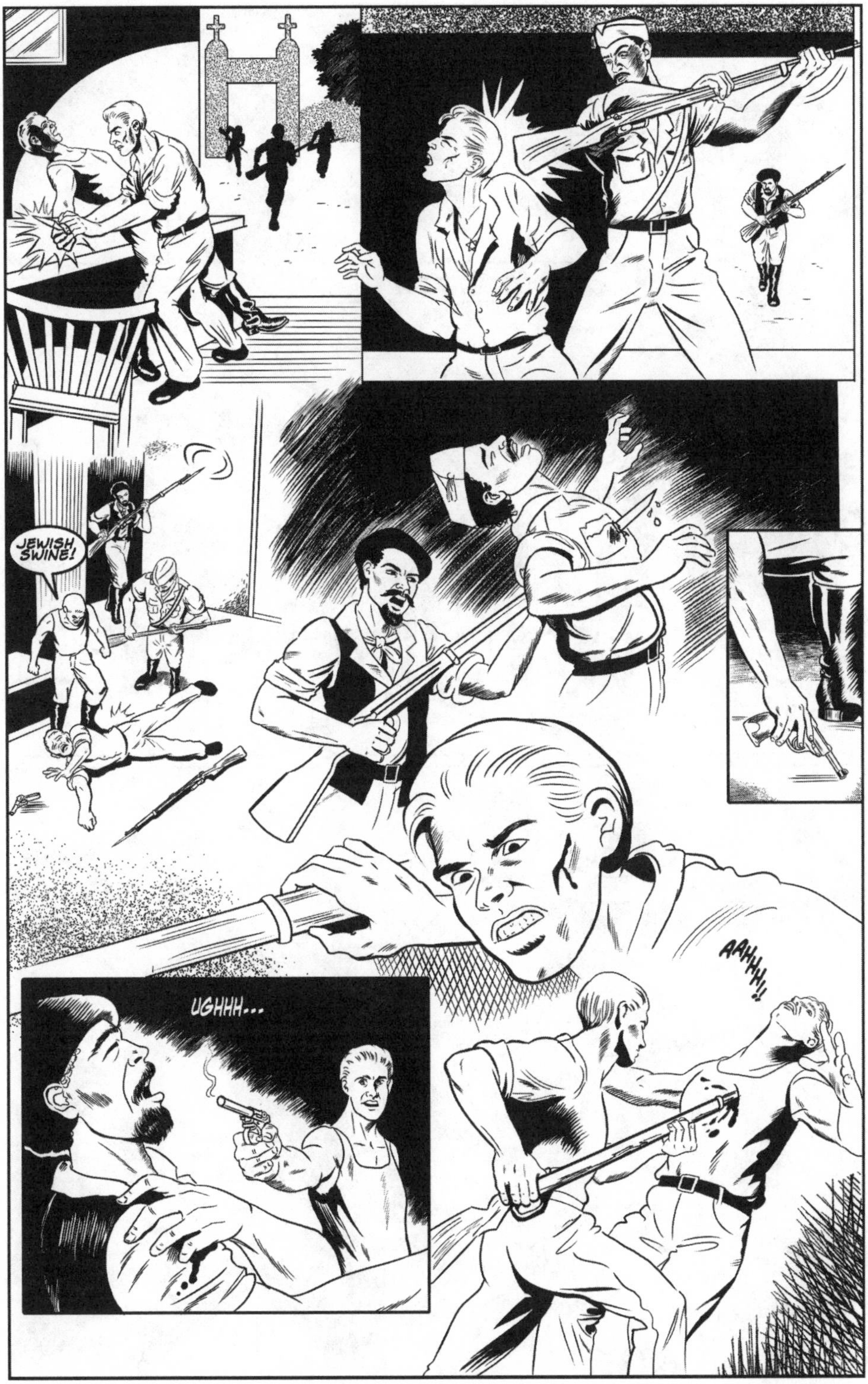
JEWISH SWINE!
AAHHH!!
UGHHH...

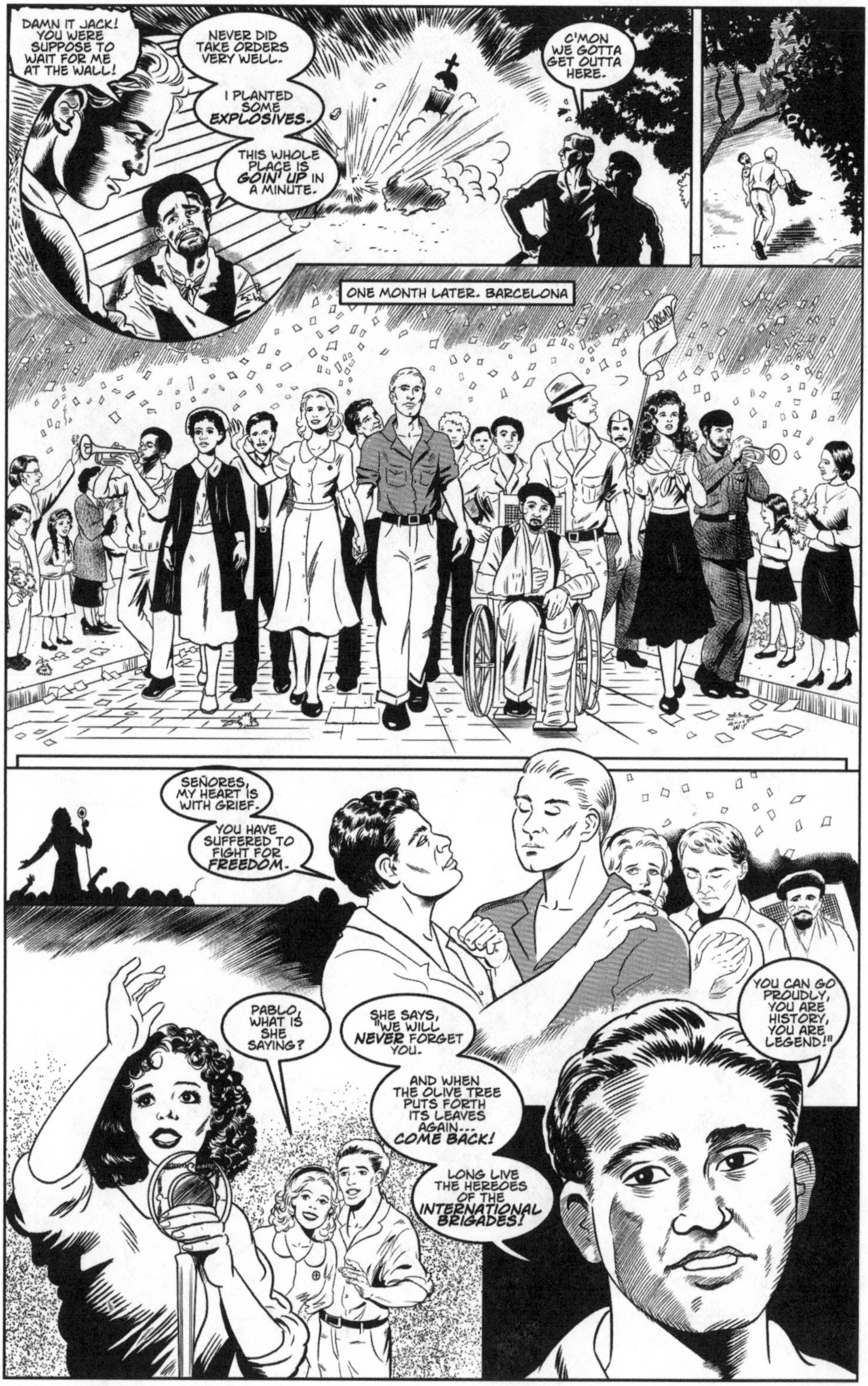

DAMN IT JACK! YOU WERE SUPPOSE TO WAIT FOR ME AT THE WALL!
NEVER DID TAKE ORDERS VERY WELL.
I PLANTED SOME EXPLOSIVES.
THIS WHOLE PLACE IS GOIN' UP IN A MINUTE.
C'MON WE GOTTA GET OUTTA HERE.
ONE MONTH LATER. BARCELONA
SEÑORES, MY HEART IS WITH GRIEF.
YOU HAVE SUFFERED TO FIGHT FOR FREEDOM.
PABLO, WHAT IS SHE SAYING?
SHE SAYS, "WE WILL NEVER FORGET YOU.
AND WHEN THE OLIVE TREE PUTS FORTH ITS LEAVES AGAIN... COME BACK!
LONG LIVE THE HEREOES OF THE INTERNATIONAL BRIGADES!
YOU CAN GO PROUDLY, YOU ARE HISTORY, YOU ARE LEGEND!"

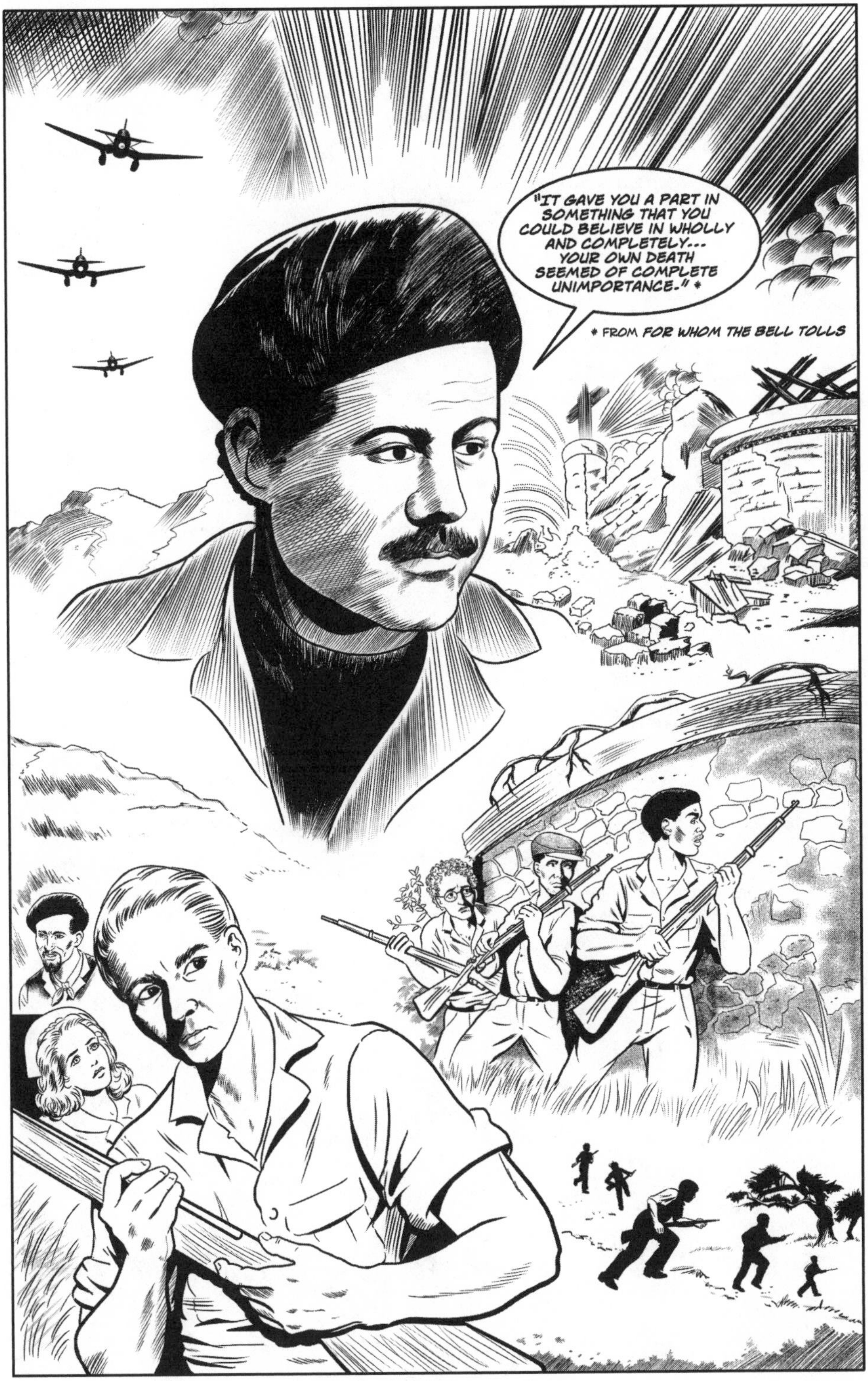
"IT GAVE YOU A PART IN SOMETHING THAT YOU COULD BELIEVE IN WHOLLY AND COMPLETELY... YOUR OWN DEATH SEEMED OF COMPLETE UNIMPORTANCE." *
* FROM FOR WHOM THE BELL TOLLS

The Comic and the Spanish Civil War

by Paul Buhle

The emergence of nonfiction comic art as a medium in which to describe historical events and personalities is recent, by most measures, and within the culture of people under thirty, the genre has taken on new and important roles. The depiction of wars has also found a global audience, especially for the widely translated works of Joe Sacco. More recently, *March*, a three-volume graphic work on the life of John Lewis, has won multiple prizes, reaching large audiences with direct sales and assignments to college classes, and may be said to have set a precedent for nonfiction comics. The heavy sales of the *Black Panther Party* comic of 2021 reminds readers (and publishers) that somewhere to the left of the mainstream other potential subject matter beckons and readers await. For the purposes of our book, the struggle against fascism offers a parallel to the struggles against racism, white privilege, and police killings that led to the largest sustained political demonstrations in U.S. history during the summer of 2020. Now more than ever, that struggle is very much a factor in American life.

SINCE GOYA IN MODERN HISTORY, art has been employed to make antiwar statements, even against the greatest odds of governments and broad sectors of society intolerant of dissent. It is a truism that artists do not protest because their protests are likely to be successful but because the artist must speak, or lose the claim to be a real artist. Exiled Germans made art of all kinds against Hitlerism, Picasso painted *Guernica*, and on the U.S. scene, the varied artistic expressions against the Vietnam War set the tone for a generation, throwing off the politically indifferent "free enterprise art" mood of the Cold War 1950s. We can conveniently turn to comics as a long-maligned subset of the larger fields of art, as we grapple with the particulars of a form of protest that has fought its way, across more than a half century, to being taken seriously.

It is notable that comic books first seized public attention at the late 1930s moment of global dread. The market for this new pulp product skyrocketed, among troops overseas as well as adolescent and preadolescent readers at home. So long as the Second World War lasted, "war comics" swept the field, with any popular comic reaching a quarter million or even a half million in sales, issue after issue. Most were mere star-spangled action, with no purpose other than hailing the bravery and predicting the victory of the Allies, too often against Japanese "Yellow Devils," with the occasional Arab or African as helpmate to the heroic forces.

Boy Commandos (1942) is counted among the first war comics to hit the newsstands. Multicultural, non-racist by implication, *Boy Commandos* was written by one of the coming giants of superhero comic books, Joe Simon, himself the son of a union organizer. Here we find, alongside Americans, British, and Irish, the youthful Partisans exiled from their German, Italian, and Spanish home countries, often family members of the murdered or imprisoned parents or relatives, taking their revenge against fascism. If other comics rarely reached this kind of articulation—too often, blond American superheroes won the war without much assistance—the anti-fascist sentiment did not disappear until late in the 1940s.

After the surrender of Japan, war comics lost much of their vaunted popularity and took an unpleasant turn toward Cold War themes. Now, sneaky and unpleasant-looking Russians sought to manipulate clueless natives, while images of exotic temptresses (especially of the Asian variety) played upon the innocence, and doubtless the pure lust, of American boys who found themselves overseas. The Korean War, naturally, extended these themes, with some slight corrections since South Koreans were allies.

Amid that widely unpopular war—or "police action," as it was known—something important changed within comic narratives and comic art. Scholars largely agree that realistic action comics, especially war comics, arose in the form of EC Comics in the early 1950s. Harvey Kurtzman, best known as the founder of *Mad* magazine, worked with artists in stories ridiculing the adventure and glory of war in the daily newspapers' "funny pages." Meanwhile, Kurtzman had developed for EC a successful series of mainstream comics about military conflicts across the ages. The most vivid issues recounted the Korean War through stories that returning GIs told to Kurtzman. In contrast to earlier war comics, these stories romanticized nothing, neither the suffering of the GIs nor their opponents, nor the tragedy of civilians caught in the middle. They were fundamentally antiwar comics.

Meanwhile, a different trend in the field of comics took shape. Almost since their inception, comic books were attacked by some critics as damaging the minds and morals of young people. Congressional hearings held in the same Foley Square Manhattan courthouse where Communists had effectively been put on trial only a few years earlier marked a gloomy turn in a comics industry already facing competition from the appeal of television to the young. To be accepted for sales at newsstands, comic books needed a Comics Code Seal of Approval, which required self-censorship by writers and artists under threat from politicians and Catholic Church–based enforcers. Few companies bucked the trend. EC chose to abandon comics altogether for a black-and-white magazine format: thus, *Mad*, free from censorship.

This censorship left a lasting mark on the creators of comics in the generations to follow. If previous writers and artists had self-censored, straying from accepted standards only in crime and horror comics, later generations would regard themselves as opposed to censorship on principle. The path had been laid for war comics to become "political" in new and radical ways. Even some of the war comics continuing into the Vietnam era, showing righteous Americans making their way against the totalitarian enemy, bore a sort of "no more wars" sentiment just beneath the surface. But other comic book series reflected upon the uncertainties of the self-conscious warrior in the age of mechanized warfare. Moral uncertainties lurked close to the surface.

The generation of comic artists coming of age at the end of the 1960s took up these uncertainties and turned them into opposition. The new rebels of the "underground comix" genre reflected the local underground newspapers that sprang up on campuses and in communities, offering a dramatically new style of journalism, comics that had never been seen before. The artists, antiwar, anti-military and taken with the dramatic issues of the day rather than history, did not often touch upon the Spanish Civil War. But one of the most admired of the artists, a gifted specialist in action-style comic art, marked a notable exception.

Spain Rodriguez, a half generation older than other underground artists, is rightly considered one of the masters of the field and certainly the one most devoted to the war-and-action traditions of Harvey Kurtzman and EC. Rodriguez had a special claim on his father's homeland, having adopted it as his given name in his teenage years. Veteran of a motorcycle gang in Buffalo and no stranger to violence, Rodriguez, moving to the West Coast, could be described as *sui genesis* among the peaceniks of the Bay Area circles of artists. He did not set a tone so much as provide one for a very particular kind of comic art, with tough left-wingers fighting a cruel and destructive social system. And enjoying the action.

By the early 1970s, Rodriguez began to draw a series of historic war stories. These included the saga of the Spanish anarchist Benventuri Duruti, stories of the Red Army's defeat of the Germans, and of the particular heroism of a doomed Soviet female pilot. In the years shortly before his death in 2011, he devoted himself to a book-length graphic biography of Che Guevara, who might rightly be considered a child of the earlier anti-fascist fighters. Here, Rodriguez reached new heights in his depiction of idealists throwing caution to the wind. Facing a field of contradictions within the Cuban Revolution, Guevara makes a glorious, self-sacrificing exit: "Shoot, Coward!" he dares his CIA-hired assassin. "You are only killing a man." With a driving narrative and action art depicting military conflict and the bravery of revolutionary soldiers, this graphic story of Che is the precursor to the current volume.

We must look beyond the United States to find comic art counterparts to Rodriguez, such as the multivolume *Le cri du peuple* (The Cry of the People) by Jacques Tardi on the struggles of the Paris Commune against overwhelming military force. Among those relatively few artists actually drawing in Spain, Carlos Giménez is assuredly unique. Having survived the Francoist slaughter of his parents and the brutal repressions that followed, Giménez commenced after the dictator's death to draw and publish his own personal saga and that of the children he grew up with in the period between the end of the war and the 1950s. Giménez's masterwork, *Paracuellos*, which first appeared in Spain in 1981, was recognized almost immediately as important, both artistically and politically. Lamentably, and despite winning practically all the major comic art prizes in Europe, more than thirty years passed before an English-language version arrived. The Foreword to *Paracuellos* is a one-paragraph personal tribute by Will Eisner, one of the deans of U.S. comic book storytelling and art, written a few years before passing.

Comics in Spain have increased in number and popularity since Gimenez, with a small but growing number using the Civil War as a topic. *Un largo silencio* (The Long Silence) by Miguel Angel Gallardo is regarded as a classic of sorts, treating the life of his father as "ordinary"; rather than acting in some heroic fashion against Franco, it is about how he survived. *Los Surcos del Azar* by Paco Roca, also considered a classic by Spanish comic artists, addresses the Republicans who manage to escape and go on to struggle against the Nazis in occupied France. *El Arte de Volar* by Antonio Altarrib, regarded as the "Spanish *Maus*," offers another survival narrative of his father, who lived through a long stretch of the twentieth century. In the past year the Spanish comic *The Lincoln Brigade*, authored by a cast of collaborators, joined these Iberian productions in reaching English audiences with a story centered on African-American labor organizer Oliver Law.

Gimenez's work was autobiographical, and in this way he offered a counterpart to the wave of autobiographical comic writers and artists more famous in the United States, such as Art Spiegelman, Harvey Pekar, Lynda Barry, and Alison Bechtel, to name just a few. Their work is largely responsible for raising critical awareness and approval of comics as a distinct art form. Spiegelman's *Maus*, based upon recollections of his father, a Holocaust survivor, anticipated *Persepolis*, a best-seller by Marjane Sartrapi about a young person's life in Iran at the time of the Shah's overthrow and the assumption of power by the Ayatollahs. These hugely popular war and conflict stories were in a decidedly new vein. Joe Sacco, wandering through the Balkans, then Israel and the occupied West Bank as a sort of journalist-reporter, added another dimension of what comic art could do, what some comic artists were driven to do, under the most extreme circumstances.

And so, arguably, we have reached another new stage. *!Brigadistas! An American Anti-Fascist in the Spanish Civil War*, scripted by Miguel Ferguson and drawn by Anne Timmons, returns to the what we might call "truer-than-fiction" writing. In expressing the life experiences of Abe Osheroff, enthusiastic volunteer for the Abraham Lincoln Brigade, we see and feel the lives and fortunes of the youthful idealists determined to stamp out fascism before it set the world on fire. That they did not succeed was no surprise, even in the years when the vision of anti-fascism united whole generations of radicals across many lands.

That the Brigade members used every ounce of their courage, energy, and determination finds a unique expression in these pages. Anne Timmons's style is both realistic and something beyond realism. It rejuvenates, we think, comic art styles from the 1940s Golden Age and goes far beyond them.

Acknowledgments

Thanks go to the Harburg Foundation, whose early grant helped to get the project off the ground. Thanks to our many friends at ALBA— the Abraham Lincoln Brigade Archives—who encouraged this project from its inception. We also wish to thank Michael Yates for his initial work encouraging MR Press to publish our book, and Martin Paddio for the many tasks needed to reach its completion.

Finally, huge thanks are due to Gunnel Clark, Abe's partner and an activist in her own right, for opening her house and generously sharing Abe with so many students, activists, and professors over the years.

————

Extend Abe's legacy of social justice activism with a contribution to the Abe Osheroff and Gunnel Clark Endowed Fund at the Center for Human Rights at the University of Washington. The fund provides financial resources for undergraduate and graduate students to support human rights projects that promote social change through direct action and adhere to the principles that guided Abe's lifelong activism.

https://jsis.washington.edu/humanrights/funds/abe-osheroff-and-gunnel-clark-fund/

Further Reading

The Boy Commandos, vol. 1. Introduction by Paul Buhle. New York: DC Comics, 2000.

Chute, Hillary L. *Disaster Drawn: Visual Witness, Comics and Documentary Form*. Cambridge, MA: Harvard University Press, 2018.

Dore, Mary, Noel Buckner, and Sam Sills, directors. *The Good Fight: The Abraham Lincoln Brigade and the Spanish Civil War*. Narrated by Studs Terkel. 98 minutes, 1984.

Hochschild, Adam. *Spain Is In Our Hearts: Americans in the Spanish Civil War, 1936–1939*. New York: Houghton-Mifflin, 2016.

Yoe, Craig, ed. *The Unknown Anti-War Comics*. New York: IDW, 2018.

Contributors

MIGUEL FERGUSON is an award-winning professor, author, and educational entrepreneur. As the founder of the company OfCourse!, he creates innovative curriculum and provides training on public policy and social justice topics.

ANNE TIMMONS is a Portland-based painter and illustrator whose work has appeared in a range of national magazines. In addition to teaming up with Trina Robbins on illustrated biographies and adaptations, she has worked Paul Buhle on *Studs Terkel's Working* and *Bohemians*.

PAUL BUHLE, retired Brown University Senior Lecturer, has authored and edited more than forty books on the American and Caribbean Left, and is the editor of more than a dozen nonfiction graphic novels.

FRASER M. OTTANELLI teaches the history of U.S. radicalism and immigration at the University of South Florida.